MEMOIR OF KOREAN WAR POW

T.I. HAHN

PublishAmerica
Baltimore

Softcover 9781630047283
PUBLISHED BY PUBLISHAMERICA, LLLP
www.publishamerica.com
Baltimore

Printed in the United States of America

Acknowledgement

I would like to Thank firstly all mighty God for saving my life sixty three years ago and for giving me the strength, ability to be able to share my story. I have written this book as a way of thanks to my loved ones. My mother who saved my life without her knowing it, my father, my loving wife and four children who inspired me and made me happy and fulfilled as a family man. I want to thank the people who have pulled me up when I stumbled. My colleagues and fellow anti-communist POWs, I want to thank everyone who helped me to make this book published, especially Senator Harry Reid, general John K. Singlaub, Warren Sessler, D. Rocky Hanson, Kenny Kang, Daniel Lee, martin Kim and my children, Judy, Kathryn, James, Thomas Han and Jim Koo.

이동휘 장로에게
나의 一生의 친구에게 증정합니다.
2013년 5월 27일 (Memorial Day)
저자 한동상 증정
Donald Han

United States Senate
Washington DC 20510-7012

September 2, 2010

Dear Mr. T. I. Han

Thank you for sending me a copy of your book on the Korean
War. It was a compelling account, and I was pleased to have read
it. I particularly enjoyed the parts that chronicled your Korean War
experiences.

I want to thank you for your service to the United States Army in
Korea, and I am pleased to hear that you have lived happily in Nevada
since immigrating to the United States. I hope to hear from you in the
near future about your book published.

My best wishes to you.

Sincerely,

HARRY REID
Majority Leader
United States Senator

FOREWORD

The Author, T. I. Hahn is a Korean American and a good friend of mine. He helped me a lot in writing my book by translating the Korean languages into English. I am a Korean War Veteran. In the year of 1953, I fought against the Chinese and the North Korean Army at "Out Post Harry" with the US Army, 3rd Infantry Division, in the battle of "the Iron triangle". I was awarded the "Silver Star Medal" by the US Government for my distinguished services in the battle field.

Mr. Hahn was one of the leaders of Korean War anti-communist POW. During three years of Koje-do UN POW camp's life. He had organized and struggled hard to fight against the compulsory repatriation of all POWs which the Communist truce delegation had tenaciously demanded. He and his friends had devoted great contributions to oppose the compulsory repatriation of POWs to communist North Korea. He had fervently supported the voluntary repatriation that the United States had strongly insisted. He and his comrades had organized POWs many harsh demonstrations to oppose the compulsory repatriation. Consequently, the Communists negotiators abandoned their insistence and 30,000 anti-communist North Korean POWs refused to return to the North Korea and remained in the South Korea. They all joined into the ROK Army and strengthened the ROK Army's fighting power during the Korean War.

Mr. Han had later worked for US Army Provost Marshal Office as an Interpreter/Investigator for 19 years before immigrating to the United States. He was sponsored and invited by the Department of the State as a Special Immigrant status. He has lived in the United States for 38 years and is an outstanding citizen. He lived 18 years in North Korea, 25 years in South Korea prior to immigrating to the United

States where he has spent most of his life. He states "the USA is the best country in every respect" He has four children who grew up and were educated in the United States. They are all satisfied and enjoying their happy lives as productive citizens.

Warren Sessler
US Army Military Historian

CONTENTS

FOREWORD...7

PREFACE...13

PART I OVERVIEW OF THE KOREAN WAR............................15

PART II THE ORIGIN OF THE KOREAN WAR......................22
  CHAPTER I HISTORICAL BACKGROUND OF KOREAN CONFLICT.......22
    1. JAPANESE COLONIZATION OF KOREAN
       PENINSULA...22
    2. THE YALTA CONFERENCE AND KOREAN
       PENINSULA...24
    3. THE JAPANESE' DEFEAT AND KOREAN
       LIBERATION..27
    4. THE COLD WAR BETWEEN TWO SUPERPOWERS 31
    5. PARTITION OF KOREAN PENINSULA ALONG THE
       38TH PARALLEL...34
       a) Drawing the line..34
       b) Dean Rusk's testimony......................................37
    6. THE EMERGENCE OF TWO GOVERNMENTS........40
       a) The Emergence of the Republic of Korea....................40
       b) The Emergence of North Korea Regime (DPRK)...........42

  CHAPTER II THE OUTBREAK OF THE KOREAN WAR....................48
    1. THE SOVIET UNION, CHINA AND THE KORAN
       CONFLICT..48
    2. SECRET LETTERS OF USSR FOREIGN MINISTRY 51
    3. THE TESTIMONY OF NORTH KOREAN GENERAL
       YU SUNG-CHOL...56
    4. NORTH KOREA'S WAR PREPARATION..................57
    5. DEAN ACHESON'S SPEECH............................59
    6. STALIN'S APPROVAL.................................60
    7. N. KOREAN FORCES ATTACKED S. KOREA...........62
    8. U.S. RESPONSE TO N. KOREAN AGGRESSION......67
       a) President Truman's Decision................................67

    b) United Nation..69

    c) General MacArthur did an on-site Inspection..............70

  9. FALL OF SEOUL......................................71

  10. NORTH KOREAN FORCES SQUANDERED THREE DAYS IN SEOUL...................................74

  11. MASS SLAUGHTER OF POLITICAL OPPONENTS 75

  12. U.S. FORCES ENTERED THE KOREAN CONFLICT 77

    a) The Smith Task Force and Daejon Battle.....................77

    b) General Dean's missing.......................................79

  13. INCHON AMPHIBIOUS LANDING..............82

  14. RE-CAPTURE OF SEOUL.........................84

  15. UN FORCES ADVANCED TO 38ᵀᴴ PARALLEL........87

  16. WAKE ISLAND CONFERENCE..................89

  17. KIM IL-SUNG ASKED URGENT HELP TO STALIN 92

  18. CHINESE WARNING.............................93

CHAPTER II The Chinese Intervention....................96

  1. UN FORCES CROSS THE 38ᵀᴴ PARALLEL...............96

  2. CHINESE VOLUNTEER ARMY CROSSED THE AMROK RIVER..97

  3. CHINESE ARMY OFFENSIVE....................102

  4. TRUMAN SUGGESTED THE USE OF ATOMIC BOMB..108

  5. THE CHOSIN BATTLE AND THE HUNGNAM WITHDRAWAL OPERATION......................109

  6. MACARTHUR WANTS TO EXPAND THE WAR......113

  7. THE WAR OF ATTRITION.........................114

  8. GENERAL RIDGWAY'S WAR....................115

  9. KOREAN WAR COULD BE ENDED IN THREE MONTHS..118

  10. GENERAL MACARTHUR SACKED.............121

  11. MAO AND VAN FLEET LOST THEIR SONS.........124

CHAPTER IV Armistice Talk.............................129

  1. ARMISTICE TALK PROPOSAL..................129

  2. REPATRIATION OF POWS.......................131

  3. CONCLUSION OF ARMISTICE..................133

  4. THE GAIN AND LOSS OF THE WAR PARTICIPANT COUNTRIES...136

    a) North Korea (People's Republic of Korea)..................136
    b. South Korea (Republic of Korea).......................138
    c. United Sates.......................................139
    d. China (People's Republic of China)...................142
    e. Soviet Union......................................142
    f. Japan...143
  5. CONSEQUENCES OF THE KOREAN WAR............144

PART III Koje-do UN POW Camp............................150
CHAPTER I Drafted to North Korean Army.....................150
  1. THE OUTBREAK OF KOREAN CONFLICT........150
  2. DRAFTED TO NORTH KOREAN ARMY..............152
  3. FINAL FAREWELL TO MY MOTHER.................153
  4. ADMISSION TO N. KOREAN ARMY OFFICERS
    SCHOOL.......................................157
  5. THE UN FORCES CAPTURES PYONGYANG........159
  6. SURRENDER TO THE U.S. ARMY......................161
CHAPTER II The Beginning of my POW Life...................167
  1. MOVE TO PYONGYANG PRISON...................167
  2. JAPANESE HELLISH CARGO SHIP................169
  3. BUSAN POW CAMPS............................170
    a) Seomyon Compound............................170
    b) Busan Koje-ri POW Compound...................172
    c) Call from Camp Headquarters...................176
  4. BECOME POW LEADER............................178
  5. MOVE TO KOJE-DO POW COMPOUND.................179
  6. EXODUS FROM THE RED 76TH COMPOUND........180
  7. MOVE TO 83RD COMPOUND..........................181
CHAPTER III The Truce Meeting and POW Camps.............184
  1. OUTSET OF THE TRUCE CONFERENCE.............184
  2. THE REPATRIATION OF POW ISSUE...................187
  3. SGT COON'S SURPRISE OFFER.....................192
  4. YI, BECAME THE C.I.C INFORMANT...............192
  5. YI'S ANTI-COMMUNIST COUP D'ÉTAT (ROD
    COUP)...193
  6. CONCILIATION OF POWS...........................194
    a) North Korea's Appeasement....................194

b) UN's Conciliation..............196
7. WOMEN POW COMPOUND................196
CHAPTER IV Interesting Stories in POW Camps................198
a) Grandfather and his Grandson....................198
b) Woman Company commander....................200
c) Volunteer Soldier and His Horse....................202
d) The Civil Service Agent Choi....................204
2. A STORY OF ROKA DROP-OUT POW....................206
a) ROK Army retreated by the Chinese Voluntary Army..206
b) Execution of Chinese POW....................209
CHAPTER V Pro And Anti-Communist POW Camps:............212
1. PRO-COMMUNIST CAMPS................212
2. CLASH BETWEEN POW AND ROK ARMY SECURITY GUARDS................213
3. UNLUCKY N. KOREAN ARMY COLONEL LEE, HAK-KOO................214
4. COMPOUND 62 RIOT (2:18 RIOT)................216
5. RIOTS AT 76TH, 77TH, 78TH RED COMPOUNDS........218
6. POWS SEIZED GENERAL DODD, CAMP COMMANDER................218
7. SCREENING OF PRO AND ANTI-COMMUNIST POWS................223
8. AT THE SCENE OF SEGREGATION SITE................225
9. MASSACRE IN THE 83RD COMPOUND....................227
10. THE STALEMATE OF THE POW REPATRIATION ISSUE................231
11. 76TH RED COMPOUND RIOT................233
CHAPTER VI Repatriation of POWs....................235
1. EXCHANGE OF SICK AND WOUNDED POWS......235
2. ZHOU EN-LAI'S NEW PROPOSAL................236
3. RHEE RELEASED ANTI-COMMUNIST POWS......238
4. POWs ISSUE................242
5. THE FINAL POW REPATRIATION AT THE PANMUNJOM................245

PREFACE

In Korean modern history, it may be safe to say that the Korea's most tragic event was the Japanese armed invasion and colonization of the Korean Peninsula., The tragic Korean War mainly caused by the division of Korea into north and south. After the World War II, Korea was liberated from the Japanese colony by two super powers, the United States and the Soviet Union. But unfortunately they divided into two parts North and South at the 38th parallel. Accordingly, the Soviet army stationed in the north and the US Army stationed in the South Korea. They had established two different ideological governments; the North was Socialistic Communism and the South was Capitalistic Democracy. The Korean Conflict which started on June 25, 1950, mainly caused by the division of the Korean peninsula and formation of two different political governments formed in the North and the South.

The United States and the Soviet Union, two major powers of the post World War II, had a political showdown for the world's hegemony over capitalistic democracy and socialistic communism. The Korean peninsular was destined to the fate of a shrimp caught in the battle of whales, as the old Korean proverb.

After the Second World War, communism spread rapidly all over the world especially in Eastern Europe and Asian pacific area. Under these circumstances, the North Korean Army attacked South Korea in an attempt to unify the peninsula under Kim Il-sung's control. Subsequently the United States armed forces entered the conflict to stop the North Korean army's invasion. The sixteen countries joined the United Nation's Army fought against North Korean army and the Korean civil war eventually became an international global conflict.

United States president Truman then made a prompt resolution to stop the Soviet expansion throughout the far eastern countries, especially after Chinese Communists won the civil war and established the communistic state just one year ago in September 1949. The war which Kim Il Sung launched to unify the Korean peninsula did not bring about his intended object, like the Syngman Rhee and MacArthur did subsequently.

The Korean War was the first military conflict of the Cold War, and in a sense, the Korean War was a miniature of World War, in which military forces from seventeen anti-Communist nations (including South Korea) fought against the North Korea and the Chinese Communist. The figure rises if we count those UN members who sent Medical units and ships to Korea. In addition, we must take into account those non-belligerent countries, such as Soviet Union, Japan, West Germany, Formosa and other countries. In this sense, the Korean War was a miniature of the world war. In spite of its limited nature, the Korean War was tremendously destructive. Korea's industrial base was wiped out and several millions people killed by the war. There was great suffering and sacrifices of the Korean people by the global Cold War. I want to describe my experiences of the Korean War and a POW life with various stories for the readers interested in the tragic Korean War without any political prejudice and bias.

The Korean War is now called "the forgotten war" among the American people and I want to make the forgotten war as "the memorable war." As a witness of the Korean War, intend to describe in detail how the war started, who started first, the process of three (3) years of fierce battles. I hope to help readers to understand more in detail about the Korean War.

On the occasion of 62nd anniversary of Korean War this year, I want to pray for the souls of the soldiers of all related countries and the Korean civilians who were killed in the Korean War. I honor the memory of those who were killed in the War. May their Soils rest in peace in Heaven!.

PART I

OVERVIEW OF THE KOREAN WAR

On August 15, 1945, Korea was liberated from the Japanese colonial occupation at the end of World War II. However, unfortunately Korea was divided into two parts North and South at the 38th parallel line by the two superpowers, the United States and the Soviet Union. The Soviet Union occupied above the 38th parallel and below that line by the United States. Consequently the Korea was divided politically and ideologically, and two different governments established in the North and the South Korea, by the support of the United States and the Soviet Union.

On a drizzling Sunday, at 4 am, on 25 June 1950, North Korean army launched a full-scale invasion across the 38th parallel into South Korea.

Dean Acheson, the Secretary of State, informed the North Korea's attack to President Harry S. Truman. He did not hesitate. He took prompt action by approving a proposal for an emergency meeting of the United Nations Security Council. The Security Council quickly met the next day and approved a U.S. resolution which demanded for the end of hostilities and the withdrawal of North Korean forces above the 38th parallel. Over the next three days, as the North Korean army continued to advance further to South and captured Seoul, South Korean capital, in three days. President Truman immediately instructed General Douglas MacArthur in Tokyo, Japan, to supply South Korean forces with ammunition and equipment. On 26 June Truman then authorized MacArthur to use U.S. air and naval units against North Korean targets. Next day, he extended the range of those targets to include those in North Korea. He also authorized the use of U.S. ground forces. On 30 June, after MacArthur had gone to Korea to assess the situation, Truman authorized MacArthur to use all of his available forces to repel the invasion. On June 30, he authorized the sending of a regimental combat team to Korea. Since then, over the next three years, total of 1.4 million American soldiers served as part of a United Nations Command, fought against North Korean and Chinese voluntary forces in a conflict that dramatically changed the complexion of the Cold War, between United States and the Soviet Union.

On January 12, 1950, Acheson had described in his speech at the National Press Club in Washington that Korean peninsula was out the part of U.S. defense perimeter in East Asia and stated that the U.S. defense perimeter line was from Leukyu island-Japan-Okinawa-Philippine and Taiwan, excluding Korea. His speech might give the North Korean Communists an impression that the American forces might not enter the Korean civil war when they would attack the South Korea.

After Japanese surrendered on August 15, 1950, the American occupation forces under the command of Lt. General John Hodge landed in September 10, 1945. General Hodge did not recognize any political group including the "Shanghai exiled Korean provisional government" led by popular Korean nationalist Kim Koo as the legitimate government of Korea. Instead he established an American military government. Disturbed by the political and social chaos he found in Korea, Hodge was soon working closely with Dr. Syngman Rhee, rightist Korean nationalist who had spent most of his adult life in the Untied States working for Korean independence. He received a doctor degree at the Princeton University. Hodge believed that Rhee could do the best chance to restore order and stability in the South Korea. But Rhee's goal of immediate Korean independence conflicted with American policy.

At the Cairo Conference of 1943, U.S. President Franklin Roosevelt, Stalin of Soviet Union, Winston Churchill of Great Britain, Chiang Kai-shek of China declared that "in due course Korea shall become free and independent." The Potsdam Conference of July 1945 re-affirmed the Cairo statement. But what Roosevelt had in mind at Cairo was a multi-power trusteeship, which would include the United States, the Soviet Union, Great Britain and China and which could last up to forty years. He did not think that Korea was ready for immediate independence after the war. After Truman took office in 1945, he adopted the basic outlines of Roosevelt's policy for Korea.

At the Moscow meeting of foreign ministers in December 1945, both the United States and the Soviet Union agreed to an American proposal providing for the election of a provisional government and the establishment of a trusteeship lasting for as long as five years. A joint Soviet-American commission was established to prepare Korean election of the provisional government. But all the Koreans opposed the proposed five year trusteeship and demanded an immediate independence. The five year trusteeship did not have friendly sentiment to the Korean people who wanted the immediate independence after the release of 35 years of Japanese colony. Koreans made fierce demonstration throughout Korea. Although the commission met several times, Korean election for the establishment of a provisional government were never held. Even more importantly the failure of the election made the hardening of relations between Washington and Moscow. The United States and the Soviet Union had been at odds with each other politically and ideologically since Bolshevik revolution since 1917.

At this juncture, the United States wrote about the need to contain Soviet expansionism. This doctrine of containment became the basis of the "get tough" policy that President Truman adopted toward the Soviet Union by the spring of 1946; it was also the foundation of American foreign policy throughout most of the Cold War. The onset of the Cold War directly affected developments in Korea. American policy within the South Korea became one of supporting rightist elements and limiting leftist political activity. Several Korean nationalist and leftist members were killed by assassins. Among them were popular nationalist Kim Koo, Yeo Woon Hyoung and Jang Deok Su, Song Jin-woo, An Jae Hong, etc,.

In May 10, 1948, the election was held only in South Korea under the auspice of the United Nations, and three months later the newly established legislative assembly elected Dr. Rhee as the first president of the Republic of Korea (ROK). Four month later, a separate regime, the Democratic People's Republic of Korea (DPRK), led by Kim Il-sung, was established in the north, on September 9, 1950, but the United Nations declared the South Korean government as the lawful government in the Korean peninsula.

During the two years that followed, political situation in South Korea remained very unstable. Civil war raged in South Korea as political leftists engaged in various guerrilla activities in the mountains like Jiri-san and Odae san, with the support of the North Koreans.

In the meantime, the Communists victory in China would certainly be encouraged Kim Il-sung's ambition to unify the country militarily under his control. Meanwhile, Kim had built a military force outfitted by the Soviet Union and made plan for an invasion of South Korea for the unification of Korean peninsula. He and his vice Premier Pak Hon Yong made first visit to Moscow in September 1949, and again in April 1950 to get permission of his plan for an invasion. In April's visit, Stalin finally agreed to the invasion under the condition that South Korea should be defeated within a month as Kim assured him.

The North Korean forces' attack on June 25 was a smashing success. The North Korean army had captured the South Korean capital Seoul in three days. When North Korea attacked South Korea, President Truman felt that he had little choice other than a military response. President and his administration officials believed that North Korea was merely serving as a proxy for the Soviet Union for their worldwide expansion strategy.

The United States was committed to resurrecting Japan as a major power in East Asia to cope with the Soviet-Chinese power. The loss of Korea to the communists would pose a real danger to Japan located next to Korean peninsula.

The North Korean forces continued their advance defeating the ROK army and American forces. By mid-August 1950, the North Koreans captured almost 90% of the South Korean territory. The only part of Korea not captured by the North Koreans was Daegu and Busan. On September 15, UN forces successfully conducted an amphibious landing operation at Inchon port, about 25 miles west of Seoul. About the same time UN forces broke out of the defense perimeter line established around Daegu and Busan. It was the moment of the shift for the US and ROK Army to offensive from the defensive.

By the end of September, Seoul had been retaken, and the North Korean army had retreated north of the 38th parallel. Had the UN Command forces been ordered to stop at the 38th parallel, and if it did not cross the 38th parallel, the United States would have been able to declare victory in the Korean War at the time. And the Korean War would be ended in three months instead of three years of fierce battle. There was no Chinese forces entered the Korean War at the time.

General MacArthur dismissed the Chinese entry and continued the UN march northward, even promising on November 24 to have American troops home for Christmas. Two days later, the Chinese struck in massive numbers against the overextended UN troop, inflicting heavy casualties, what military historian 'Roy Appleman' has called "one of the worst defeats an American army has ever suffered." At the end of January, the Eighth U.S. Army had withdrawn more than 300 miles, the longest retreat in American military history. Once more the South Korean capital of Seoul was in the enemy's hands on January 4, 1951. Instead of having as its objective the liberation of North Korea from communist control, the purpose of the war returned to the original one of Keeping South Korea from falling to the north Korean communists.

The Chinese offensive, however, had not been an unqualified success for the Chinese. As the Chinese advanced below Seoul, they faced an increasing barrage of artillery fire and air raids, which took a heavy toll on them. Their supply lines also grew thin, and they began to run out of supplies. U.S. Air force jets and bombers provided indispensable ground support for troops fighting along the front line. Despite the Chinese intervention into the war, General Douglas MacArthur had continued to oppose strongly President Truman administration's policy. On April 11, 1951, Truman relieved him of all his commands after House Minority Leader Joseph W. Martin made public a message in which the general publicly challenged the president's foreign policy. (Refer to Part III, Chapter IV, article 9, MacArthur sacked, for more detail)

In March 1951, when UN forces were driving the communists once more out of most of South Korea, President Truman had planned to announce that the UNC was ready to enter into armistice talks. The president was under great pressure from America's European allies, especially from England, to launch a peace initiative. With the war having reached a military stalemate by June, and still under great pressure both at home and abroad to end the conflict, the White house decided to try to get armistice talks started using quiet diplomacy. The talk, which began on July 10, stretched over two more years at the small village of Panmunjom about five miles east of Kaesong. Many occasions, the negotiations were broke off by the UN and/ or Communist negotiators because of lack of progress or alleged violation of the neutral zone where the negotiations were taking place.

Although the bargaining was hard, most of the issues were settled expeditiously. But the only issue that held up signing of a truce agreement was the issue of the repatriation of prisoner of war (POW). The communist negotiators insisted that all POWs should be repatriated all for all, as provided by the Geneva Convention of 1949, which called for quick and compulsory repatriation of all POWs at the end of a war. The Truman administration was determined that no prisoners should be forced to return against their will, insisting the voluntary repatriation. For President Truman, the issue of returning POWs was a moral issue.

However, both sides finally agreed the anti-communist POWs not wanting to be repatriated would be given to a Neutral Nations Supervisory Commission for 90 days to make their decision. This issue delayed armistice agreement almost two years. On June 18, 1953, the Korean president Rhee abruptly released 25,000 anti-communist POWs under his control without an approval of UN command. The communist negotiators made a strong protest and demanded to re-intern them immediately. The Chinese troops attacked only the South Korean's positions in retaliation for release of the anti-communist POWs. As the result, both side lost more number of their soldiers than 30,000 POWs released.

On July 27, at Panmunjom, the truce agreement was signed by both sides and the Korean conflict which lasted three years one month two days was ended. The negotiators had agreed to hold a political conference to discuss a Peace treaty and Korean unification within 30 days. But the meeting, which was held in June 1954 in Geneva, became quickly deadlocked. No agreement was ever reached, and Korea remains a divided nation North and South for 67 years for now and still remains technically at war. The peace treaty would be only solution for the peace of the Korean peninsula and for the solution of the North Korean nuclear program. The 1950-1953 Korean conflict ended with an armistice, not a peace treaty and another Korean War could be destined to break out at any time by either side. (For further detail on Korean War, Please read Part II, III)

PART II

THE ORIGIN OF THE KOREAN WAR

CHAPTER I

HISTORICAL BACKGROUND OF KOREAN CONFLICT

1. JAPANESE COLONIZATION OF KOREAN PENINSULA

Korea known as "The land of Morning Calm" is one of the oldest nations in the world. Its history began five (5) millennia ago when the early settlers formed tribal societies in the Korean peninsula. It consists of the peninsula that separates the East sea of Korea from the West sea, and the Korean peninsula located geographically like a land bridge between the Asian continent and Japan, thereby Korea always possessed a great strategic geopolitical significance. Its neighbors are the three big powers of East Asia; Japan to the east, Russia to the north east, and China to the north and west. Korea was and is one of those nations with the misfortune to lie at a crossroads of world power politics, repeatedly stomped over, brutalized, and occupied by the strong neighbors. In Korea's instance, the perpetual antagonists were China, Japan and Russia. When the Japanese launched their periodic imperialistic adventure on the Asian mainland, Korea was the most convenient invasion route, served as a geographic bridge located between Japan and China. As an ancient Korean

proverb accurately laments, "A shrimp is crushed in the battle of the big whales."

Due to the defeat of the British-Chinese Opium War, Chinese national strength fell into a decline to a considerable extent, and thereby its influence on the Korean peninsula was much diminished. The Korean peninsula then turned into an arena of politics of imperialism as the powers immediately surrounding the peninsula, such as Japan and Russia. However, Japanese succeeded in getting a treaty with Korea in 1876 opening Korean ports and providing for diplomatic relations, and that proved to be the fatal foot in the door. Japan was determined to replace China as the paramount power in the yellow sea area.

Japan's imperial expansion gained momentum in 1890s. The Sino-Japanese War of 1894-95 was a direct result of rivalry between the two powers for control of the Korean peninsula. The efforts made by Koreans to modernize their country and to preserve the independence of their nation could not achieve their goals. To make matters worse at the time, the Korean politics divided into two factions and the parties argued and dispute each other between pro-Japanese and pro-Russian faction. In 1904, Japan won the Russo-Japanese War. The war was officially ended by the Treaty of Portsmouth, and it explicitly acknowledged Japan's predominant interest in Korea and its right to intervene in the internal matters of the country. Japan consequently annexed Korea and Korea became a victim of Japanese imperialism, suffering in many years under the humiliating Japanese colonial rule for 35 years. There were widespread up-risings, and guerrilla war against the Japanese occupiers that went for years. On March 1, 1919, there was a large scale rebellion throughout the Korean peninsula, demanding freedom and independence, but the Japanese imperialist put it down with extreme brutality. However, none of these resistances worked out. Korean people were suffering badly until the Japanese imperialist offender was defeated by the US Army and Soviet Union Army in the Pacific War. Thanks to the United State and Soviet army and people of the both countries. However, they divided Korea at 38th parallel, that eventually caused the miserable Korean War.

2. THE YALTA CONFERENCE AND KOREAN PENINSULA

February 4, 1945, when Roosevelt, Winston Churchill, and Stalin, met in Yalta in the Russian Crimean coast of the Black Sea, to consult the solution of Germany problems and treatment of the spear of influence after the World War II. The atomic bomb was far from ready to be tested, and although a successful test would be made sometime in the summer. But there was neither any guarantee that the bomb would work nor a consensus about how quickly the war would be ended. For one thing, there was much disappointment over how powerful the bomb would prove to be. And the simple fact was that allied military planners couldn't afford to base their strategy on an untried weapon. They had to be prepared for the worst-possible-case scenario, which predicted that Germany might hold out until the end of the year and that Japan might be able to fight on for as long as another year and a half after the German defeat until the middle of 1947. The allied plan called for a primarily American force to undertake an amphibious invasion of the Japanese home islands, beginning early in November 1945. Japanese would fight to their last drop of blood to defend their home and it estimates of probable Allied casualties ranged as high as one million. The allied planners' worst fear was that the Japanese Kwangtung Army, which was occupying Manchuria, might be transferred to the defense of the home islands. American intelligence believed that this army numbered upward of seven hundred thousand troops and was extremely well equipped. As early as November 1944, the American Joint Chiefs of Staff had prepared a report stating that to prevent such a transfer the Soviet Union must engage the Kwngtung Army in Manchuria at least three months before the Allied invasion of Japan was scheduled to begin. That meant that Soviet would have to declare war on Japan and launch their attack on Manchuria early in August. At Yalta, Stalin promised Roosevelt that the Soviet would enter the war against Japan within three months after Germany's surrender.

From the outset of the Pacific War against Japan, General MacArthur wrote a letter and urged Washington superior to find a way to persuade Russia to enter the Pacific war. On December 10, 1941, only three days after Pearl Harbor, MacArthur sent a pleading cable to General George C. Marshal, the army chief of staff, from his headquarters in the Philippine.

In February 1945, General MacArthur himself again felt that it was absolutely essential to get the Russians to promise to take on the Japanese Kwangtung Army. MacArthur was thus willing to see Russia rewarded for its services with far more than Roosevelt had just promised Stalin at Yalta. He was even willing to let the Russians have Korea. In their November 1944 report, the Joint War Department Intelligence officer asserted that Japanese strength were such that Russian intervention was imperative. The Joint Chiefs' estimate was that the Pacific war would last eighteen months beyond the collapse of Germany and that allied casualties would be reduced by 200,000 men if the Soviets entered the war before the U.S. forces invasion of Japan. Chiefs of Staff had observed that self-interest would "inevitably bring the Soviet Union into the war in Asia sooner or later". At the Teheran, two years earlier, Stalin had promised vaguely to enter the Pacific war at proper time." Now the JCS urged that Roosevelt hold him to the pledge.

But there were considerable grounds for wondering whether even Soviet Union had the power to rally its devastated and exhausted nation to take on the Japanese. Perhaps as many as twenty million Russian soldiers and civilians had died in the war against Germany and thousands of Russian towns and villages had been completely destroyed by flow of the battle; and the nation's agricultural and industrial productivity had been decimated.

It was, however, precisely the ruination of European side of Russia that made Stalin so determined to develop Soviet power in Asia. Manchuria and Korea constituted one of the world's greatest industrial, agricultural, and transportation complexes, and this valuable region was already connected to Siberia and western Russia by the Trans-Siberian Railway. Stalin's dream was to incorporate Siberia, Manchuria and Korea into a single great economic system that could sustain the Soviet Union while its western areas recovered from the war. Siberia remained a largely undeveloped frontier whose stupendous mineral resources could be effectively exploited after the war only if the Soviets had unlimited access to the factories, the food supplies, and the ice-free ports of southern Manchuria and Korea.

Russia had suffered so grievously in the west, during World War II, Stalin set his sights on the East for the resurrection of the prostrated Soviet nation. But he could make the necessary gains in the East only if the Soviet Union contributed to the defeat of Japan. Russia's horrendous suffering by the German invasion put Stalin in an excellent position for bargaining with his allies at Yalta. Stalin declared the war against Japan for only the last week of Second World War. An atomic bomb was dropped on Hiroshima on August 6, 1945, and on the tenth the Japanese offered to surrender under the condition that the emperor be allowed to remain in power. President Truman was prepared to agree to that condition but could not do so explicitly, since the American public wanted an unconditional surrender, and majority of American wanted the emperor to be deposed and tried as a war criminal. Japan announced its surrender on the 15th August, 1945. The war was over, but the role in Far Eastern Asia affairs to which Stalin's declaration of war against Japan entitled him. His hasty occupation of Manchuria and northern Korea by his troops led to the Korean war five years later.

At the Yalta conference, Stalin promised that the Soviet Union would enter the war against Japan in return for four (4) major concessions:

1) Outer Mongolia would remain a Soviet satellite, independent of China.

2) Sovereignty over the Kuril Islands and the southern half of Sakhalin Island (both lying north of Japan and offshore from Siberia, Sakhalin having been divided between Russia and Japan since 1905) would be transferred from Japan to the Soviet Union.

3) A joint Sino-Soviet company would be formed to manage the Manchurian railways; and

4) The commercial port of Dairen, terminus of the South Manchurian branch of the Trans-Siberian Railway, would be internationalized, and the Soviet Union would be permitted to lease neighboring Port Arthur as a naval base from China.

Although many historians and politicians have expressed outrage over Roosevelt's having "sold China down the river" at Yalta. But Roosevelt was pleased because he felt that the agreement formally and clearly limited the Soviet Union to a minor role in Asia while promising to spare the United States hundreds thousands of casualties.

To the Roosevelt inner circle, such a saving of life warranted the political risks inherent in giving the Soviets an opportunity for expansion into Japanese held areas. To the State Department officials planning the Yalta Conference, Korea was to be a bargaining pawn. According to Yalta planning papers, U.S. was willing to share postwar occupation of Korea with Great Britain, China and the USSR (provided it entered the Pacific war). But the papers stressed that the United States should play a leading role in the occupation and military government. But it had no long-range interest in Korea; what it wished was a buffer against any Russian thrust against Japan. (Extract from "Korea and Yalta" written by Richard Whelan).

Once again the Korea became a "shrimp was caught between the whales."

3. THE JAPANESE' DEFEAT AND KOREAN LIBERATION

Talking about the Korean War, it is deemed necessary to evaluate the cause and origin of the conflict. As we all have known the fact that the Japan conducted the surprise attack on Pearl Harbor in Hawaii and the pacific war started between the United States and Japan. But following the German surrender on May 8, 1945, and having suffered a string of defeats in the South pacific islands, such as Philippines, Okinawa, Iwo Jima and in China by the US forces. Japan turned to

Moscow to mediate an end to the Pacific war. However, Soviet leader Joseph Stalin had already secretly promised Washington and London that he would attack Japan within three months of Germany's defeat. He thus ignored Japan's plea, and mobilized 1.6 million troops along Manchuria and North Korean borders. August 7, 1950, United States dropped an atomic bomb in Hiroshima and inflicted heavy casualties and property damages. At this time, the Soviet Union declared the war against Japan and 1.6 million troops started to attack the Japanese Kwangdung army stationed in Manchuria, and Korea. The soviet forces landing on Rajin and Chongjin, North Korea, and advanced south with overwhelming power. 12,000 Soviet soldiers died in two weeks of fighting. The Soviet troops ended up just 30 miles from Japan's main northern island, Hokkaido. Consequently Japan surrendered unconditionally to the United States and Soviet forces under one condition that they wanted to preserve the royal family. Consequently, the Korea was finally liberated from Japanese Colonial rule after 35 years.

On September 10, 1945, General MacArthur, the Supreme Commander of the U.S. forces of the Pacific has received the Japanese surrender on a U.S. Navy ship in Tokyo Bay. After 65 years later, in recent years some historians including history professor at University of California, Santa Barbara, and Hasegawa Tsuyoshi, a Russian speaking American scholar have argued that the Soviet surprise attack on the Japanese army occupying eastern Asia served as effectively with the dropping of atomic bombs in ending the war. The impact of the lightning Soviet advance comes through in the words of Japan's wartime prime minister, Kantaro Suzuki, urging his cabinet to surrender. Dominic Lieven, a professor of Russian at the London school of Economics, said anti-Soviet sentiment in the West tended to minimize Soviet military achievements.

As a result of Japanese defeat, the Korea was liberated but was unfortunately divided into two parts, North and South, at the 38th parallel arbitrarily by the United States and Soviet Union. At first, it was intended to be no more than a temporary and facilitative demarcation line, simply for the purpose of disarming the Japanese troops and accepting their surrender, and not in sense a political boundary. As a result, Soviet troops were stationed in the North and U.S. troops in the South, thereby, two different political systems of government formed respectively in the South and North Korea. This is considered to be the main factor that contributed to the Korean conflict. With the close of World War II, Koreans were looking forward to their long cherished dream of independence. The Koreans were simply ecstatically happy to see the last of the hated Japanese occupiers. At the time, they have jumped and danced up and down with great joy all over the Korea, celebrating their liberation. But they never expect and even thought of their forthcoming national tragedy due to the separation of the Korean peninsula. After 35 years of Japanese occupation, they did not want any more of it. However, seeds of dissension were already sprouting because of the division. No one could ever predict the future at the time that the Korean War would occur within five years because of the division and two different ideological governments.

I was born in Hamhung city located in the north east coast of Korean peninsula. I was an 8th grade middle school boy at that time. I still remember that I joined and followed the crowd who fervently welcomed Soviet troops. They were air transported to Hamhung air field and there I saw for the first time in my life the mysterious Soviet army who had different features than Koreans and Japanese. It was very strange and amazing for me to see the tall westerners with high noses and yellow hair! Their military discipline appeared to be very relaxed compared to the strict disciplined Japanese army. The private soldiers were freely talking with high ranking officers and hugged women soldiers, which the Japanese armies were never allowed to do so. The Soviet army officer's insignia of rank looked to me more stylish and splendid than the Japanese army's and that impressed me at that time. Anyway, we all welcomed the Soviet troops by showing our "thumbs up" and greet them saying "Harosho, Harosho" means "good/wonderful" and they greeted back to us saying "Haroshio." Anyway, that was my first impression of the Soviet soldier's outward appearance.

At the Yalta Conference in February 1945, Roosevelt and Stalin discussed the Korean question only briefly and informally. Roosevelt made the point at that time that because Korea had been under Japanese rule for long time, the Koreans had very little political experience and would need a period of tutelage. This should be supplied by a trusteeship government composed of representative of U.S., Soviet, Britain and China. This government would acquaint the Korean people with the principles and procedures of democracy and would train Korean politicians and administrators, who, as they gained experience, would gradually assume more and more responsibility. Roosevelt cited as his paradigm the American "tutelage of the Philippines", which had lasted more than fifty years, since the Spanish-American War. After forty years of American colonial rule, the Philippines had been allowed to set up a republic government in 1935, with the understanding that the new government would remain under close American supervision for another ten (10) more years; at the end of this time the nation would be granted full independence. Since the Koreans are somewhat more advanced than the Filipinos had been in 1898, the trusteeship over Korea would not have to last longer than about twenty to thirty years. According to US Ambassador 'Averel Harriman', Stalin replied that in his opinion, the period of trusteeship should be as brief as possible.

Indeed, Stalin said, he really didn't see any need for a trusteeship at all, since the Koreans would be perfectly capable of governing themselves once their nation had been liberated from the Japanese. Harriman took this to mean that Stalin assumed the Koreans, left on their own, would form a Communist government friendly to the Soviet Union. That was precisely what Roosevelt wanted to prevent and place the government friendly to the United States. His conception of trusteeship for Korea was based on the assumption that the United States, supported by Britain and China, would dominate the arrangement and would thus be in a position to direct Korean policy until such time as the Koreans themselves had adopted American ways and could be trusted to act consistently in a manner optimally favorable to American interests, which would in turn greatly benefit Korea. Once the Soviets had occupied Korea, they would never allow a four-power trusteeship to be set up. Korea would, instead, become yet another Soviet satellite. The American goal, then, was to keep the Russians out of Korea, or at least out as much as possible.

Unfortunately, American troops were so exhausted and depleted, and so dispersed over vast areas of the Pacific, that no substantial forces could possibly be hastily dispatched to Korea. Indeed, the American Joint Chief of Staff, estimated that it might be the end of September—more than six weeks away—before they could send any troops at all to occupy even part of Korea. The United States, at the time, had no intention whatsoever of fighting the Japanese Army in Korea, and Washington had hoped only that once Japan had surrendered, American troops could swiftly occupy all of Korea before the Russians had a no chance to move in, but the Soviet forces had already attack the Japanese forces. If once the United States was firmly in control, then perhaps the Russians could be allowed to assume their subsidiary role in the four-power trusteeship. The United States didn't really want anything to do with Korea except to prevent the Russians from occupying the entire Korean peninsula and installing a Communist puppet government.

The United States was not wrong in wanting to prevent entire Korean peninsula from becoming a Soviet satellite.

4. THE COLD WAR BETWEEN TWO SUPERPOWERS

After the Second World War, the United States and Soviet Union were the two remaining great super powers. The USA and its allies, known as the West, promoted American style democracy and capitalism, while the Soviet Union and its supporters countries sought to expand so called socialism and communism. Therefore, their interests began to contradict each other in the postwar world. With the declaration of the Truman Doctrine in 1947, the USA adopted a policy of containment: opposing Communist expansion in the world. US President Harry Truman implemented the Truman Doctrine, which stated that the USA would oppose aggression against democratic countries. This was the basis of the containment policy that guided American diplomacy. NATO (North Atlantic Treaty Organization) was established in 1948, to defend Western Europe against possible Soviet aggression. Nevertheless, the degree of the Soviet threat was not clear and become reality. Therefore, the West had not undertaken significant military preparations to confront Soviet or Communist expansionism. Actually, the most western people were fascinated by and enjoying the victory of the Second World War. NATO was only a skeletal organization without the conventional and nuclear strength that would be associated with it later in the Cold War. The Republican Congress had drastically cut American defense expenditure at less than 3 percent of the gross domestic product (GDP), and the American armed forces were also in a low state of combat readiness.

The Cold War represented a new military situation as well as a new international one. After 1945, warfare underwent a revolution. Before 1945, most wars had been fought with the goal of decisively annihilating an enemy's armed forces. Warfare continued until one side unconditionally surrendered. After 1945, such total warfare became prohibitively costly.

There were three basic reasons for this. First, the advent of atomic weapons multiplied the destructiveness of warfare. Therefore, seeking a total victory became a very dangerous endeavor when an opponent might use atomic or nuclear weapons if faced with a major defeat on the battlefield.

Second, the First and Second World Wars showed conventional warfare was an exhausting affair. Third, even small country's conflicts were often of concern to the superpowers. Therefore, there was a risk that any conflict involving a superpower or one of its allies could escalate into a Third World War.

Ever since the Russian Proletariat revolution, the Democratic and capitalistic system of the Western Europe and North American states had been opposed by the totalitarian approach adopted by the Communists in the Soviet Union.

Lenin in Russia had preached world revolution, and his successor, Joseph Stalin, had combined the revolutionary claims of Communism with traditional Russian expansionism and fear of its neighbors. The basic antagonism of these two social systems had been submerged by the common danger of Nazi Germany, and the temporary necessity of alliance to defeat Hitler's Germany and his followers in World War II. Under the stress of that cataclysm, Russia and the West had helped each other survive. However, once the menace was removed, the old differences surfaced again, and within a tragically short time after 1945, it was obvious that the world had entered on old and dangerous paths once more.

In fact, they were even more perilous in the late forties than they had been in the thirties. For now most of the earlier players had been swept from the board; now instead of a series of "great powers" and potential balances among them, there were really only two, the "Superpowers," the United States and the Soviet Union. Great Britain, France, Italy, Germany, Japan, and China were all pale shadows of their former selves, reduced to satellites of the two giants. Not only that, but the two remaining states possessed, if they chose to use it, power that was immense even by the standards of the mid-twentieth century: The Russian had the greatest armed forces in the world, and the United States had the atomic bomb.

Korea was but a small part of this, far less important to either than events in Europe or in China, but very much influenced by what was happening elsewhere.

In Europe, disagreements surfaced even before the end of World War II.

The former colonial countries mere struggle for survival released most of their colonies. From India all the way around to Korea, there was disruption and discord. India wanted the British to get out, and became independent in 1947;

Burma became a republic 1948, the British Malaya and the Indonesia, fought against the Dutch and in 1946 in Indochina, the returning French, later replaced by the Americans, got involved in a full-scale war with Ho Chi Minh.

All of these events were bad enough for the colonial powers. In the late forties the worst was what happened to China, There the

Nationalist government of Chiang Kai-shek had waged a long bitter, and sometimes hopeless struggle against the Japanese, and Mao's Communist forces. The nationalists already worn down, driven by corruption and internal dissension, could not stand before the Communists despite American efforts first to mediate and then to help them. By the end of 1947 the communists held all of Manchuria in the north; by 1948 Chiang was clearly failing. Most Chinese people's minds were away from the nationalists and turned it to the side of Communists. By 1949. it was all over, the Communists controlled the China and the Nationalists had withdrawn to the island of Formosa. Mao Tse-tung's government immediately signed treaties of friendship and assistance with Soviet Russia, and when the United Nations, at American insistence, refused to oust Nationalist China and replace it with the Communist government, the Russian indignantly walked out of the Security Council in January 1950, in the means of protesting for it.

The Communist victory in China was a bitter blow to the Americans who supported arms supplies and other assistance for many years to Nationalist Chang's government. The Democratic Administration in Washington was lambasted with charges that it had lost China, and a demagogic Republican senator named Joseph McCarthy terrorized government and much of American public life with wild, unsupported, but widely believed charges about Communists in high places.

5. PARTITION OF KOREAN PENINSULA ALONG THE 38TH PARALLEL

a) Drawing the line

Korea has been under the colonial control of Japan for 35 years, as I described previously, and the Korean people had suffered under Japanese occupation. During the time, many Korean independence movement activists were executed miserably by the Japanese army and police. Koreans severely resisted Japanese occupation and demanded independence. However, they could not achieve their freedom and independence. Some Korean nationalist and communist fought against the Japanese authority both inside Korea and Manchuria China, and they formed a National provisional government in Shanghai. Dr. Syngman Rhee was the leader of the government for a short time period in the early 1920s, and then he went to America, where he lived most his adult life (43years). He received Doctor Degree at Princeton University and vociferously condemned Japan. His actions earned him popular recognition in Korea. Kim Ku, a famous Korean Nationalist independence activist succeeded the president of the provisional Korean government until the Korean liberation in 1945.

US President Franklin Roosevelt wanted to place Korea under international trusteeship when Japan would be defeated. At the Teheran Conference in 1943, the Soviet Union, the United Kingdom, and the USA agreed that Korea should be run under an international trusteeship before becoming fully independent. However, the details of trusteeship were not determined before the Soviet Red Army annihilated the Japanese army in Manchuria and pressed into Korea in August 1945. Initially, the United States proposed the division of Korean peninsula to the Soviet and the Stalin agreed, without any modification, the US proposal along the arbitrary line of the 38th parallel. Korea was liberated from the Japanese rule, however, unfortunately, the division of Korean made the peninsula an ideological battle ground of the cold war between the East and the West, as well as between the North and South Korea. A bloody war was fought there and millions of lives were sacrificed in order to prevent the spread of Communism.

Korea has become a focal point of world politics, one of the most sensitive spots in the scheme of balance of power and ideology. Therefore, many Koreans think that the Korean Peninsula along with its people are victims of the Cold War between the two superpowers. If the world in 1948 had not been separated into two super powers opposing sides and if Korea had not been geographically located between these two sides, the conflict in the "Land of the Morning Calm" ultimately would have been resolved within the parameters of a Korean solution. But Korea was to become, by the accident of history and geography, a pawn in a great power play between the United States and the Soviet Union. The cold war division of the country between Communist North and Capitalist South Korea was manipulated by both sides for purposes wholly outside intervention to the peninsula.

According to the U.S. government files released by the U.S. archives, in Washington on the evening of August 10, just hours after the receipt of the Japanese surrender offer, the State-War-Navy Coordinating Committee-Liaison between the diplomatic and the military branches of the U.S. government-convened an all-night meeting to discuss the problem of assigning allied commanders to accept the surrender of Japanese forces in various regions of Asia and the Pacific. Among those present was Dean Rusk, a thirty six year old colonel on the war Department General Staff who had recently returned from serving under General Joseph Stilwell in China and who would later serve as secretary of state under President John F. Kennedy and Lyndon B. Johnson. Around midnight, as Rusk later recalled, he and Colonel Charles H, Bonesteel who were asked by Assistant secretary of War, John J. McCloy "to retire to an adjoining room and came up with a proposal which would harmonize the political desire to have the U.S. forces receive the surrender in Korea as far north as possible and the obvious limitations on the ability of the U.S. forces to reach the area."

The paramount concern was to reserve for the United States the prestige of having the Korean capital within its zone and thus of receiving the surrender of the Japanese colonial governor-general. American military forces could then take over the centralized administrative apparatus and the communications system of the entire nation. American occupation of Seoul would both symbolize and make possible American domination of the trusteeship. They settled instead on the line of latitude 38th degrees north because it had the great virtue of already being on most maps of Korea. The line, approximately halfway up the peninsula, divided Korea into a northern sector of 48,000 square miles and a southern of 37,000. It was intended to be no more than a temporary and facilitative demarcation line, simply for the purpose of accepting the surrender of Japanese troops in the beginning and not in any sense a political boundary. Rusk and Bonesteel recommended the 38th parallel and they choose this line because they felt it important to include the capital of Korea in the area of responsibility of American troops.

To Rusk's surprise, the Russians accepted the 38th parallel without any modification. Although the South Korea contained twelve of Korea's largest cities—including Seoul, the capital, with 20 million people. South was primarily agricultural and historically supplied rice for the entire country. The northern zone, although larger with 48,000 square miles, had only about 12 million population. But because of its highly developed hydroelectric plants, the North had most of Korea's industrial plants—chemical, steel, cement, and fertilizers, products that complemented the South's agrarian economy. Washington hoped that the Russians would be willing to trade exclusive domination of northern Korea for shared access to the entire peninsula. What concerned the Soviets most, however, was in the north: the railways line and a number of warm-water ports as well as mineral resources and hydroelectric power vital to Manchurian industry. Furthermore, as they apparently saw matters, exclusive control of a North Korea buffer was greatly preferable to any arrangement that would bring an American presence right up to the Soviet border near Vladivostok. (From The Korean War, by Richard Whelan)

b) Dean Rusk's testimony:

In January 1990, Dean Rusk who drew the 38th parallel line on the Korean peninsula had an interview with the Korean Daily Newspaper (Chosun Il-bo) in Seoul and stated as follows; [It was the result of an agreement between the State department and the department of Defense with our recommendation to divide Korea at the 38th parallel. It was relatively easy and simple as there weren't any problem or obstructions. After we found the 38th parallel on the Korean map, we came back to the conference room and advised that the 38th line should be a demarcation line between the U.S. and Soviet forces. It was good thing that Seoul, the capital city, was within our jurisdiction. Our recommendation was immediately adopted and the line became the permanent division line of the Korean peninsula.] Because of the demarcation line, the Korean peninsula was separated into two parts, geographically and ideologically, it later contributed to cause the miserable Korean War which claimed several millions lives, the huge property loss and gave great anguish to the Korean people.

The proposal to divide Korea into two temporary occupation zones was included nonchalantly in the middle of the lengthy text prepared in Washington to be issued as General Order Number One, specifying responsibilities for accepting the Japanese surrender in areas throughout the Far East and the Pacific. On August 15 Ambassador Harriman in Moscow received the text of the order and submitted it to Stalin for his approval. In his reply the next day Stalin agreed to the U.S. proposal, not even singling out Korea for any special comment. But he had two requests, which were surely meant as tacit exchanges for his acceptance of the division of Korea. First, he wanted Soviet troops to accept the Japanese surrender in the Kuril Islands, which was to become Soviet territory in accordance with the Yalta agreement. Second, and more important, he wanted Soviet forces to occupy the northern half of the Hokkaido, the northernmost of the four major Japanese home islands.

Even after Stalin had approved General Order Number One, there was no certainty that Soviets forces would actually halt when they reached the 38th parallel to comply with the American proposal. Korea would provide an interesting and important test of Soviet willingness to cooperate and to abide by agreements, which was, after all, the fundamental issue that was precipitating the Cold War. It must consistently be borne in mind that the emergence of the Cold War was not sudden and decisive.

If the Russians didn't stop voluntarily, there would be very little else to stop them. They had assembled 1,6 million men along the Manchurian and Korean borders for their invasion. Such a force would have been necessary to subdue the full-strength Kwantung Army. But as it turned out that the Russians had from the outset overwhelming superiority of force, with more than twice as many men and five times as many tanks as the Japanese. The Soviet forces would encounter some fanatic resistance, but the Kwantung Army simply couldn't hold in the face of such might. Americans feared that the Russians would keep right on going until they reached Busan, in the extreme south of Korea. But when the Soviet troops had reached the 38th parallel, on August 20, Stalin had all that he really needed—all, but except northern Hokkaido, and that he still hoped to win by halting his forces at the appointed line in Korea, thereby demonstrating how cooperative he was prepared to be.

John Allison of the US State Department wrote a memo to Secretary Rusk in 1950 in which he strongly made such announcement "I am convinced that there will be no permanent peace and stability in Korean peninsula as long as the artificial division at the 38th parallel continues." And his assessment was right and correct vision.

A group of Koreans, mostly the nationalists and all other factions, excluding the pro-Japanese faction, formed "the Preparation Committee for the Establishment of Korean Government" led by Nationalist Yeo Woon Hyung who proclaimed their interim administration of the government of the Korean People's Republic. This group began as a very broad coalition, with adherents across the entire political spectrum, from rightists through moderate leftists. They all agreed on only one issue: that Korea must achieve immediate and complete independence. Many Korean intelligentsia youth and students had jointed the organization. Beyond that, all was confusion, controversy, factional rivalry, personal opportunism, and out-and-out hatred. However, General Hodge did not acknowledged the committee and also the Shanghai Korean provisional government led by Kim Ku, but only he supported Dr. Syngman Rhee who spent most of his adult life in the U.S. and had received doctor's degree at the Princeton University. General MacArthur has ordered to General Hodge to support Syngman Rhee as a Korean leader.

6. THE EMERGENCE OF TWO GOVERNMENTS

a) The Emergence of the Republic of Korea.

In spite of the Communists terrorism, the election preparations were carried out, and by April 9, the last day of registration, 7,837,504 eligible voters, or 79.7 percent of the Koreans above the age of 21 had registered. Of this number, 51 percent were men and 49 per cent were women in 200 electoral districts with 13,407 voting places. Each district was to elect one member of the constituent assembly, and 842 candidates, including 17 women, ran for the office.

Although some 44 persons, including many candidates, were killed, more than 100 wounded, and 68 voting booths were attacked by leftist terrorists and opponents of the separate election. The UNTCOCK indicated that the actual mechanics of voting was generally satisfactory and the secrecy of the balloting was, by and large, ensured.

In the midst of widespread corruptions and even violence, Syngman Rhee and his party gained majority in the National Assembly. No party won a clear-cut majority. But Dr. Rhee's Party won 54 seats, the Korean Democratic Party of Kim Song-su, 29, the Taedong Youth Corp, 13, National Youth Corps 6, the People's Unity Party 10 and the remaining 83 seats were Independents. The National Assembly held its first meeting on May 31, and Dr. Rhee was elected as its Chairman. On June 12, a Democratic constitution was adopted, and June 20, Dr. Rhee was elected as the first president of the Republic of Korea, and he formed a government that claimed to represent all of Korea, but it was mostly the former pro-Japanese factions, on August 15, 1948. The UN General Assembly recognized the new Republic of Korea (ROK) in October 1948. But it was given diplomatic recognition just by the western powers, as the People's Democratic Republic of Korea received recognition solely from the eastern block, and the Soviet veto in the Security Council prevented the ROK from actually joining the United Nations. The UN then set up a permanent commission to try to unify the country. Both Soviet and American troops withdraw from the North and South Korea, leaving behind a government which each denounced as illegitimate and both claimed to represent all of Korea. As all moderate leaders in South Korea opposed the UN election which meant a right-wing government would be established in the South; and it would be countered in the North with a communist government.

The moderates, nationalists who doubtless represented a majority on both sides of the 38th parallel, were thereby excluded completely, and Korea was divided into two extreme political camps, South and North. Thus Korea found itself in May 1948, split with an ideological and geographical clarity. The conditions were consequently ripe for civil war. Now, in a house divided, the only means of achieving unity would be war. Within six months there was occasional raiding by the North and South across the 38th parallel, and major exchanges of gunfire were conducted. South Korean president Rhee was vigorously calling for war against the north, and Kim Il Sung was equally busy forming trouble, and openly boasting of the thousands of guerrillas North Korea was supporting in South Korea. Civil disorder and armed riots spread to the coast and mountainous regions of South Korea. The South Korean government imposed a marshal law to contain the riots and uprisings. The guerrilla war in South Korea came to a head in April 1948 when a major rebellion exploded on Cheju-do, an island off the southern coast, to oppose the UN election only in South Korea. The ROK Army was sent to suppress the rebellion, but they themselves rebelled against the government, around the Yosu and Sunchon in October 1948, and later they were suppressed and fled to the mountain to join the guerillas. It's called "Yosu-Sunchon ROK Army Rebellion." President Rhee instituted harsh measures to suppress the Cheju rebellion and subversion throughout Korea, including purging his own police force. By the time that fighting finally ended after January 1949, more than 30,000 people were killed in Cheju-island. At the time, the former Korean president, Park Jeong Hee was arrested and sentenced a death penalty because of involvement of the Army rebellion as an instigator and the leader of Communist ring in the ROK Army. In short order, the rebellion spread to Taegu and other areas. The political context of South Korea was marked by authoritarian government by President Rhee and Military ruler Park Jung Hee. The violent students protest and demonstration Rhee himself was overthrown by the student's demonstrations.

b) The Emergence of North Korea Regime (DPRK)

The Soviets in their zone turned to Kim Il Sung and other Communists of similar background. From the expediencies of 1945, the stage was set for confrontation and tragedy in the future. In North Korea, the Soviet Army stationed and Stalin was not ready to risk a major conflict against America and preferred to protect Soviet security by establishing North Korea as a buffer. The KPR then encouraged peasants to seize Japanese landholdings, advocated the takeover of Japanese factories by their workers, and set up local governments (The People's Committee) to assume police duties and to supervise food distribution. The significant difference between the northern and southern Korea was that the Russians, unlike the Americans, chose to recognize the People's Committee as legitimate local governments. The People's Committees dealt harshly with the Japanese and with the vicious Korean collaborators, executing or imprisoning many, impounding their wealth, and confiscating their holdings of land and basic key industries. Land reform and the nationalization of key industries were the cornerstones of the policy designed to win the loyalty of the people.

Unlike the Americans in South Korea, the Russians did away at once with the Japanese colonial bureaucracy, turning the Japanese out of office and scrapping the old structure altogether. In marked contrast to what the Americans would do in the south, the Russians did not set up a military government but instead of having the North Koreans Central Peoples Committee in Pyongyang operated, which became the de facto government of the Russian occupied zone. This was terribly important, for what the Koreans wanted more than anything else was independence—and although the Soviets certainly did not grant them that, they managed to create an illusion of independence that the great mass of unsophisticated Koreans found persuasive and satisfactory. For the most part the Russians remained relatively inconspicuous and operated skillfully behind the scenes, moving cautiously but persistently to remove their political rivals. The power in the North Korea was in the hands of genuinely pro-Soviet Koreans, there was "considerable evidence to indicate that the Russians actually did permit the Koreans of their choice to exercise real authority, whereas in the American zone, the Korean employees, mostly pro-Japanese collaborators, of the American military government were allowed a little power and no authority." Unlike the North Korea, the South Korean Rhee's government employed all the vicious pro-Japanese factions who should firstly be punished by the Korean people for their treasonable acts. Thus the Korean government unfortunately constituted by the pro-Japanese factions.

To head the pro-Soviet government the Russians installed thirty four years old Kim Il Sung, who throughout the 1930s had been the leader of a band of several hundred Korean guerrillas whose forays from their bases in Manchuria into northern Korea had been so vexatious to the Japanese that the colonial government had organized a special squad to hunt Kim and his guerrillas against Japanese occupation of Korean peninsula.

In the early 1940s, he and his men had sought refuge in south eastern Siberia from the intensive Japanese crackdown against Manchurian guerrillas. He then evinced his loyalty to the Soviet Union and to the Communist cause in hope of enlisting Russian aid in the fight against Japan. He was the battalion commander of the Special reconnaissance unit which would serve for the future possible Japanese War. Realizing that Kim could be very useful to them in Korea, the Russians groomed him for leadership. Like Tito, Kim put the interests of his own nation before those of the Soviet Union. But unlike Tito's, Kim's goals did not conflict with Stalin's, though Kim was self-reliance person.

Unlike the South Korean government, the North Korean Communists purged successfully all pro-Japanese sympizers and anti-Communists from leadership positions in North Korea. The

North Korean Communist Party was officially established in July 1946. With Soviet support, Kim Il-sung established authority over other prominent figures within the party. With these developments, North Korea was progressing toward cohesive statehood. In turn, the Soviets proceeded with their own elections in North Korea. On August 25, 1948, the Supreme People's Assembly was elected. One month later, the North Korean Communists formed their own government (DPRK), with Kim Il Sung elected as the premier, and thus Korea, in fact, was divided ideologically and politically between the North and the South.

Both governments considered themselves to be the only legitimate rulers of all Korea, calling each other a "puppet regime", and violent skirmishes and small raids happened very often at the 38th parallel line. North Korea had been attempting to subvert South Korea internally and guerrillas in South Korea received direction and support from North Korea. Many North Korean leaders including Park Hon-yong (Vice prime minister), Kim Du-bong (Assembly Chairman) were the leaders of Communist party in the South. North Korea was inaugurated on September 9, 1948.

The North Korea claimed that the territory of the DPRK covered the entire Korean peninsula, and called South Korea "the southern half of the republic", as same as the South Korean government claimed representing whole Korean peninsula. Even N. Korea designated Seoul as the nation's capital in 1948, and Pyongyang as a temporary national capital, and Seoul as special city administered directly by the central government. North Korea's population in 1948 was about 12 million. The Supreme People's Assembly (SPA) was established on August 25, 1948, as the supreme organ of the state, and its delegates were elected by all citizens 18 years of age and over for a four year term. The number of the delegates of the first Supreme People's Assembly in 1948 was 572 (212 representing North Korea and 360 representing South Korea). They also eliminated the Nationalists in election. Various measures implemented by the Korean Communists government during the period of the Allied occupation initiated the communization of the northern half of Korea.

Following the establishment of the Communist regime in 1948, the new government discarded many traditional systems, changed the people's way of life, and North Korea became one of the most regimented and closed societies in the world, as intended and was isolated by the United States, politically and economically. Nevertheless, they insisted that their social goal and policy was especially for the welfare of workers, peasants, and all classes of people. And therefore, they promulgated the following new laws and systems which were then insisted the most advanced system for the Korean people as their propaganda.

1. The Land Reform—the free confiscation of farm land from large landowners and free distribution to the poor tenant farmers.
2. Promulgation of the Equality Sex law.
3. Nationalization of large basic factories.
4. Enforcement of Eight Hour Working rue and Annual leave system.
5. Free Compulsory Education given to children, up to middle school. And free education for High School and college and university.
6. Free medical treatment and expenses.
7. Free Taxation system.
8. Social Clean-up campaign. (Clean-up

The Korean Workers Party: In 1949, the North Korean Workers' Party and The South Korean Workers Party merged and formed a new party named the 'Korean Workers Party' (KWP) with a membership of about 79,000. The KWP, whose General Secretary was Kim, Il Sung, became the most powerful political institution in North Korea. Kim Il Sung said that the workers party was a combat unit and a vanguard of the working class, and said "we must fight with our utmost to maintain the party's purity, iron unity, and the Party will exercise an absolute power in order to complete the Korean revolution." All top ranking Party members, who had also occupied top positions in the Supreme People's Assembly and the State Administration Council concurrently, were members of the so called Partisan (Kapsan) factions of the Korean Worker's Party until about 1973. The members of the Korean faction, such as Choe Hyun, Kim Chaek, Park Sung-chol, Oh Chin Woo, and Choe Yong gon were those who were with Kim Il-sung in Manchuria and Siberia before their return to Korea. Two exceptions were Nam Il and Heo Ka-I, Russian born Koreans who elected to stay in North Korea when Soviet troops withdrew from North Korea in December 1948.

North Korean Military. The People's Army was a powerful instrument of the Korean Worker's Party through which it absolutely controls the state and the people. The North Korean Communists consciously fostered strong militarism and created a huge military machine in order to carry out what they called the "liberation of the southern half of the Republic" and to complete so called Korean revolution and reunification. The North Korean Army was created in February 1948 with some 20,000 Members of the security force who were trained by the Soviets. Kim Il-sung had some 300 seasoned fighters who constituted the partisan group. There were also about 2,200 Communists who had been with the Chinese Communists at Yenan group and returned to Korea in late 1945, and about 3,000 Koreans returning from Siberia under Heo Ka Yi and An Kil.

In March 1948, a Soviet-China-North Korea Joint Military Council was established in Pyongyang, and both the Soviet and the Chinese Communists helped North Korea's military. Sometime in 1949, about 20,000 Chinese Korean Communist troops who fought against Chinese nationalists in Manchuria under Communist Commander Lim Piao, entered Korea and formed the three strongest divisions in the Korean People's Army. Among the top military leaders, in addition to Kim Il Sung, were Kim Il, Mu Jeong, Kim Chaek, Choe Yong Gon, and O, Jin Woo as well as Soviet born Korean generals Such as Nam Il, Heo Ka Yi, and An Kil. The number of troops in the North Korean Army increased rapidly after 1948 as they were intensely indoctrinated with political ideology and militarily trained. At the same time, increasing quantity of Soviet weapons were brought into North Korea.

The North Korean Army had consisted of volunteers who were recruited under a quota system. Each district had a quota to meet, and these "volunteers" were actually conscripted into military service. From March 1948, some 20,000 young men between ages of 18 to 22 were recruited annually into the military. As a result, the people's army grew from two divisions and one mixed brigade in 1948, to 24 infantry divisions of 135,000 troops, 4 mixed brigades, and two tank brigades by June 1950. The tank brigade of 8,000 troops had 150 Russian built T-34 and the 2,300 man Air Force had 211 Yak and MIG planes built in the Soviet Union, and the Navy of 15,270 men had 35 military craft of various kinds.

The allied occupation achieved its primary aim that of defeating and disarming Japanese troops in Manchuria and Korea. However, it failed to implement Korean unification. They divided the Korean peninsula at the line of 38th parallel and when they withdrew their troops from the both side of Korea, they left a nation which was still divided and confrontation which had subsequently contributed to onset of the Korean conflict.

CHAPTER II

THE OUTBREAK OF THE KOREAN WAR

1. THE SOVIET UNION, CHINA AND THE KORAN CONFLICT

March 5, 1949, Kim Il Sung and Park Hon Yong (Vice premier) visited Moscow to sign an agreement of the 'Economic & Culture Treaty' in April 1949, two countries had concluded a 'Military alliance Agreement' to give a way for building up N. Korean Army.

At this time, Kim had implicitly expressed his desire for the armed unification of Korean peninsula to Joseph Stalin, Soviet Premier, and requested his support and approval. But then Stalin did not agree Kim's idea. Stalin stated at that time that 38th parallel line was established by the agreement between the United States and the Soviet Union. He did not want to break the agreement and have a military hostility against United States, especially under the present situation that 500 US military advisors are still stationed in the South Korea.

The United States and soviets were both victorious allied countries of World War II, and he did not want to confront with Americans and have another war that might lead to nuclear war. And Stalin advised Kim to be more cautious in the matter. On the contrary, Stalin then suspected and worried about the S. Koreans, supporting by the Americans and Japanese, might invade North Korea. Stalin also said, if the South Koreans invade the North Korean then, it would be much reasonable and better position to repulse the south Korean invaders and proceed south to achieve reunification.

Following Secretary of State Dean Acheson's speech to the National Press Club in January 1950, to exclude Korea from the U.S.

defense perimeter, Kim renewed his overtures to Moscow and Beijing. Although Stalin approved Kim's plan to reunite Korea and even promised to supply North Korea with arms and military equipment, he did so reluctantly and only after Kim Il Sung promised that he could defeat S. Korea within a month.

Stalin was genuinely concerned that the war in Korea could lead to a world war involving the United States and the Soviet Union. But he did not want to put himself in the same embarrassing position that he did not give the Chinese Communists the support during their civil war against the Nationalists. Indeed, according to several authors, Stalin waited until the Chinese agreed to support the invasion before he gave it his unequivocal backing. Should the United States intervene in the war, he anticipated that the Chinese would enter the conflict, thereby diminishing the need for Soviet intervention while forcing Beijing to be more dependent on Moscow, something he preferred. At the same time, he hoped that a war in Korea might force the United States to redefine its resources away from Europe and offset America's efforts to re-establish Germany and Japan as major economic and political powers.

Chinese Mao Tse-tung also did not agree the Kim's idea at the time and he thought the same idea with Stalin. Mao said that it would be more righteous to repulse South Korean's attack and if the US Forces, Japanese and S. Koreans united forces would attack N. Korea, then Chinese Army would have better position to enter the Korean War to defend N. Korea. As for the Chinese, they had cooperated with Kim for more than a year in repatriating Korean soldiers who fought with them against the Nationalists. Mao Tse-dung also deeply resented America's support of Nationalist leader Chiang Kai-shek in the Chinese civil war. He was angered and worried by U.S. efforts to turn Japan into a major regional power that could once more pose a threat to China, just as it had before World War II. But he was also concerned that the North Korean invasion might become entangled with his own plan to attack Taiwan.

As for the reason why the PRC decided to send its troops into Korea in late October and November 1950, clearly concern for its own national security was a major consideration. Even after the United States entered the war in July, Chinese leaders proceeded cautiously. Although they transferred 90,000 of their best troops close to the border between China and North Korea, they believe that the United States lacked the military strength to counter the Soviet Union's military power in Europe and fight a war against China and North Korea in Far East Asia. By the time General MacArthur visited Formosa and the continued buildup of American forces in Korea, and growing concern that the United States would seek to unify Korea led the Chinese in August to prepare for military intervention. The Inchon landing of September 16 and the American decision to roll back communism by marching to the Amrock river (Yalu) almost certainly weighted heavily in Beijing's decision to enter the Korean War.

Kim and Park had subsequently continued to persuade Stalin. Park assured Stalin that if their Army would capture Seoul, 200,000 communists and guerillas in South Korea would up-rise and overturn the Rhee's government.

Stalin started to understand the Park's explanation. Consequently, the Politburo of Central Communist Commission had held and discussed the matter. Stalin considered the following affirmative facts and circumstances.

1. The Communist Chinese victory over the main land civil war made encouraging the world's Communism movement.
2. The Soviet's successful test for atomic bomb in 1948, made a come back from an inferior position in the possible future war against the USA.
3. It would mitigate the strained relations with the NATO, which was established by the United States.
4. US Army might not enter the Korean Conflict.

An American author named "Carter Malkasian" wrote in his book "The Korean War" that Kim Il Sung was one of an anti-Japanese guerilla and fought in Manchuria and later he fled to the Soviet Union when he and his comrades were attacked and chased by the Japanese Kwangtung Army." At 'havarobsk' it was known that he was trained and served in the Soviet Army.

2. SECRET LETTERS OF USSR FOREIGN MINISTRY

The opening, in recent years, of archives from the former Soviet Union reveal the reluctance of the Soviet Union—and the people's Republic of China—to support an invasion of South Korea by North Korea at least through the winter of 1950. Although North Korean leader Kim Il Sung proposed in the fall of 1949 only an attack on the Ongjin Peninsula, on the west coast of Korea extending both above and below the 38th parallel. Soviet leader Joseph Stalin understood that such an attack could result in a full scale war that might involve the United States; this he was anxious to avoid at all costs.

Kim also argued that partisans in South Korea were waiting for the opportunity to overthrow its leader Syngman Rhee, and he even seemed to suggest that the Chinese would support him even if the Soviets did not. But the Soviet leader had doubts that a popular uprising against Rhee would happen without more support of the partisans in the South or that Kim could defeat South Korea in short order as he promised. Stalin also raised questions about the military superiority of North Korean over South Korean forces. At the same time, however, he never excluded entirely the possibility of a North Korean invasion, and he promised military assistance in order to build up North Korean forces. What is also striking in the documents that follow-all from the Soviet Foreign Ministry Archives is the economic and political dependence of North Korea on the Soviet Union.

Thanks to the end of the Cold War and a growing exchange of historical information between Beijing, Moscow, and Washington. These records have become increasingly available to historians, although the materials from Russia and China still have to be studied with considerable caution because they remain incomplete. But they do provide much essential information.

In order to give readers a more clear understanding who had initially started the Korean War, it is necessary to transcribe the primary documents of the Korean conflict, Since the North Koreans have constantly insisted that the South Koreans had initially invaded the North Korea and S. Koreans started the war.

Document 1

Ciphered Telegram from (T.F.) Shtykov [Soviet Ambassador to Democratic People's Republic of Korea]
To [A.IA] Vyshinsky [Soviet Minister of Foreign Affairs], September 3, 1949

On September 3, the personal secretary of Kim Il Sung, Mun Il (A Soviet Korean), came to me and at the commission of Kim Il Sing reported that they had received reliable information that in the near future the southerners intend to seize the part of Ongjin peninsula which is located to the north of the 38th parallel, and also to bombard the cement plant in the city of Kaesong. In connection with this, Mun Il said, Kim Il Sung asks permission to begin military operations against the South, with the goal of seizing the Ongjin peninsula and part of the territory of South Korea to the east of the Ongjin peninsula, approximately to Kaesong, so as to shorten the line of defense. Kim Il Sung considers, Mun said, that if the international situation permits, they are ready to move further to the South. Kim Il Sung is convinced that they are in a position to seize South Korea in the course of two weeks, maximum 2 months. I asked Mun to transmit to Kim Il Sung that this question is very large and serious, it is necessary to think it through carefully and that I therefore urgently recommend to Kim Il Sung not to be in a hurry and not to take 'any measure' while there is no decision on this question. Kim Il Sung will probably raise this question again soon.

It has been established that the North Koreans truly did seize an order to the commander of troops on the Ongjin peninsula to begin artillery fire on the cement plant in Kaesong on September 2 at 8:00 and destroy it. From the order, it is clear that the southerners consider this plant to be military. The period indicated in the order has past but so far there has been no shelling. The northerners have taken the necessary measures in case of firing on the plant, Regarding the intentions of the southerners to seize the part of the Ongjin peninsula to the north of the 38th parallel, we have only indications of this from deserters from the South Korean Army. There have not been any serious incidents at the 38th parallel since August 15. Small exchange of fire has taken place. There have been instances of artillery firing on the territory of North Korea on the Ongjin peninsula, trespassing of the parallel. The southerners are carrying defensive work at the 38th parallel at a fast tempo. I ask your order. [Gregori Tunkin] [charge d'affaires of the Soviet embassy in Pyongyang]

Document 2

Ciphered telegram from Gromyko to Tunkin, September 11, 1949

You must meet with Kim Il Sung as soon as possible and try to illuminate from him the following additional questions:

1. How do they evaluate the South Korean army, its numbers, arms and fighting capacity?
2. The condition of the partisan movement in the South Korea and what real help they think they will receive from the partisans.
3. How do the society and people regard the fact that northerners will be the first to begin an attack? What kind of real aid can be given by the population of the South to the army of the North?
4. Are there American troops in the South of Korea ? What kind of measures, in the opinion of Kim Il Sung, can the Americans take in case of an attack by the northerners?
5. How do the northerners evaluate their possibilities, i.e., the condition of the army. its supplies and fighting capacity?
6. Give your evaluation of the situation and of how real and advisable is the proposal of our friends.

Document 3

CIPHERED TELEGRAM FROM TUNKIN TO SOVIET FOREIGN MINISTRY
(IN REPLY TO TELEGRAM OF SEPTEMBER 11)
SEPTEMBER 14, 1949

Kim thinks they should not count on substantial help from the partisans, but Park Hon-yung has a different opinion. He thinks the help from partisans will be significant. At any rate, they hope that the partisans will help in actions against the communications of the enemy and that they will occupy the main ports of South Korea, though they will not be able to do this at the beginning of the campaign. With regard to the question of how the population will regard the fact that the northerners will begin a civil war, Kim Il Sung oscillates. During the conversation on September 12, he definitely stated that if the northerners begin military action, this will produce a negative impression in the people and that it is politically disadvantageous to them to begin it. In connection with this he recollected that during the conversation between Mao Zedong and the Korean representative Kim Il [Chief of the political Administration of the North Korean Army] in the spring of this year, Mao stated that in his opinion the northerners should not begin military action now, since in the first place, it is politically disadvantageous and in the second place, the Chinese friends are occupied at home and cannot give them serious help. The thinking of Kim Il Sung amounts to waiting until the conclusion of the main military operation in China.

In the conversation on September 13, Kim Il Sun does not propose to begin a civil war, but only to secure the Ongjin peninsula and a portion of the territory of South Korea to the east of this peninsula. They consider that in case of a civil war the people of South Korea will be sympathetic toward the northern army and will help it. In the case of successful military actions they hope to organize a number of uprisings in South Korea.

According to official data, there are 500 American military advisers and instructors in South Korea. According to a secrete service information, which need confirmation, there are 900 American military advisers and instructors and 1,500 soldiers and security officers in South Korea. In case of a civil war in Korea, the Americans, in the opinion of Kim Il Sung and park Hon-yung, could send Japanese and nationalist Chinese soldiers to the aid of the Southerners; support the South Koreans from the sea and air with their own means; American instructors will take immediate part in organizing military actions.

The proposal of Kim Il Sung amounts to the following; at the beginning to strike the South Korean Army on the Ongjin peninsula, to destroy the two regiments stationed there, to occupy the territory of the peninsula and the territory to the rest of it...and then to see what to do further. After this blow, the South Korean army may have become demoralized. In this case move further to the south. If the South Korean army is not demoralized as a result of the Ongjin operation, to seal the borders seized, to shorten in that way the line of defense approximately by one third. It is not possible to hurry with the operation on the Ongjin peninsula. It is necessary to wait until additional arms arrive from the Soviet Union. Meanwhile, we must consolidate the defense on the remaining portions of the 38th parallel. Kim Il Sung admits the possibility of the Ongjin operation turning into a civil war, but he hopes that this does not happen, since the southerners, in his opinion, do not dare to attack other positions of the 38th parallel.

Moreover, a drawn out war in Korea could be used by the Americans for the purpose of agitation against the Soviet Union and for further inflaming war hysteria. Therefore, it is inadvisable that the north begin a civil war now. Given the present internal and external situation a decision about an attack on the south would be correct only in such cases as the northerners could count on ending the war quickly; the preconditions for it are not there.

We propose that under the indicated conditions to begin the partial operation conceived by Kim Il Sung is advisable.

3. THE TESTIMONY OF NORTH KOREAN GENERAL YU SUNG-CHOL

Lieutenant General Yu, Sung-chol who was the Chief of Staff of the North Korean Army (NKPA), and was one of the key member of the Korean war planners. He defected in 1950s from North Korea to Russia. He wrote his testimony in November 1990, for the 'South Korean Daily News paper' about how they prepared the South Korea invasion plan. He stated in his testimony titled "My Testimony" as follows:

[We started to prepare the attacking plan in May 1950, after Stalin had agreed to Kim Il-sung's invasion plan. In fact, the initial attack plan was made by the Soviet Army advisors under the supervision of Lieutenant General "Vacilief" who was a war hero having had abundant war experiences during the World War II, against Germany.

The initial war plan has included combat orders, movement of each combat unit, and army supply plan including the camouflage of troop movements as like a normal military training. Originally two North Korean Army Corps were scheduled to attack the South Korean Army at the 38th Parallel line. Seoul, the capital city, was the final occupation destination as planned. They had judged if they'd capture Seoul, 200,000 of South Korean Communists and the Partisans would start riots and overturn the South Korean Rhee's government. I, myself, translated the attack plan that was written in Russian, into Korean and we made the final plan with cooperation of Major general Kim, Bong Yul (Artillery Commander), General Jung, Hak-jun (Chief of Staff of Artillery Command), and Colonel Park, Kil-nam (Chief of Army Engineer Corps) under the supervision of General Kang Kon, Chief of Staff of the North Korean Army.

The goal of operation plan was originally limited to the capture of Seoul mainly due to vice premier Park Hon Yong's assertion that the South Korean partisan and anti-government Communists would support to overthrow the South Korean government when they'd occupy Seoul. That was then the North Korean leader's optimistic view of the liberation of South Korea. Kim Du-bong (South Korean born) who was the Chairman of the North Korean National Assembly also insisted that the main forces of the South Korean Army were mainly stationed along the 38th parallel line to defend Seoul and there should be no problem about the remaining South Korean Army because they were nothing but a reserve army. Therefore the North Korean army could easily unify Korea without giving any chance for the US Army intervention. These facts had fully reflected the operation plan we prepared for the capture of Seoul.]

As we have read above Yu's statement, it is obvious and indisputable evidence that the North Koreans had started the Korean War first, as contrary to the North Korea's allegation that the South Koreans had initially invaded to North.

4. NORTH KOREA'S WAR PREPARATION

As I mentioned before, North Korean premier Kim Il Sung wanted to unify Korea militarily and then he tried to consent Soviet leader Joseph Stalin and Chinese leader Mao Tse-tung to approve his plan of an invasion. But Neither leader was anxious to give him the green light. Both Stalin and Mao Tse-tung were concerned that an attack on South Korea might lead to an American response and intervention. The Soviet leader, moreover, was preoccupied with the West, whereas the Chinese leader was fearful of any action that might divert his attention away from his own plan to attack Formosa (Taiwan). Stalin did not want an armed clash with United States, as America and Russia had mutually agreed to establish the 38th parallel line on the Korean peninsula. Moreover, there were more than 500 US Army advisors stationed in South Korea. In the spring of 1950,

Kim Il Sung and Pak Hon-yong visited Moscow again and they both tried to convince Stalin to support their plan, and if they invade South, Communist guerrillas would also attack the South Korean Army in the rear and S. Korean people would start riots against Rhee's regime. Stalin was finally persuaded and agreed to Kim's invasion plan after being reassured that South Korea could be defeated within a month, and Mao had little choice except to go along with him.

After persistent efforts made by Kim & Park, Stalin began to consent his plan and took his consideration. At this juncture, North Korea took the following actions:

1. To replace 38th Parallel Security brigade with the regular North Korean Army.
2. Move all the N. Korean residents near the 38th parallel line to rear zones.
3. Reassign Korean soldiers of the Chinese Communist's army, to N. Korean Army.
4. Transfer all the heavy arms on trains towards the south.
5. Relocation of the major N. Korean Army to the 38th demarcation line.
6. Encourage students to join Army and Air force.
7. Give military training to all school students and young labor workers.

Meanwhile, Kim Il Sung, who had built an impressive military force outfitted by the Soviet Union, made plans for an invasion of South Korea. He was allowed to build such a force because Moscow viewed North Korea as part of security blanket around its borders. Ironically, the United States refused to equip South Korea in a similar way because it feared that South Korea might use its military strength to invade North Korea, as president Rhee used to insist, thereby preventing a major conflict between the United States and the Soviet Union. In March of 1950, Kim and his vice premier Park Hon-yong visited Moscow and finally received Stalin's approval and Kim sent an envoy to Beijing where he tried to get an assent of Mao Tse-tung for their plan to attack South Korea and then they finally obtained Mao's consent also.

5. DEAN ACHESON'S SPEECH

On January 12, 1950, U.S. Secretary of State 'Dean Acheson's' famous speech to the National Press Club just six months earlier, repeated the president's views, and again he excluded South Korea from the U.S. defense perimeter in East Asia. He said the American "Defense Perimeter" ran along the Aleutians to Japan, thence to the Ryukyus (Okinawa) and the Philippine islands, and those positions would be defended militarily by the United States if necessary. Acheson's speech derived its importance from the fact that authorities on the Korean War have tended to regard it as a green light to North Korea. Kim Il-sung was "much excited" when informed of the Dean Acheson's speech and he also learned that the U.S. Congress had cut off Korean aid. Acheson's speech was viewed as a green light by North Korean communists. These might caused the leaders of North Korea to lure to take a chance for Korean unification under his control.

It was thought that Dean Acheson's intention was to test the will of the Soviets. Acheson, when he was Under Secretary of State, was one of those who in 1947 strongly voiced the importance of securing Korea for free world and he drawing of a line between "the Russians and Americans." There was no consensus among the policy makers behind the containment policy as of early 1950. If North Korea started a war, then the containment policy would be justified and it would create a consensus supporting the policy. Whatever Acheson's motives may have been, many argue that he deliberately misled Kim Il-sung and lured the North Korean Communists into launching a war against South Korea. Some believe that Acheson "wishing to shape defense in Asia, created a situation in which the offence would blunder." This probably overemphasizes the impact of the speech, given the already existing hostility of both regimes in Korea, and the fact that each was determined to be rid of the other. It was one thing to decide rationally that South Korea was not vital to American interests more than Soviet Union at that time.

Realizing that North Korean guerrilla movements in the south were virtually wiped out and there was no hope of the South Korean government being overthrown by the subversive activities of the South Korean Worker's Party and guerrillas. The North Korean Communists decided to launch the war, for by the spring of 1950. Conventional military attack was the only alternative left to Kim Il-sung for achieving Korean unification. All his policy options including the south-north political meeting for peaceful unification had been tried and had failed in the past.

6. STALIN'S APPROVAL

Even though the Korean Conflict drastically upped the ante of the Cold War and led to twenty years of especially bitter relations between the United States and Communist China, neither the Soviet Union nor the PRC had been particularly anxious to have North Korea invade South Korea. Kim renewed his overtures to Moscow. In March, 1950, Kim and his vice Premier Pak Hon Yong, visited the USSR again to meet Joseph Stalin and discuss his plan for attacking South Korea. Kim and Pak both assured Stalin that they could win the war within a short period of time, and the North Korean army would occupy Seoul within three days, then South Korean guerrillas would attack the south Korean army in the rear and about 200,000 South Korean communists would riot against the South Korean government, as they stated before, and thus it would easily overthrow the Rhee's South Korean government and achieve Korean unification under Communists control.

At the time, the new born Chinese government had a lot of domestic problems after the long civil war, and they could not afford to assist North Korea. Since Stalin was somewhat persuaded, ambiguous approval, but then he advised Kim to discuss his plan with Chinese leader Mao Tse-tung, who had little choice except to go along with him.

Although Stalin approved the plan to reunite Korea and even promised to supply North Korea with arms and other military equipment, he did so reluctantly and only after Kim Il-sung promised that he could defeat South Korea within short period of time. Stalin was genuinely concerned that the war in Korea might lead to a world war involving the United States and the Soviet Union. But he did not want to put himself in the same embarrassing position that he had found himself a year earlier by not giving the Chinese communists the support they expected in their successful civil war against the nationalists. Indeed, Stalin waited until the Chinese agreed to support the invasion before he gave it his unequivocal backing. Should the United States intervene in the war, he anticipated that the Chinese would enter the conflict, thereby diminishing the need for Soviet intervention while forcing Beijing to be more dependent on Moscow, something he preferred. Stalin approved the war with following conditions attached:

1. You must win quickly, should the war start.
2. The Soviet Union would never join the war at any time, and did not want expansion of the war, but would support the arms and military equipment.

As for the Chinese, they had cooperated with Kim Il-sung for more than a year in repatriating Korean Chinese soldiers who had fought with them against the Chinese nationalists. In the year of 1948, one-time, Mao's army retreated by Chiang's Nationalist from Manchuria to North Korean territory and so Mao owed Kim some debts before. Mao Zedong also deeply resented Washington's support of Nationalist Leader Chiang Kai-Shek, and like Stalin, he was angered and worried by U. S. efforts to turn Japan into a major regional power that could once more pose a threat to China, just as it had before World War II.

Therefore, the PRC decided to send its troops into Korea in late October and November 1950, clearly concerned for its own national security was a major consideration. Even after the United States entered the war in July 1950, Chinese leaders proceeded cautiously and they transferred 90,000 of their best troops close to the China and North Korean border.

The Opening of Soviet Diplomatic Archives in the 1990s shed new light on the origins of the Korean War. The initiative for the North Korean attack on South Korea came from North Korean leader Kim Il-sung incited by Park Hon-young, who over a period of months in 1949-50 won over a skeptical Joseph Stalin to support the invasion plan. Kim first discussed the topic during a meeting with Stalin in Moscow in the spring of 1949. As late as January 1950, Stalin remained unpersuasive, although he did approve stepped-up military assistance to North Korea. "I understand the dissatisfaction of Comrade Kim Il-sung, he cabled the Soviet ambassador in Pyongyang, but he must understand that such a large matter in regard to South Korea such as he wants to undertake needs large preparation. The matter must be organized so that there would not be too great a risk." The risk that Stalin feared the most was the possibility of a direct military confrontation with the United States.

Stalin did not reveal his intentions to Chinese Leader Mao Zedong, whom he met in Moscow in February 1950. Mao had complained several years later to the Soviet ambassador to China that "when I was in Moscow there was no talk about conquering South Korea."

While approving the invasion, a still cautious Stalin warned Kim that "if you should get defeated, you could not expect to be bailed out military by the Soviet Union. Kim would have to turn for help to China instead."

7. N. KOREAN FORCES ATTACKED S. KOREA

On early Sunday morning, 4 AM, June 25, 1950 (Korean time), the North Koran forces launched an attack against South Korea, and over 96,000 North Korean troops, supported by Soviet-built tanks, crossed the 38th parallel. The North Korean army's prime assault troops of seven divisions and three independent units, attacked south from the 38th parallel boundary. The North Koreans had one additional manpower advantage in the short run: about one-fourth of their army was made up of Korean Chinese who had served in the Chinese Communist forces in China and had been demobilized and returned to Korea after the Nationalists fled to Taiwan. These men gave the North Korean army a degree of battle experience and combat hardness which the South Korean army at the outset largely did not enjoy. They achieved total tactical and strategic surprise. Facing them were four Republic of Korea (ROK) Army divisions and one regiment totaling 38,000 men. South Korea's other four (4) divisions were spread out in various places. Since no one had predicted the attack, large numbers of South Korean soldiers were away on weekend passes. High ranking officers were invited to the new opening ceremony party of the Army Officers Club located in Yongsan district of Seoul. However, North Korea as well as other socialistic countries alike, have been insisting that the South Korea started to invade North Korea at first and advanced 4 to 6 kilometers all along the 38th parallel. Then the North Korean Army Supreme Command had to order to repulse the enemy, which had later been proved to be a false accusation. There is no ground and the logical contention that the South Korean forces started to attack N. Korea at first. The war lasted for three years, one month two days, but Kim Il Sung failed to accomplish his objectives. The tragic war caused tremendous hardship for the Korean people in both North and South. It destroyed a vast number of lives (4 million) and properties, and it made the peaceful reunification of Korean peninsula more difficult. The unification rhetoric from both North and South was belligerent, each threatening to take over the other side and each insisting that unification of the nation must be achieved. However, the problem was both sides wanted it to be their own social system under his rule and control, instead of a peaceful reunification through earnest negotiations of mutual conciliations. It seems that the problem could not be solved and are still the same extent today. The two sides understood and insisted that as long as the 38th parallel was not dismantled, true independence of Korea and true peace between two Koreas would be impossible.

In the war, North Korean's general pattern of the attack was as follows. First heavy artillery bombarded the attack zones. Next the infantry and tanks moved forward, smashing the bewildered South

Korean defenders. Finally the mechanized North Korean units pressed on to their objectives pursuing defeated units. The North Koreans possessed three times as much artillery as the ROK Army. Nearly all of it outranged the South Korean guns. The superior numbers and guns were not the decisive factors for the North Koreans because they possessed an ultimate weapon: the 'tank.' It is a bizarre fact, but five years after a world war which proved beyond all doubt the surprise attack capability of the tank to break great gaps in enemy defenses, the American-equipped South Korean possessed nothing to stop a tank-neither a single tank of their own, nor armor-piercing artillery shells, nor combat aircraft, nor antitank land mines.

The North Koreans themselves had only 150 tanks, but little to stop them. The only weapons the South Koreans had possessed with even remote potential for stopping the T-34 tanks were American 57 mm antitank guns and rocket launchers (bazookas). The first ROK Division defended the approach to Seoul via Kaesong, Col. Paik Sun-yop commanded the division. At only 29 years of age, he was the youngest divisional commander in the ROK army. On 25 June, the veteran 6th North Korean division overwhelmed Paik's forward regiment and captured Kaesong, the ancient capital of Korea, in four hours. Paik put up a fierce fight with his remaining two regiments. He withdrew to a pre-arranged defensive line on the Imjin River. Artillery fire supported counterattacks and was directed against North Korean penetrations. Nevertheless, unable to stop the North Korean tanks, Paik was pushed back. He wrote in his memoirs that many soldiers acquired "T-34 disease" and panicked at the sight of tanks, Some of Paik's men laden with high explosives, threw themselves upon oncoming tanks.

The 6th ROK Division, under the able Kim Chong O, also fought well and managed to halt the 2nd and 7th North Korean Divisions for three days at Chunchon. At the ROK Army military headquarters in Seoul, there was disorder. With communications disrupted, Chae Byong-deok had no idea of the situation at the front. By the end of 26 June, the North Koreans had invaded Uijongbu and looked upon an open road to Seoul. Consequently, Paik sought to withdraw across the Han River, but Chae Byong Deok ordered him to "Fight to the death in your present positions." The roads and trains out of Seoul were clogged with people trying to flee. In the confusion, the only one bridge across the Han river was prematurely blown up, and hundreds of civilians, soldiers who were crossing the bridge at that moment were blown up. Forty four thousand soldiers and most of the army's heavy equipments were now cut off to the north. Although in a disorganized state, Paik managed to pull his division across the Han river near the western outskirts of Seoul. Thus by 28 June, Seoul had fallen into the hands of North Korean army, in three days after start of the war.

Major General Chung Il Kwon, Chae's successor, decided to withdraw and preserve the ROK army rather than engage in further last-ditch defensives. Major General Kim Hong Il took charge of delaying actions as the ROK army withdrew to the Nakdong-river. Kim Hong Il had been a senior officer with the Chinese Nationalists in the Second World War and had experience of commanding large formations. His steady efforts provided much help to postpone the North Korean Army's advance.

The North Koreans obviously knew the ROKs had no effective antitank weapons, because they adopted tactics that under normal conditions of warfare would have invited annihilation: they line up their armor in columns, one tank behind the other, on the narrow Korean dirt roads and headed south, their infantry strung out behind them. In the past, the South Koreans asked the Americans for tanks, but were refused because of the appraisal of Korea's mountainous terrain, plus a judgment (largely erroneous) that Korea's one-lane bridges over small streams were too weak to support the tanks, that U.S. military advisors cited in 1949 in denying a South Korea request for tanks. Perhaps the advisors, more likely, Americans used the terrain as an excuse to turn down the request for tanks because they feared South Korea's president, Syngman Rhee, would use them to attack the North, as he had occasionally threatened in the past. The United States deliberately provided only defensive weapons to South Korea. President Rhee expressed his determination to "move into North Korea" to American ambassador John Muccio in February

1949. Rhee regularly advocated using force to bring about Korean unification.

Meanwhile, the North Korean Communists emphatically stated that without the "Liberation of the southern half of the Republic, the Korean revolution would not be completed. On June 28, 1949, the Democratic Front for the Unification of the Fatherland was founded in Pyongyang. It announced so called "peaceful unification formula" advocating the formation of an election committee of representatives of political parties and social organizations of the South and North to conduct the general elections throughout the peninsula for the establishment of a unified national legislature. Between May and August 1949, many border clashes between the troops of the South and North occurred at such places as Ongjin, Kaesong, as well as Paekchon in Hwanghae-do and near Chunchon in Kangwon province. Meantime, The leaders of the South Korean Workers' Party who migrated to the North, formed the Democratic Front for the Unification of the Fatherland in June 1949. They sought cooperation of anti-Rhee elements in the South, and initiated a guerrilla war against the south in cooperation with the remnants of the rebels who had brought about the Yosu-Sunchon ROK Army soldier's rebellion in South Cholla province in October 1948.

The North Korea's Democratic Front for the Unification of the Fatherland sent several guerrilla units into South Korea in the fall of 1949. The North Korean guerrillas established their eastern base in the 'Odae san' mountain area in Kangwon-do. The second guerrilla base was established on the 'Chiri-san' area in the North Cholla-do. In October and November, North Korean guerrillas, supported by their allies in the South, launched a large scale winter offensive at Andong, JinJu, and Pohang, and the fighting continued throughout the winter months. But the counterattack launched by South Korean troops and police destroyed most of the guerrillas and their allies by March 1950.

President Rhee of South Korea is used to mention openly for the commitment of the Korean unification by the armed invasion to North as well as Kim Il Sung of North Korea. Kim had planned and sought

Soviet support for the invasion and later he started the war on June 25, 1950, as we all know and the various historic facts proved it.

8. U.S. RESPONSE TO N. KOREAN AGGRESSION

a) President Truman's Decision

The North Korean attack on June 25 was a smashing success. Equipped by the Soviet weapons with more than 1,400 artillery and 150 modern tanks, the N. Korean force of 98,000 soldiers quickly drove the South Korean forces into hasty retreat. Three days later, North Korean troops captured Seoul, and aggressors quickly demolished South Korean's resistance as they occupied more than a half of the territory of the Republic of Korea, and tens of thousand South Korean Army soldiers were captured as Prisoners of War in the early stage of the war. President Truman, who received the report from Acheson about North Korean's aggression on Sunday, June 25 1950, was on a vacation at hone in Independence, Missouri. He responded immediately by approving a proposal for an emergency meeting of the United Nations Security Council. Later that day, President Truman had flown back to Washington D.C., and sent a survey team to Korea. Despite President Truman's decision to commit U.S. forces to defend South Korea, there was really little that he could do immediately to halt the N. Korean advance.

The U.S. government that had "lost China" had to do something, and the initial response was diplomatic an appeal to the United Nations. On June 27, the United States won approval from the United Nations, which the United States still dominated, of a resolution calling from military sanctions against North Korea, and immediate retreat their troops out of South Korean territory, up to above the 38th parallel. But even while that was prepared, it was obvious that North Korea might not respond positively, and therefore further steps had to be taken. Even though the Pentagon had expressed major reservations about the military and strategic value of Korea, once North Korea attacked

South Korea, the US president felt that he had little choice other than a military response. Truman and most foreign policy makers believed that North Korea was merely serving as a proxy for the Soviet Union.

The Truman administration also believed that its credibility both at home and abroad, both among U.S. allies and its enemies, was at stake in Korea. The spread of Communism throughout the world and United States, for many Americans, the United States was imperiled by the threat of Communism both at home and abroad. The Soviet Union's successful testing of an atomic bomb in September 1948, the Chinese communist's victory a month later, the conviction of Alger Hiss, a former high State Department official of perjury that he had been a communist, and the admission by Karl Fuchs, a high-level atomic scientist that he had given atomic secrets to the communists. Secretary of State Dean Acheson was blamed by McCarthy and his followers, who held Acheson and other high-ranking State Department officials largely responsible for the loss of China. The Communist victory in China was a bitter blow to the Americans, who for many years support arms and military equipments and had some sort of special relationship with each other. The Democratic administration in Washington was lambasted with charges that it had lost Nationalist China, and a demagogic Republican senator named Joseph McCarthy terrorized government.

President Truman put it best when he commented soon after the North Korean invasion of South Korea that "the attack upon Korea makes it plan beyond all doubt that Communism has passed beyond the use of subversion to conquer independent nations and will now use armed invasion and war." Truman believed that the world was in a state of crisis. He was concerned with maintaining the international credibility of the United States and his own credibility at home.

Faced with such an international and domestic crisis, Truman concluded that he had no other alternative but to respond to what he regarded as naked aggression in Korea sponsored and directed from Moscow. President Truman later wrote; "if the Communists were permitted to force their way into the Republic of Korea without opposition from the free world, no small nation would have the courage to resist threads and aggression by stronger Communists neighbors."

b) United Nation

To allow South Korea to fall to the communists so soon after China had fallen would also damage American prestige in Europe and other parts of the world. At the same time, taking the matter to the Security Council let the world know just how seriously it regarded the fighting in Korea. It was also a way to achieve a collective response to the invasion rather than a unilateral action by America. The most important of them came out of a conference held between officials of the State Department and the Army, late on the morning of Sunday, June 25. There was a suggestion that if North Korea kept on fighting and if the United Nations called on member countries for assistance, the United States should authorize General MacArthur, in his role as Commander in Chief Far East, to use American forces to stabilize the situation.

Throughout this period, the initiative was taken by the State Department, and the military people rather hesitantly went along. War may be the main reason for the soldier's existence, but he seldom wants it. The suggestion for assistance was soon to come into force, for that afternoon the American deputy ambassador to the UN, 'Ernest A. Gross' presented a resolution to form a U.N. force that was passed unanimously after a short discussion, without a Soviet veto. The Soviet Union was still boycotting the UN since January 1950, protesting the UN Security Council's seating of the new Peoples Republic of China (PRC) in place of Nationalist China's seat. Thank god, God helped the Republic of Korea to survive for the Soviet's delegate not attending the UN Security Council meeting. It was a Lucky day for the Republic of Korea's fate without a Soviet Union's veto.

c) General MacArthur did an on-site Inspection.

On June 27, two days after the war began, MacArthur sent a fifteen-man mission headed by Brigadier General John H. Church to Suwon, thirty miles south of Seoul, to observe and report on the combat situation and the logistical needs of the ROK Army. The next day Church relayed to Tokyo MacArthur's office the dismaying news that Seoul had fallen and North Korean divisions had achieved major breakthroughs on the central front. Church further advised that the South Korean defenses were collapsing fast and that American forces would be needed to stop the North Korean offensive.

On June 29, MacArthur flew from Tokyo to Suwon to investigate the situation himself. In a small schoolhouse he met with Korean president Rhee, Ambassador Muccio, top ROK officers, and American military advisors. After listening to the disheartening reports of a number of the conferees, MacArthur remarked, "Well, I have heard a good deal theoretically, and now I want to go and see these troops that are straggling down the road."

According to Lieutenant General Edward Almond, MacArthur's group went to a point on the south bank of the Han River at Dongjak-dong, Yongdungpo, Seoul, where they could see "the enemy firing from Seoul." He remembered MacArthur's comment about the ROK soldiers they observed for about an hour. "It is a strange thing to me that all these men have their rifles and ammunition, they all know how to salute, they all seem to be more or less happy, but I haven't seen a wounded man yet." While watching "the pitiful evidence of the disaster I had inherited." MacArthur came to several important conclusions before leaving the scene of chaos and devastation at the Han river: His divisions in Japan would have to be dispatched to Korea after getting the President's authorization.

The next day, June 30, he reported to the Joint Chiefs of Staff:"... The Korean army and coastal forces are in confusion, have not seriously fought, and lack leadership through their own means...The Korean army is entirely incapable of counter action and there is grave danger of a further breakthrough. If the enemy advance continues much farther it will seriously threaten the fall of the Republic…To continue to utilize the forces of our Air and Navy without an effective ground element cannot be decisive.

If authorized, it is my intension to immediately move a US regimental combat team to the reinforcement of the vital area discussed near Suwon and to provide for a possible buildup to two-division strength from the troops in Japan for an early counter-offensive."

Truman quickly gave MacArthur "full authority to use the ground forces under his command, such use was qualified by the need to protect Japan." Acheson observed, "We were then fully committed in Korea." He and the President saw the sending of American ground troops into action as potentially the first stage of a global conflict. President Truman approved General's recommendation and appointed General MacArthur as Commander in Chief of the United Nation Forces.

9. FALL OF SEOUL

The North Korean attacking forces advanced at a rapid pace towards Seoul and captured it in three days on June 28, Kim Il Sung said then in his speech to the soldiers on August 15, 1950 that: [The national liberation struggle, which the Korean people are waging for the freedom and independence of their fatherland against the U.S. imperialists who attempt to enslave them, does not arise from a transient of temporary course, but from the fundamental national aspiration of the Korean people who do not wish to become slaves again to foreign imperialists…].

President Truman, over the next three days, as the North Korans continued to advance further south and occupied Seoul, Truman ordered American ground, air and naval support for South Korea and escalated America's military commitment in Korea. On June 29, he authorized the sending of a regimental combat team to Korea. Thus, Korean's civil war escalated to become a global war and over the next three years, approximately 1.7 million American soldiers, serving as part of a United Nations Command (UNC), fought against North Korea and Chinese communist forces in a conflict that dramatically changed the complexion of the Cold War and served as a precedent for U.S. involvement in the Vietnam war a decade later.

The great irony of the Korean conflict was that at the time the North Koreans invaded South Korea, most Americans had never heard of Korea and its location. Yet most Americans never really understood why the United States had to fight in Korea. Why more than 1.7 million Americans served in the armed forces there between 1950 and 1953 or why some 33,000 of US soldiers died there in battle fields. They understood, of course, that the United States was determined to halt the spread of Communism. However, that truism didn't go very far toward answering the fundamental question, Why Korea? Why did the Truman administration decided to intervene militarily in small and remote Korea after having done nothing more than protest as all of Eastern Europe and all of China fell under Communist domination ? Why was the U. S. government willing to go to the brink of World War III in order to save the repressive and only nominally democratic South Korean regime of Syngman Rhee ? Those are among the questions that this book attempts to answer.

In doing so, it will focus more on the political than on the pure military aspects of the Korean war and will examine "The Korean conflict," as it was officially designated by Washington, within the context of the global Cold War. The Korean peninsula is geographically located between Japan and Northern China, Russia and performs as role of a land bridge. Therefore, it is safe to say that Korea and its people were sacrificed and suffered a big calamity by the global Cold War induced by superpowers.

The primary reason for the Truman administration to intervene militarily in a Korean domestic civil war was that the Korean conflict was the United States national extension of the policy of containment that the U.S. had adopted this strategy for fighting the Cold war. Essentially this policy rested on the assumption of an implacable foe-the Soviet Union, whose ultimate aims were the expansion of Communism all over the world. Secondly, the Truman administration was then criticized by the republican congress for the loss of China to Communism, and they were feeling, more or less, a remorse about it. Thirdly, the United States supported the establishment of the South Korean government and was recognized by the United Nation and could not sit still, watching the Communist North Koreans capture all of South Korea and achieve Korean unification under the control of north communists who would come under the Soviets sphere of influence.

The Korean War had now begun as the first open war between the USA and a proxy of the Soviet Union. For the two Koreas, their political identity and the very survival of their peoples were at stake. But for the superpowers, influence within East Asia was at issue and Korea was a regional battleground for their global competition.

In Seoul. the North Korean invaders established a Seoul People's Committee which was made up of South Koreans, many of them public officials and assemblymen president Rhee had imprisoned as Communists. The Communists next began "recruiting" men for military service and a compulsory labor draft, primarily for emergency transport work to replace facilities damaged by U.S. air strikes. The People's Committee started a census to find families of ROK military, police, and government personnel.

More than half of Seoul's students are actively aiding the Communist invaders, with many voluntarily enlisting in the North Korean army. Apparently attracted by the glamour of a winning army, the morale of these recruits may suffer rapidly if they going get rough time. The similar disaffection in other segments of the Seoul population: The working class "generally supports the Northern Koreans, while merchants are neutral and the intelligentsia and the government officials continue to be pro-Southern."

With the North Koreans clearly in the ascendancy during July, Pyongyang Radio drummed at the theme that forty eight former members of the National Assembly still in occupied Seoul, announced to withdraw their support of Rhee and come over to the side of the "People". But whatever chances the North Koreans had for massing broad popular support were soon squandered. Because of the NKPA's logistical problems, the army literally lived off the land. Soldiers went through Seoul house to house, collecting rice, and thus food price skyrocketed consequently; by late July, Seoul rice prices were seven times higher that in Busan, eleven times more that in Daegu.

With the continuing American bombings, the leftists who initially endorsed the Communist regime "are being demoralized" by the bombings and are removing their identification armbands and modifying their behavior" because of doubts about a final North Korean victory.

10. NORTH KOREAN FORCES SQUANDERED THREE DAYS IN SEOUL

The North Korean army captured Seoul within three days after the outbreak of the conflict and suddenly stopped the assault. It appeared to be waiting for further new combat orders from higher command. Before the war, Pak Hon-yong (former leader of the South Korean Communist party, and vice premier of DPRK) insisted that if North Korean forces capture Seoul, the Partisans in the South would fight against the South Korean army unit from the rear. The 200,000 Communists in South Korea would revolt against Syngman Rhee's government. Thus, the North Korean forces waited for three days in Seoul, for the South Korean people's revolt. However, nothing had happened as they expected. They were later ordered by higher command to keep advancing further to the south. This event was a lucky auspicious one for the South Korean army for allowing sufficient time to reorganize and to array the formation of troops. And it also gave the time for the U.S. forces stationed in Japan to land safely at Busan port without any obstructions. Both U.S. and ROK Army could be able to construct the defense line of the Busan Perimeter at Nak-dong River to defend Daegu and Busan. The three days of wasting time by the North Korean invaders was a decisive factor and benefited for the U.N. forces to build a resistance line at the Busan perimeter. Later the UN forces successfully landed Inchon port and re-captured

Seoul and consequently made the UN forces repulsed all the North Korean army out of South Korean territory.

If the North Korean forces should continue to attack and advanced further south from Seoul to Busan, when they captured Seoul, Kim Il Sung might be able to achieve his goal of unification easily within a month or two as he initially planned. The Korean civil war might have ended in a month. If it was so, the American forces had little chance and justification to enter the Korean domestic civil war and might have given up the landing operation at Busan which would cost many casualties and costly fighting against enemy occupation forces. Thanks to the "Delay of three days in Seoul". Those three days gave the Eighth US Army stationed in Japan an enough time to quickly move and land on Busan port and built the defense perimeter on the Nak-dong River to defend Taegu and Busan city. Therefore, it is no exaggeration to say that the North Korean's three days squandered in Seoul saved the destiny of South Korea, and it was the blessing of heaven for the survival of the Republic of Korea. After the war, it was known that Kim Il-sung bitterly regretted the waste of three days in Seoul, and blamed severely Park Hon Yung for it. On December 23, 1954, at the joint meeting of N. Korean government officials and military authority, Kim severely criticized and reprimanded Pak Hon-yong, his vice premier for his misjudgment and put all the blame on him for the defeat of the war.

11. MASS SLAUGHTER OF POLITICAL OPPONENTS

The South Korean police and military Police massacred in large scale the South Korean leftist people who were once members of the Labour party but later they gave up their political ideas by the placation of the South Korean government before the Korean conflict started. The South Korean police and Army military police killed many leftists of convicted prisoners, Communist suspects and the people who were former members of leftist political parties, right after the North Korean's invasion to the South. Those incidents happened many different places like Inchon, Taejon, Taegu, Busan, Kwangju, Jeonju, and Yesan etc,. They brutally killed those people without fair justice or trials. They killed and threw the bodies into one big dirt hole or into the sea water. At Inchon they killed many people by firing squad at the Wolmi-do and threw into the sea, when the North Korean people's army launched the attack.

There were many partisan guerrillas in the mountains of South Korea in 1948 and 1949, supported by probably five times as many South Korean communist and sympathizers. Six thousand insurgents and suspected sympathizers in South Korean jails and most of them were killed.

When the North Korean army advanced up to Taegu and Masan, the South Korean army and police tried to kill more than thousand leftist prisoners in Busan prison. At this time an American colonel of the US Army advisory Agent assigned to ROK Army stopped them and prevented a mass execution in Busan. He wrote in his own memoir later. Journalist Alan Winnington sympathetic to the Communists, saw a mass grave near Taejon with 1,000 to 1500 victims and the US Army advisors verified that South Koreans had executed those buried there.

When the US and ROK Army recaptured and restored Seoul, one of the US Army and the British army officers witnessed at the massacre scene just before their execution. The ROK Army and the police tried to execute those over a thousands people who had helped and co-operated the North Korean army when they captured Seoul. At the same time those two army officers convinced the polices to stop and prevented the attempted slaughters.

On the other hand, the district that the North Korean troops occupied, the local South Korean families of leftists and communists who were sentenced and killed by the Korean police previously also revenged the high ranking officials of the Korean government, police and ROK Army officers with the help of the North Korean Army. The North Koreans also killed many political opponents. They killed hundreds political prisoners in the Hamhung Prison, put their bodies into a water well, when they retreated.

When the UN forces and ROK army returned back, police and ROK Military police killed the leftists and North Korean army's collaborators too. And thus the revenge of the political opponent continued constantly in the vicious circle of the retaliations.

During the Korean War, both South and North Korean people lost control of their mind to become a devil and killed their ideological opponents each other exchanging the constant retaliations.

During the war, the Korean government had empowered the ROK army soldiers and police the authority of immediate execution of enemy or communists.

12. U.S. FORCES ENTERED THE KOREAN CONFLICT

a) The Smith Task Force and Daejon Battle

The Eighth US Army was sent to Korea, right after the decision to commit ground forces. The USA hurriedly ferried formations into South Korea, commanded by General Walton Walker. Korean president Rhee placed the ROK army under the UNC command. The first reinforcements, the 24th and 25th US infantry Divisions, arrived in Korea directly from Japan. Their men had been enjoying the comforts of occupational life in Japan and were not ready for combat. Like the ROK army, the two divisions were not equipped to combat T-34s. On 1 July, a detachment of the 24th US Army divison, known as Task Force Smith, arrived at Busan and was dispatched to Osan. North Korean armor pressed the Americans back to Daejon where the 24th division was stationed.

Daejon is an important road hub, and there the entire Division, attempting to make a stand, was overrun. Its commander, Major General William Dean, was personally involved in the front line combat and was captured by the North Koreans. One North Korean officer, Lieutenant Ok Hyung-uk, later told that many Americans were too frightened to fight and had no fighting will. At first, the North

Korean soldiers did not know Americans GIs were fighting against them until they captured some American prisoners near Osan.

Most of Task Force Smith was destroyed with heavy casualties and forced to retreat to Daejon. The Kum River Line was broken. The 3rd and 4th N. Korean Divisions crossed it, Daejon lay wide open. Daejon with five highways, General Dean did not plan to hold it long. Then the Eighth Army commander, General Walker, flew into the Daejon airstrip on July 18 to talk with General Dean, and everything changed.

Walker had a great problem: he had to find a line quickly that could be defended to stop the North Korean advance. For the previous twenty four hours, Walker's chief of staff, Colonel Eugene M. Landrum recommended to lead Walker to decide that the no-retreat position had to be the North-south line of the Nakdong river and then east to Yongdok on the east coast. If the North Koreans penetrated over the Nakdong River as they had the Kum-river, the vital road and railway center of Daejon would be lost, and the Americans and ROKs would be forced back to Busan; an untenable situation.

American reinforcements were just arriving in quantity, but they needed time to get into position and to set up a line on the Nakdong-river. This meant the much-battered 24th Division, still the only force available on the battle line, had to delay the North Korean advance as long as possible. That effectively is what Walker told Dean at their July 18 meeting at the Daejon airstrip. "Hold for two days.!" Walker said. That would give him time to get the 1st Cavalry Division into position behind the 24th at Okchon and south of Daejon along the Kunsan road. The 1st Cavalry division was unloading that day at the south and west of Taejon, the Americans' retreat could be slowed. That was the plan. General Dean nodded and changed his orders: Daejon would be defended. But by July 18, the 24th Division was very near the end of its strength. The primary defense of Taejon fell on the 34th Regiment, which General Dean hastily called on from the vicinity of Nonsan. New defensive positions were established along the Kapchon river three miles west and northwest of Daejon. The division was extremely low on artillery, not only because each battalion had only two firing batteries, but because the 63rd Battalion had been overrun south of Kongju. The 52nd Battalion had been cut off near Taepyong-ri and had brought out only one 105mm howitzer. General Dean consolidated all of his 105mm howitzers into one composite battalion and emplaced it at the Daejon airstrip to defend the city and to back up the 34th Regiment. That composite unit, along with the 11th Battalion of 155mm howitzers, meant Dean had just two battalions of artillery to meet the assault of two North Korean divisions.

Daejon had been another disaster for the 24th Division. Of the nearly 4,000 men engaged there on July 19-20, nearly 30 percent (1,150men) were dead, wounded or missing (most of them dead). At noon on July 22, the division turned over the front-line positions, now back at Yongdong, to the 1st Cavalry Division. The 24th Division's strength that day was 8,600 men. In the seventeen days since Task Force Smith had first engaged North Korean forces at Osan, two NK divisions had driven the 24th back a hundred miles and had killed, wounded or captured three out of ten of the 12,200 soldiers in the division when it was committed to Korea. It lost enough equipment to provide for a division, its losses of officers had been high. On July 22, with General Dean still missing, Eighth Army ordered Major General John H. Church to take command of the division. There were many heroic actions by American soldiers of the 24th Infantry Division in these first weeks in Korea.

b) General Dean's missing

The Commanding Officer of the 34th Regiment, Colonel Beauchamp was missing. He never returned to Taejon where he was supposed to be. About 5 p.m., when General Dean discovered no one knew where Beauchamp was, he turned command of the 34th over to Colonel Washington who was the executive officer. He told him to get the withdrawal under way with speed.

Enemy fire now was increasing greatly in Taejon itself, wounding many men and spreading panic among Americans and Koreans alike.

Colonel Washington got the convoy together, placed General Dean in it and put himself at its head, they started off just before 6 p.m.

By now Daejon was in flame. Debris and walls were falling into the streets. Many buildings not ablaze had enemy snipers in them. At one intersection a military police vehicle had been destroyed. A dead MP lay behind the steering wheel. Two dead North Koreans lay in the road. Now leaderless, the convoy rushed through the city, drawing sniper fire all the way. Fifty vehicles of the convoy took a wrong turn and ended up in the same dead-end schoolyard. Men in these trucks abandoned their vehicles and they started off through the hills away from the sound of firing. Some of these men came back but many others never were heard from again. The remainder of the convoy continued on through one street with buildings on both sides burning fiercely. General Dean's vehicle and an escort jeep mistakenly sped past the turnoff to the Okchon road. When enemy fire prevented the two vehicles from stopping and turning around, they continued on south-down the Kumsan road. Other convoy vehicles also missed the tricky turn and went down the Kumsan road behind General Dean, as did the rear guard, Company L, under Captain Jack E. Smith. The rest of the convoy got on to the Okchon road, but just outside the city an enemy mortar shell hit the lead vehicle and it began to burn. A half-track pushed it out of the way. Enemy fire now struck the half-track, killed the driver and set the vehicle a fire. Machine-gun fire ranged over the road. Everyone rushed for cover in the ditches. Some Americans saw North Koreans rise from rice paddies and spray the column with burp guns. The 21st was the only force now holding up the North Korean advance. It had to withdraw on July 21 to a position four miles northwest of Yongdong.

Company L under/Captain Smith, the last unit out of Daejon, went down the Kumsan road where the enemy had lain in wait all day. Smith found the road littered with abandoned American vehicles and equipment. At one enemy road block Smith organized about 150 men, including about 50 wounded, salvaged some vehicles and joined the group with this company. And then he led the whole party through a series of small roadblocks, getting past the last one just before dark.

And when Smith got through, he kept right on going-all the way through Kumsan to Chinju, almost at the southern tip of Korea. Smith left the wounded at Busan, then continued with the rest back up to Daegu, where on July 23 Colonel Wadlington had assembled about 30 men of the 34th Regiment.

General Dean's story was less happy: one mile south of Daejon on the Kumsan road, Dean stopped his jeep, there a wrecked truck lay with several wounded men. He loaded these men onto his two jeeps and told them to go on. He and two other soldiers got on an artillery half-track that followed behind. A mile down the road, Gen. Dean's aide, Lt, Arthur M. Clarke, riding in one of the jeeps, was hit in the shoulder by small-arms fire. One mile farther on the group, with the half-track following came to a stop where a destroyed truck blocked the road. N. Korean troops with rifles and machine guns were laying down fire. Dean and the rest of the group crawled down to the bank of the Daejon River, which ran beside the road, and waited until darkness. During this time, Smith's party fought its way down the road and passed on. After dark, Dean with his group crossed to the west side of the small river and started climbing a mountain.

A little after midnight, Lieutenant Clarke, leading the group, found no one behind him. He went back and found several men asleep, but not Dean. Clarke did not know what had happened to his boss. He waited two hours, then awakened the men, and all climbed to the top of the mountain, where they waited all day, hoping to see Gen. Dean. That night, Clarke led the group eastward into the mountains, then south, eventually reaching U.S. lines at Yongdong on July 23.

Dean actually had gone down for water for the wounded men. On the way he fell down a steep slope was knocked him unconscious. When he came to his senses, he had a broken shoulder, bruises and a head gash. General Dean wandered through Korea for thirty six days, before he was captured by North Koreans. He was betrayed by two South Koreans who were pretending to help him. The North Korean soldiers who captured him, thought then his rank was only a first Lieutenant, because two stars on his cap, similar to the rank of N. Korean 1st Lieutenant. Gen. Dean was the highest ranking American

POW. He spent more than three years as a North Korean prisoner. He was released October 1953 through the repatriation of the Prisoner of War at Panmunjom, Korea. He was presented the Medal of Honor, both by the Korean and United States presidents.

The two betrayed Koreans were later captured by Korean police and they were both sentenced to put into prison. One suspect was sentenced to death and the other suspect, Han was imprisoned for 15 years, but he was released later by General Dean's petition submitted to Korean president Rhee.

13. INCHON AMPHIBIOUS LANDING

The Inchon Landing operation was a stunning and brilliant victory for the UNC forces. With this landing, the N. Korean's invasion was completely overturned. The N. Korean Army was virtually annihilated and started to retreat. While General Walker halted the North Koreans around the Busan perimeter, the US last Defense line, MacArthur was planning a more decisive action to the North. MacArthur is one of the great figures of the Korean War. At the beginning of the war, his reputation was gigantic from his victories in the Pacific war against the Japanese army. After the war, he had governed the occupation and reconstruction of Japan. So great was his influence that Washington made few attempts to control his actions. MacArthur was devout exponent of decisive warfare. Throughout the Pacific War, he had engaged in a series of amphibious assaults to outflank the Japanese, get behind their supply lines, and bypass their strong points. Thus, in Korea he did not want to continue a frontal battle at Busan, but sought to annihilate the North Koreans in one swift stroke.

In New Guinea and the Philippines he ran the most successful series of amphibious operations in history, a string of hard-won battles that carried Allied forces more than 2,500 miles into the heart of the Japanese empire. The landing at Leyte was the most famous of them, in October 1944, but a year earlier around the Huon peninsula of New Guinea. MacArthur had achieved the greatest of military victories, the destruction of a field army without fighting it, by cutting off its supplies and leaving it isolated and starving. In these great battles, MacArthur's relations with the U.S. Navy had not always been entirely harmonious, but they had always been effective. As he said when he was pushing the Inchon idea, "The Navy has never turned me down yet." MacArthur proposed an amphibious landing at Inchon, the port for Seoul. A landing there offered the opportunity to sever North Korea's lines of communication and trap its army to the south. Aside from its military achievement, MacArthur's Inchon scheme might be judged by the quality of the opposition it aroused, for almost everyone was opposed to it. Gen. Omar Bradley, Chairman of the Joint Chief of Staff and Gen. J. Lawton Collins, "Lighting Joe" of World War II fame, now Chief of Staff of the U.S. Army, thought the proposed operation was too deep in the North Korean rear which might well leave the invaders stranded and contained. Most other commanders agreed with the idea of a landing, but wanted it in some other, less difficult place, such as perhaps Kunsan, the smaller west-coast port, 100 miles south of Seoul.

Inchon was an extremely dangerous and risky point to attack. City-fighting is costly under the best of circumstances; it is even more so when soldiers must first disembark from assault craft directly under defending fire. Additionally, the Inchon harbor had deep tidal shifts, high sea walls, a narrow channel, broad mudflats, and fortified islands. The tide fell 20 feet (6m) twice per day. MacArthur, though, believed that these could be overcome and this was the point to attack. The North Koreans would never expect it. The JCS initially were skeptical about the attack. But MacArthur won them over through skillfully presenting his plan to them at a strategic planning conference in Tokyo.

The 1st US Marine and 7th US Infantry Divisions would mount the assault as part of the newly formed X US Corps. Lieutenant General Edward Almond, MacArthur's chief of staff, was given command of the Corps. Circumventing Walker, Almond answered directly to MacArthur. The X US Corps represented the last of MacArthur's reserves. He gambled, if his gamble failed and disaster struck at Inchon, there would be no troops left to retake Seoul Korea. The troops were to be put ashore on 15 September in a tidal 'window'-the period when the tide was high enough for landing craft to reach the shore. First, the Marines would seize Wolmi-do, the island controlling the harbor. Then, they would press into the city and on to capture Kimpo Airfield, Next, Seoul, the most important rail and road hub in South Korea, would be assaulted. Finally, both divisions would block the enemy retreat from the Busan perimeter. Ironically, Kim Il Sung and Kim Chaek were aware of the likelihood of an American amphibious attack at Inchon. However, they decided to stake everything on the Second Battle of the Nakdong Bulge and left Inchon relatively undefended.

Early on 15 September, UNC naval and air forces bombarded Wolmi-do. MacArthur was personally present aboard the flagship of the amphibious assault force, the USS Mount McKinley. At 6:33 am, the first battalion of the 5th Marine/regiment landed and took the key point on the island without a single fatality. The remaining battalions of the regiment assaulted Inchon itself at the next tidal window at 5.30 pm. The disembarking marines clambered over the sea wall and through enemy bunkers to capture the dominating ground surrounding the beachhead. Meanwhile, the 1st Marine Regiment landed on the city's southern outskirts. Thus the Inchon amphibious landing operation was successfully completed. (Extract from A short History of the Korean War written by James L. Stokesbury)

And therefore, most of the Korean general public very adore General MacArthur and Koreans later erected his bronze statue at MacArthur's Park in Inchon in commemoration of his meritorious service for the Korean war.

14. RE-CAPTURE OF SEOUL.

By morning the US Marines had pressed 6 miles (10Km) inland and controlled the Inchon-Seoul supply route. The North Koreans, facing the X US Corps, retreated to Seoul where 20,000 held out in a last-ditch stand. Major General O.P. Smith, commander of the Marine division, planned a two-pronged attack to take Seoul from the north and southwest. Kimpo fell to the northern group on 18 September, 1950.

Anxious to capture Seoul, General Almond threw the 7th US Division's 32nd Regiment into the attack from the southeast. The fight for Seoul was ferocious. UNC artillery fire and close air support struck the city heavily. Napalm and incendiary bomb caused big fires. Many civilians died in the fighting. The North Koreans fought fanatically, using suicide squads to destroy American tanks. They were finally defeated by 27 September when the Korean, American and UN flags were raised over the capitol building. Next day, a congratulation ceremony was held at the Korean government building. General MacArthur made a speech to congratulate the recapture of Seoul and he transferred it to Korean President Rhee. He also said that the fifty three countries of the world had promised to support the Republic of Korea. President Rhee then awarded the order of Military Merit medal (Taeguk medal) to General MacArthur.

In the meantime, Gen. Walker broke out from the Busan perimeter on 23 September. Three days later, the 1st US Cavalry and 7th US Divisions linked at Osan, trapping large numbers of N. Koreans. The NKPA (NK People's Army) fell into a rout. Trapped the North Korean forces west of Osan were smashed. Those to the east collapsed as they retreated north. Many soldiers took refuge in the Taebaek-san as guerrillas. Ranking officers frequently surrendered to the American and ROK forces. The battered 13th North Korean Division's chief of staff, Colonel Lee Hak-ku, even shot its commanding general (Major General, Hong, Young-jin), who wanted to continue reckless assaults—in order to allow the men to retreat. By the time they were back across the 38th parallel, the North Koreans had lost over 150,000 men. The UNC captured 125,000 prisoners. UNC losses in the offensive, including Inchon, were 18,000.

The Inchon landing was a stunning and brilliant victory for the UNC. The threat to South Korea was completely overturned and the NKPA virtually annihilated.

Therefore, Kim Il Sung's efforts for the unification of Korea seemed to be futile and fell through. However, while MacArthur's maneuver warfare was outstandingly effective in annihilating the North Koreans, it did not create a stable basis for peace. Rather, the decisiveness of the victory greatly threatened the Security of the Soviet Union and the Peoples Republic of China.

On October 1, MacArthur broadcast a surrender-now message to Kim Il-sung, the North Korean leader, to read as follows; "The early defeat, complete destruction of your Armed Forces, and war-making potential is now inevitable. In order that the decision of the United Nations may be carried out with a minimum of further loss of life and destruction of property, I, as the United Nations Commander-in-Chief, call upon you and the forces under your command, in whatever part of Korea situated, forthwith to lay down your arms and cease hostilities."

Two days later, Chinese premier, Chou En-lai warned that China would intervene if UN troops crossed the 38th parallel. When the Americans crossed it, Kim Il-sung exhorted his troops to fight to the last man, assuring them they did not stand alone but had "the absolute support of the Soviet Union and the Chinese people." In Beijing the Ministry of Foreign Affairs declared that the "American war of invasion in Korea has been a serious menace to the security of China from the very start, and now that American forces are crossing the 38th parallel on a large scale, the Chinese people cannot stand idly by."

MacArthur's intelligent chief, Major General Charles Willoughby, issued the following statement in response: "Recent declaration by Chinese Communist Forces leaders, threatening to enter North Korea if American Forces were to cross the 38th parallel, are probably in the category of diplomatic blackmail." Three days later the Central Intelligence Agency delivered an assessment of the situation to President Truman. "Despite statements by Chou En-lai," it read, "troop movement in Manchuria and propaganda charges of atrocities and border violations, there are no convincing indications of an actual Chinese Communist intention to resort to full-scale intervention in Korea."

At their meeting on Wake Island on October 15, Truman asked MacArthur his opinion on the likelihood of Chinese intervention. The general assured him it was unlikely, and added that North Korean resistance would end by Thanksgiving. Before the 90 minute meeting ended, the president asked him once again what the chances were for Chinese intervention. "Very little, and had they intervened in the first or second months, it would have been little bit active resistance, but we are no longer fearful of their intervention.", and the president was reassured.

15. UN FORCES ADVANCED TO 38TH PARALLEL

Upon re-capture of Seoul after the successful Inchon landing, US and ROK Army forces continued to advance up to the 38th parallel line. ROK soldiers had arrived there September 30, one day before the Americans. The initial goal of UN resolution of Jun 27 on the Korean War, by calling only for action "repel the North Korean armed attack back to 38th parallel and to restore international peace and security in the area", seemed to imply that military operations would cease once the North Koreans had been driven back above the 38th parallel. The UN Command had accomplished its initial mission by driving the North Korean army out of the South Korean territory. At this juncture, General MacArthur also obsessed to have a temptation of Korean re-unification which was an ardent desire of South Korean President Syng-man Rhee. It was ever harder to be satisfied with a truncated, partial success. Always un-satisfactory status in quo. Part of the dynamic was military victory. However, Washington had worried about expansion of the war might cause a possible friction and military interventions of China and Soviet Union, if UN Forces would reach near to their national borders. The question now was whether to cross the border. To do so would clearly risk raising tensions with China and the Soviet Union.

September 8, in a private meeting with Dr. John M. Chang, the Korean ambassador, Dean Rusk refused to make any commitments on

Korean reunification pending United Nations discussion. Chang was explicit about his own government's goals: It wanted the complete destruction of KPA (Korean People's Army) and unification of Korea under the control of existing Syngman Rhee's Southern government.

In Seoul, Korean President Syngman Rhee thought the discussion about the inviolability of the 38th parallel senseless. "We have to advance as far as the Manchurian border until not a single enemy soldier is left in our country. Regardless of what the UN Command decided, we will not allow ourselves to stop. We would advance to north and achieve an unification."

MacArthur outspokenly supported Rhee as president of a united Korea. The State Department, however, was not as certain; in early September it asked MacArthur to explain what he intended to do about Rhee when Seoul was recaptured. One must sympathize with MacArthur at this juncture. His directives, both from the UN and from Washington, spoke of the restoration of peace and security; even Acheson had said publicly that America fought "solely for the purpose of restoring the Republic of Korea to its status prior to the North Korean army invasion."

The South Korean Army and the UN forces already advanced North Korean territory on October 1st and 2nd respectively, even before the Wake Island Conference with President Truman on October 5, 1950.

General MacArthur bungled a chance to win the war in October. He decided to permit X Corps and Eighth Army to continue operating as separate Commands. Even after the Inchon landing operation, both reported separately to Far East Command headquarters in Tokyo, Japan. Long after the war ended, some of MacArthur's ranking staff officers told Army historians that they felt X Corps should have been integrated into the Eighth Army once the Inchon landing was complete. Gen.Walker complained to Gen. MacArthur about and recommended for merger under his command. These included Major General Doyle Hickey, the acting Chief of staff; Brigadier General Edward/wright, the Chief planner. But in his memoirs MacArthur professed ignorance of any such dissent. So, too, did General Almond, who also stated: "It should be noted, however, that General MacArthur was at all times fully capable of making up his own mind without benefit of advice."

16. WAKE ISLAND CONFERENCE

The Wake Island Meeting: October 5, 1950, President Truman flew over to Wake Island to have meeting with General MacArthur to discuss this important matter. President Truman could call him to the White house but he himself flew 18,000 mile trip to Wake Island which is located geographically almost half way between Washington and Tokyo. He had never met his Far East commander and thought that it was time to do so. He also wanted to treat General MacArthur with courteous respect. Although Truman kept his own counsel at the time, he confessed later to Acheson he had misgivings of his own as he prepared for the journey. He was "aware of the possibility of things going wrong," and he saw the danger of unspecified pitfalls. Acheson begged off attending. "I said that as I understood my duties, it was dealing with foreign powers, and although MacArthur seemed often to be such, I didn't think he ought to be recognized as that," Acheson said.

General Marshal also declined the trip; with MacArthur away from FEC headquarters, someone of authority should be around the Pentagon in case of military emergency. Another reason, according to Secretary of the Army Frank Pace, was that "General Marshal didn't think very much of General MacArthur…and vice versa."

Edward T. Folliard of the Washington Post noted that MacArthur did not solute the President, although they just did shake hands. "I've been a long time meeting you" President Truman said with a grin. "I hope", replied MacArthur, "it won't be so long next time."

At the meeting, MacArthur said to the President that the war in Korea would be over by November 1950, and he assured the President that there would be no Chinese or Soviet's military interventions. In case the Chinese would enter the war, it should be no problem, as it would be small number of forces, if any. He dismissed out of hand the Chinese warning that they would enter the Conflict if UN forces would cross the 38th parallel line. MacArthur had then judged that the one year old China had no surplus strength for entering the Korean War. They were so weary with the fights in a long period of Chinese civil war against American backed Nationalist Chang Ke-shik and Japanese invaders. Therefore, MacArthur thought the Chinese could not daringly fight against the worlds most powerful American forces who won the Second World War.

The Chinese and Soviet Union felt a big menaces with the recapture of Seoul and the UN forces proceeded to 38th line, Chinese Premier "Chu Eun Lai" warned seriously in the radio announcement that if UN troops would cross over the 38th line, China would have to enter the Korean War.

Having heard that some government officials were advising President Truman to announce publicly that U.S. and ROK troops would not advance north of the 38th parallel, John Allison of State Department wrote a memo to Rusk in which he strongly opposed any such announcement. "I am convinced that there will be no permanent peace and stability in Korean peninsula as long as the artificial division at the 38th parallel continues. I believe the time has come when we must be bold and willing to take even more risks than we have already…I personally feel that if we can, and I am by no means certain that we can, we should continue right on up to the Manchurian and Siberian border and having done so, call for a U.N. supervised election for all of Korea.

Like the State Department extremists, the Joint Chief of Staff could be satisfied with nothing less than the unification of Korea under an anti-Communist government, but they hoped that such a result could be attained without a US/UN invasion of North Korea. General Omar Bradley wrote in his autobiography: "The JCS agreed that in order to preclude another North Korean invasion of South Korea, the North Korean Army should be utterly destroyed. It was our hope that the North Korean Army could be destroyed in South Korea. We believe that MacArthur should not be restrained at the 38th parallel. However, in order to minimize the possibility of Soviet or Chinese intervention, we felt that ground operations north of the 38ᵗʰ parallel should be conducted mostly by ROK forces, with continued American air and naval support.'

At the Wake Island meeting, MacArthur apologized for his earlier letter to the Veterans of Foreign Wars and stated that the war in Korea would be over by November. He dismissed the Chinese warning. In his view, China made the threat only because it was greatly embarrassed by the turn of events in Korea. The Chinese warning was merely a sort of threat. Encouraged by MacArthur's comments, Truman left the Wake Island meeting saying that he had never had a more satisfactory conference.

Influenced by these winds of war and displaying considerable hubris, therefore, the administration gave UN forces in Korea orders to continue their advance northward in September 1950, under the one condition that there would be no Chinese and/or Soviets military interventions. On the western side of the Korea, the Eighth Army moved northward under the command of General Walton Walker. In the east, the X Corps, consisting of the First Marine Division, ROK Army and the Army's Seventh Infantry Division, advanced under the command of General Edward M. Almond. (Excerpt from The Korean War, written by Richard Whelan)

On October 1, the ROK Army started to cross the line and US Forces crossed the next day and from there UN Forces pushed the North Korean Army all the way back to the Korean-Chinese border. Although Beijing had agreed only reluctantly to North Korea's invasion of South Korea, it had begun to prepare for entry into the war. At this time the Chinese Voluntary Forces started to attack the UN forces forcing to retreat all the way back to South of 38ᵗʰ line and lost Seoul again on Jan 4, 1951. The study of the Korean War history revealed that the War could be ended in three (3) months, instead of 3 years 1 month 2 days, if the UN forces had stopped at the 38ᵗʰ

Parallel line on September 30, 1950, as abided by the United Nation's resolution.

17. KIM IL-SUNG ASKED URGENT HELP TO STALIN

When the UN forces recaptured Seoul after the successful Inchon landing and continued to advance to 38th parallel, N. Korean Kim and Park sent the following urgent letter to Stalin, asking emergency help, on September 30, 1950, right before the UN forces cross the 38th line.

[Esteemed Comrade Stalin, On behalf of the Korean Worker's Party, We appreciate you from the bottom of our heart. You are great benefactor of Korean liberation and a great leader of world's labor class. For your grateful assistance to the Korean people who endeavor for their independence and unification. It is deemed necessary for the Soviet troops to enter the Korean War, when the enemy would cross the 38th line to invade our county, we would be unable to defend by ourselves, and therefore we are obliged to ask for your help. If the enemy forces would cross the 38th parallel line, we will absolutely need the Soviet troops. If the Soviet forces intervention would not be possible, we suggest forming an international voluntary military force organized by China and other Democratic countries to aid and support our fight. We dare to propose the above said suggestion to you and we will be expecting your favorable consideration and decision.]

Under the war situation at the time, North Korean forces could not continue to fight the war by themselves, without the help of either Chinese or the Soviet armed forces. The North Korean Army (KPA) were almost completely destroyed and smashed incoherently indeed, until the Chinese voluntary forces entered the Korean War on October 19, 1950. In the mean time, Stalin ordered 200Mig-15 jet fighters to Andong, China, located right across from Sinui-ju North Korea, and had dispatched five (5) infantry divisions near Korean-Soviet border, in preparation for a possible intervention.

18. CHINESE WARNING

From the very first day of the war American intelligence had pondered whether the Soviets or the Chinese—or both—would enter the war as active combatants. And the very beginning the analysts consistently reached much the same conclusion: Both nations had the capacity to do so but probably would not, for international political reasons.

As soon as the ROK and American forces reached to the 38th parallel, the Soviets and the Chinese were much strained and alerted. Analysts came to recognize that the major warnings they dismissed as "diplomatic blackmail" were exactly what they purported to be: a clear statement to the United States of the course of action China intended to follow of American troops crossed the 38th parallel.

The warning came through the Indian ambassador in Peking, K.M. Pannikar, pro-Communist and anti-American. The Chinese leadership treated Pannikar as a useful tool; high officials dined him, and praised him, knowing full well that the message they planted with him would swiftly pass through his foreign office to London and then to the United States.

On September 25 Paninikar dined with General Nieh Jung-chen, acting chief of the Chinese military. Then the general Nieh told Pannikar that his people "did not intend to sit back with folded hands and let the Americans come up to their border." When Pannikar protested how destructive total war would be, Nieh replied with a laugh. "We have calculated all that. They may even drop atomic bombs on us. What then? They may kill a few million people. Without sacrifice a nation's independence cannot be uphold." Nieh did not fell a war could be won by air bombardment alone, and he did not believe the United States could spare combat troops to fight in China.

Pannika immediately reported the conversation to the Indian Foreign Office. It immediately fell into British hands for relay to London and then to the British embassy in Washington. It arrived on the afternoon of September 27. The State Department consensus was that it was propagandistic bluster. A week later Pannikar was heard from again, and this time he conveyed a warning from an even higher source. The Chinese Foreign Ministry summoned him from his bed shortly after midnight on October 2 and directed that he come to the residence of Prime Minister Chou En-lai immediately. Chou greeted the Indian with tea and polite small talk and apologies for arousing him at such an hour. Then he delivered his message: If the Americans cross the 38th parallel, China would be forced to intervene in Korean conflict. Otherwise, Chou was anxious for a peaceful settlement with American. "Has Chou heard of any actual border crossings by the Americans?" Pannikar asked. "Yes," Chou replied, "he had heard they had crossed, but he did not know where. "What if only South Koreans crossed the parallel? Chou's reply was emphatic: "The South Koreans did not matter, but American intrusion into North Korea would encounter Chinese resistance." This time Pannikar's warning received considerably more attention, but again widely varying interpretations. Administration officials were clearly nervous on the morning of October 3. The Associated Press was carrying a story about a nine-mile long Chinese Army column, including artillery, stretching from Manchuria across the Amrok (Yalu) river into North Korea.

The Pannikar signals were part of intelligence studied by the CIA in preparing a briefing book for President Truman for use at his Wake Island Conference on October 5. The Chinese ground forces "are capable of intervening effectively, but not necessarily decisively," in the war. But it concluded: "Despite statements by Chou En-lai, troop movements to Manchuria, and propaganda charges of atrocities and border violations, there are no convincing indications of an actual Chinese Communist intention to resort to full-scale intervention in Korea." The CIA concluded it would not do so. The major reason: "The Chinese Communists undoubtedly fear the consequences of war with the United States. Their domestic programs are of such magnitude that their entire domestic program and economy would jeopardize by the strains." The ROK forces had already crossed the 38th parallel on October 1, and the American forces crossed next day, by the order of the UN Command.

Stalin and Chou; In early autumn Joseph Stalin received Chinese Foreign Minister Chou En-lai at the Soviet premier's vacation retreat in Sochi. Chou approached Stalin by direction of Mao Tse-tung. According to Nikita Khrushchev, "Chou asked Stalin whether Chinese troops out to be moved into North Korean territory in order to block the path of the Americans and South Koreans." Stalin and Chou at first "seemed to conclude that it was fruitless for China to intervene." But after lengthy discussion they reached a decision: China would give "active support to North Korea." Both Chou and Stalin, according to Khrushchev, "believed these troops could manage the situation completely." Chou flew back to Peking with Stalin's support.

CHAPTER III

THE CHINESE INTERVENTION

1. UN FORCES CROSS THE 38TH PARALLEL

When the ROK and American forces reached to the 38th parallel, the Soviets and the Chinese were greatly strained and alerted. Analysts came to recognize that the major warnings they dismissed as "diplomatic blackmail" were exactly what they purported to be: a clear statement to the United States of the course of action China intended to enter the war to follow of American troops crossed the 38th parallel.

The Associated Press was carrying a story about a nine-mile long Chinese Army column, including artillery, stretching from Manchuria across the Amrok (Yalu) river into North Korea.

The Pannikar signals were part of intelligence studied by the CIA in preparing a briefing book for President Truman for use at his Wake Island conference on October 5, 1950. The Chinese ground forces "are capable of intervening effectively, but not necessarily decisively," in the war. But it concluded: "Despite statements by Chou En-lai, troop movements to Manchuria, and propaganda charges of atrocities and border violations, there are no convincing indications of an actual Chinese Communist intention to resort to full-scale intervention in Korea." The CIA concluded it would not do so. The major reason: "The Chinese Communists undoubtedly fear the consequences of war with the United States. Their domestic programs are of such magnitude that their entire domestic program and economy would jeopardized by the strains." The ROK forces had already crossed the

38th parallel on October 1, and the American forces crossed next day, by the order of the UN Command.

Stalin and Chou; In early autumn Joseph Stalin received Chinese Foreign Minister Chou En-lai at the Soviet premier's vacation retreat in Sochi. Chou approached Stalin by direction of Mao Tse-tung. According to Nikita Khrushchev, "Chou asked Stalin whether Chinese troops out to be moved into North Korean territory in order to block the path of the Americans and South Koreans." Stalin and Chou at first "seemed to conclude that it was fruitless for China to intervene." But after lengthy discussion they reached a decision: China would give "active support to North Korea." Both Chou and Stalin, according to Khrushchev, "believed these troops could manage the situation completely." Chou flew back to Peking with Stalin's support.

By Khrushchev's account, there was no mention of Stalin's expressing any willingness to have Soviet troops enter the war. As had been the case the previous spring, when Stalin approved Kim Il-sung's invasion, the Soviets were to act through a surrogate state, this time Communist China.

On 19 October, the I Corps' 1st Cavalry Division and the 1st ROK Division entered Pyongyang, the North Korea capital. On the 24[th,] MacArthur ordered his commanders to advance as quickly as possible, with all forces available, so that operations could be completed before Thanks giving day. The press of the Eighth Army in the West was relentless and unreasonable, as it sent separate columns North toward the Amrok-river, the town of Chosan.

2. CHINESE VOLUNTEER ARMY CROSSED THE AMROK RIVER

American entry into the Korean War greatly concerned the Chinese Communist. An American victory in Korea would threaten their security and ideological interests. Indeed, the Chairman Mao and Premier Zhou En-lai viewed the American intervention as part of a grand plan to control East Asia. Accordingly, on 13 July 1950, four armies were dispatched to the Korean-Chinese border. It would defend China's border and support the operation of the North Korean armed forces. Historian Chen Jian describes in "China's Road to the Korean War", at a meeting of the Chinese Politburo on 4 August 1950, Mao said: "if the US imperialists win the war they would become more arrogant and would threaten us. We should not fail to assist the Koreans. We must lend them our hands in the form of sending our military volunteers there." However, Mao could not yet intervene because of the PLA was unprepared.

The Inchon landing brought the question of Chinese intervention to a head. As the North Korean People's Army (NKPA) disintegrated, Pak Il Wu, first North Korean Minister of Interior Affairs, and then Kim himself requested immediate Chinese intervention to save North Korea. For Mao and CCP, the annihilation of the N. Korean army increased the threat that the USA posed to China. The battle line was rapidly approaching Manchuria, a vital industrial region. On 24 September, Zhou protested the accidental American bombing of Andong (now Dandung) to the UN. Two days later, Nie Rongzhen, the acting PLA chief of staff, told K.M. Panikkar, Indian ambassador to the PRC, that the PRC would not passively await an American advance to the Sino-Korean border.

The American landing at Inchon also gave them a threat for their national security. The occupation of whole Korea would upset the entire balance of power in East Asia. American forces would be directly on Soviet borders as well as China's. Nevertheless, Stalin was still unwilling to risk a direct military confrontation. Therefore, Stalin asked Mao if China was in a position to interfere. He promised to supply military equipments and that the Soviet air force would provide air superiority for the Chinese armies. Mao did not respond to Kim and Stalin's requests until 2 October. At a special convened meeting of the CCP Politburo, Mao announced his intention of intervention. After the meeting, with the Politburo's tentative support, Mao sent a telegram to Stalin, comprehensively summarizing his plan. A portion of the PLA would be sent to Korea as the Chinese People's Volunteers (CPV). Although he expected American retaliation against Chinese soil, Mao's goal was nothing less than the decisive annihilation of the UNC forces in Korea. He hoped to avoid a stalemate, which would drain China's resources and stunt its economic reconstruction. Zhou was sent to Moscow to ask for large amounts of aid and weapons, as well as reconfirmation of Soviet air support. Before his departure, at midnight on 2 October, Zhou told Panikkar that "if the USA crossed the 38th parallel, the PRC would not sit still and do nothing," Nevertheless, in all likelihood, there was little the USA could have done to dissuade Mao from intervening at this point. Zhou's message was probably just meant to buy time for the CPV(Chinese People's Volunteer) to concentrate in North Korea. On 3 October, Mao appointed Peng Dehuai to command the CPV. Peng was one of the PLA's best leaders and was known for his courage in tough situations. The final orders to the CPV to enter Korea were issued on 8 October 1950. The Chinese decision to intervene gave Stalin what he wanted. When he met with Zhou on 11 October, Stalin said that the Soviet Union would provide all of the artillery, armor, aircraft, and military equipment needed, but the PRC would have to pay back for it later. It was not a free military support.

Meanwhile, the Eighth US Army approached the 38th parallel. MacArthur was hypnotized by the allure of total victory. He disregarded the repeated Chinese warnings. Not many in the American government take the warnings seriously. MacArthur and the American government sought to unify Korea under the ROK, as the Korean president Syngman Rhee eagerly wanted. In late September, the JCS and Acheson decided to pursue the NKPA north of the parallel as long as there was no threat of major Soviet or Chinese intervention. Despite the repeated Chinese warnings not to advance over the 38th parallel to cross into North Korea, on October 1st, ROK troops crossed the 38th parallel, followed by the rest of the Eighth Army on 2 October, for the increasing momentum to unify Korea.

Truman was concerned about the repercussions of crossing the 38th parallel. He arranged a meeting with MacArthur on Wake Island to discuss the situation. At the hugely publicized meeting on 5 October,

MacArthur reassured Truman that there were no signs of Chinese or Soviet intent to intervene of the Korean War.

MacArthur deployed his forces on diverging line of advance. The Eighth Army equipped with the tanks and mobile transportation advanced in the flat west, taking Pyongyang on 20 October and then moving on toward the Amrok-River (Yalu River). The ROK Army advanced in the mountainous east of Korea. The X US Corps, still acting directly under MacArthur, conducted a belated amphibious landing at Wonsan on 26 October (where the ROK Army I Corp had already occupied), and drove north. UNC front-line strength was approximately more than 200,000 infantry soldiers. In the meantime, a column of Chinese voluntary infantry was crossing the AmrokRiver into N. Korea. In October and November 1950, the Chinese Army under the name of the Chinese people's Volunteers (CPV), massed in the northern part of Korea, waiting to spring their trap against the carelessly advancing UNC forces. The Chinese CPV Army entered the Korean War in force on 25 October 1950. In the west, the thirteenth CPV Army Corps threatened to encircle the Eighth US Army. The 2nd US Division was cut off at Kunu-ri and virtually annihilated while retreating south. The entire army was forced south in a disorganized rout. In the east, the ninth CPV Army Corps encircled the 1st US Marine Division of X US Corps at the Jangjin area (Chosin reservoir). The morning of October 25 a battalion of the ROK 6th Division moved northwest from the tiny crossroads village of Onjong, the first move in a planned forty-mile push to Byokdong, on the Yalu River. Then enemy fire was encountered. The nature of the Korean conflict would now fundamentally change.

The ROK army unworriedly dismounted from their trucks and fanned out to displace what their commanders assumed was a small delaying force of North Korean army. Within a few minutes the battalion was decimated; of its 750 man strength, 350 were killed, wounded, or captured.

Another ROK battalion hurriedly moved up the same road. It could not dislodge the Chinese, but it did take two prisoners. One of them said Chinese forces had been waiting in the mountains since October 17 to ambush the advancing ROK Army. On October 28 the ROKs committed yet another regiment in the same area. It ran into a Chinese roadblock near Kojang and survived only with the aid of close American air support. At nightfall, however, the air cover ended, and the Chinese killed or captured the few men who did not flee to the mountains. Of the 3,552 officers and men in the regiment, only 875 escaped. To the west, in the area above the Chongchon toward Unsan, the ROK 1st Division also encountered the Chinese on October 25. And that afternoon a prisoner was taken. The man wore a North Korean uniform, but interrogation quickly established his true identity: Shien Chung San, thirty years old, a private in the Chinese Communist Army. He told the following story: "Shien's unit, consisting of some 2,000 men, left Tangshan, Manchuria, about eighteen miles north of the frontier. On October 19, they traveled to Antung, on the Yalu by train. They were then issued North Korean uniforms and instructed to remain silent if captured unless they could speak Korean. They then marched across the Yalu river on a newly constructed wooden bridge and into the mountains. Officers told them the United States had 100,000 troops in Korea and that China was going to send 600,000 men to defeat the U.S." The next day, October 26, even more Chinese prisoners were brought to Pyongyang for interrogation. These could be no doubt of their nationality.

Eighth Army intelligence officers collected these reports and dispatched to Tokyo with an admonition that a new enemy was definitely in the war. Tokyo did not believe it. MacArthur's headquarters airily dismissed the reports. Since the information about a Chinese presence came from POW interrogations, "the information was unconfirmed and thereby unaccepted." In a supplemental analysis the next day, with even more Chinese POWs in hand, General Charles Willoughby still spoke of the "potential" of Chinese intervention, rather than its reality. Even if the Chinese were in Korea, they should not be taken seriously. He wrote: It is to be recognized that most of the CCF troops have had no significant experience in combat operations against a major combat power. In addition, their training has been greatly handicapped by the lack of uniform equipment and assured stocks of munitions.

The CPV was composed of the thirteenth and ninth CPV Army Corps, for a total of 300,000 men. The former, commanded by General Deng Hua, contained four CPV Armies, of three divisions each. Deng had carefully trained the Thirteen CPV Army Corps. Its soldiers were of a very high caliber. For example, the 38th CPV Army of the Thirteenth CPV Army Corps was known as an elite formation from its performance in the Chinese Civil War.

General Lin Piao commanded on the western front, and Sung shin-lun commanded in the north central part of North Korea which would engage the U.S. 1st Marine Division in Jangjing (Chosin) reservoir area. The nature of the Korean conflict would now fundamentally change.

3. CHINESE ARMY OFFENSIVE

On the eve of the Chinese offensive there was not anyone with sufficient rank to challenge MacArthur's assertion that the war would be over by Christmas. On November 24, the general launched his "home by Christmas" offensive. But on 26 November, the Chinese answered by counterattacking. The Chinese launched their massive assault that day. UN troops were divided into two major commands, the Eighth Army under the command of General Walton Walker on the west, and the X Corps consisting of the 1st Marine Division led by Major general Edward M. Almond on the east. Gen, Walker didn't like that. A number of military analysts would later claim that the separation of these two forces was the major reason for the humiliating defeat the Chinese were able to inflict on UN forces; that they were able to exploit this gap to outflank both forces. Roy Appleman, a retired Marine colonel and military historian argues that the separation of command between the Eighth Army and X Corps was a mistake. Making any kind of coordinated military response to the Chinese invasion was virtually impossible.

The Chinese offensive began on the night of November 26. Hardened by just having won the Chinese Civil War, Chinese troops were also experienced and well disciplined. The CPV (Chinese People's Volunteers), unlike the NKPA, was poorly equipped in the beginning. It lacked artillery and was not mechanized.

Despite the recent increase in Soviet assistance, most of its small arms and ammunition had been captured from the Nationalist Chinese (Made in USA or Japan). Logistics were primarily organized through civilian laborers who carried supplies to the front on foot. Thus, the CPV could not advance far without suffering supply difficulties. However, tremendous manpower and a strong base of recent combat experience offset these disadvantages. Most CPV soldiers had experienced combat in the large field operations at the end of the Chinese civil war. They were hardy marchers and adept at off-road movement. Peng emphasized the quick and bold movement of infantry to encircle and overwhelm the enemy. Attacks were to be conducted at night when the element of surprise would facilitate a breakthrough. Most Chinese leaders, buoyed by their success in the Second World War and the Chinese Civil War, believed that deception, stealth, and night fighting would enable their poorly armed soldiers to overcome Western technological and material superiority.

The thirteenth CPV Army Corps first crossed the Amrok river on 14 October 1950. Two weeks later, it mounted a limited attack on the two ROK Corps in order to stunt the Eighth Army advance, this attack was known as the First Phase Offensive. After smashing a ROK and an American regiment, Peng returned to the defensive, waiting for the UNC to advance and overextend itself. Although Walker ordered a tactical withdrawal, MacArthur did not appreciate the gravity of what had occurred. He believed that only a small number of Chinese troops were actually in Korea and that a quick advance would pre-empt further intervention. On 24 November, MacArthur and Walker resumed the UNC advance, falling into Peng's trap. Expecting a quick and painless end to the war, UNC soldiers and officers advanced recklessly. Formations became strung out and did not take proper precautions against a counterattack, although General Walker, at least, proposed a fairly cautious advance.

On the evening of 25 November, Peng Teh-huai, Deputy Commander of Gen. Chu Teh, Chinese Communist Forces Commander, and his CPV sprung upon the renewed UNC advance to open the Second phase offensive. The Thirteenth CPV Army Corps, of 189,000 men, was to crush the II ROK Corps in central Korea and then cut off the retreat of the I and IX US Corps to the west. Mao and Peng hoped this offensive might unify the Korean peninsula under Communist control. The assaulting Chinese infantry moved off-road to encircle and then overwhelm UNC units. Lacking sufficient radios, Chinese used bugles, drums, and other instruments to coordinate their movements. These surprise attacks were very disorienting to the average UNC soldiers. By the end of 26 November, the ROK II Corps had completely disintegrated. The Chinese were surrounding the 42nd US Infantry Division. Meanwhile, the Chinese pressed the fronts of the two American Corps in order to pin them against the flanking movement. The I US Corps were forced to retreat hurriedly down the coast. The entire Eighth Army was threatened with encirclement.

Disregarding reports from the front, Walker and MacArthur would not permit the 2nd US Division to retreat until 28 November. By then, the 38th CPV Army had cut off the division's escape route, the road from Kunu-ri to Sunchon, South Pyongan province. The Chinese ensconced themselves on the hillsides overlooking the road and maintained a constant rain of small arms fire on to the road-bound 2nd US Division. They used satchel charges, grenades, and mortar shelling to destroy American vehicles and equipment. American troops quickly lost all cohesion. The road became filled with the wreckage of American tanks, artillery, and transport vehicles. Chinese infantry usually advanced at night. They were adept at infiltration tactics, night combat and off-road movement. Their surprise attacks accompanied by eerie sounds of whistles and bugles, disconcerted UNC soldiers. UNC air strikes napalmed the hillsides and hampered the CPV encirclement. The 38th CPV Army was unable physically to block the road, allowing the disorderly American soldiers to escape.

By 30 November, the remnants of the 2nd US Division met with the forward positions of the 27th Commonwealth Brigade, which had been attempting to relieve them. The division had taken 5,000 casualties. Meanwhile, the rest of the IX and I US Corps, with some elements of the 2nd US Division, retreated to safety via Anju on the west coast. The Chinese had not moved fast enough to block this escape route.

In the mountains around the Jangjin reservoir, the ninth CPV Army Corps of 120,000 men was preparing to encircle the X US Corps. In accordance with MacArthur's orders for an offensive to the Yalu, the 1st US Marine Division had advanced along the western edge of the Jangjin reservoir toward the Amrok river. To Almond's anger, Smith had wisely slowed the advance of the Marine division in order to concentrate his forces and maintain a steady flow of supplies. As the Marines marched north, the temperature dropped below freezing and it began to snow. It was a record breaking heavy snow and cold winter in that year of 1950. The 1st US Marine Division was an elite formation. Many of the Marines had extensive combat experience in the Pacific War. This formation of combat experience was one of the major reasons that the Marines performed well in Korea. Another was the degree to which the Marines emphasized loyalty and unit cohesion. The Marines were committed to standing together and fighting it out in difficult situations.

On the night of 27 November, the Chinese struck. They cut off the lead 5th and 7th Marine Regiments at Yudam-ri and surrounded the 1st Marine Regiment at Hagaru and Koto-ri. In mass numbers, the Chinese and North Koreans mounted frontal assaults on the Marine positions. Nearly every man took part in the fighting. All Marines, whatever their specialization, were trained to fight as infantrymen. Sergeant James H. Fearns was a mechanic who quickly departed from his duties to serve as a front-line infantryman. He found the Chinese to be much more determined opponents than the North Koreans. The North Koreans would retreat once pushed off a position. The Chinese, on the other hand, would stand and fight. However, the Chinese often made gross tactical errors. Besides frontally attacking the same strong positions repeatedly, they did not know how to exploit a breakthrough.

They would mill around on captured hills, making wonderful targets. Despite being outnumbered, the Marines inflicted hideous casualties on the Chinese frontal assaults. Every time the Chinese captured a ridge, the Marines counterattacked and drove them back off it. Napalm was dropped from F-4 fighters exploding against the Chinese blocking the retreat of Marines from the Jangjin, South Hamkyong province. In spite of being surrounded, the Marines fought their way out, destroying several CPV divisions. China's lack of technology and sophisticated military equipment and its poor lines of communication limited what Chinese could achieve on the battlefield, especially when compared to the modern technology and heavy firepower of American forces.

On 29 November, Smith ordered Colonel Litzenberg, commanding the 7th Marine Regiment at Yudam-Ri to break out to Hagaru. One battalion attacked cross-country and broke through the Chinese block at the Toktong Pass, while the bulk of the two regiments pressed down the road frontally. Steep hills and ridges lined both sides of the road. The Chinese were able to fire upon the column and wounded Marines, destroyed transportation and temporarily blocked the road. Individual Marines independently remedied problems as they arose, such as clearing wreckage off the road, assisting wounded men, or engaging the Chinese. In the daytime, US Marine Corps corsair fighter-bombers napalmed strafed, and bombed the hillsides. Through their combined efforts, the column trudged forward.

On 3 December, the vanguard of the column entered Hagaru. From Hagaru, the entire Marine force pressed on to Koto-ri. Then to the X US Corps lines and retreated safety to Sihung-ri. Smith allegedly told reporters: "Retreat, hell-we are attacking in another direction." The entire X US Corps evacuated Hungnam and left North Korea by Christmas Day. The Marines suffered 4,400 battle casualties in the fighting around the Jangjin area. The Ninth CPV Army Corps was badly damaged and had to be withdrawn to Manchuria for reorganization with. More than 20,000 casualties, most killed by the cold, littered the hillsides, frozen and covered with snow.

However, the Marines' heroism at Jangjin battle cannot mask the catastrophic results of the Chinese intervention for the UNC. The UNC fell back all the way to the 38th Parallel in the longest retreat in American military history. Even though only 13,000 casualties were suffered, the UNC ground forces, for the most part, were transformed into a disorganized mob. Captain Charles Bussey, of the 77th US Engineer Combat Company, described his recollections of the retreat in his book; [We'd been humiliated, debased, overwhelmed-routed... The news writers would slant it all to sound like a minor setback. Take it from me, however, it was carnage. Intelligence said they hit us with one-third of a million men. I believe it. They turned our Army into a leaderless horde, running headlong for Busan. Our soldiers had lost every bit of confidence in all of their leaders, from the commander in chief down to platoon leaders.]

American decision-makers now believed that they were faced the choice of either withdrawing entirely from Korea-tantamount to surrendering or escalating the conflict further. Escalation could bring the Soviet Union directly into the fighting. Thus, the Korean conflict threatened to trigger a Third World War.

One thing seemed very clear, the United States would now have to renounce, once and for all, its goal of unifying Korea militarily. Under the present circumstances, the United States would have to redefine its maximum military aim as the restoration of the status quo ante bellum. President Truman and his advisors considered the possibility of evacuating all U.S./UN forces from Korea as soon as they reached their beach heads, without waiting to see whether the defensive perimeters would hold. But that policy was rejected. The United States could not just pull out of Korea and leave the South Korea to their dismal fate. Such a cowardly and dishonorable course of action would imperil all of America's alliances. The administration feared, it would probably consign all of Asia, in the long run, to Communist domination. There was some talk of establishing Syngman Rhee's government and army on the island of Cheju-do, off the southern coast of Korea, just as the Chinese Nationalists had sought refuge on Formosa. The idea was also rejected except as a last resort.

Gen. MacArthur wanted to bomb Manchuria. He told General Lawton Collins on December 7, he wanted Washington to allow Chiang Kai-shek to send 50,000 and 60,000 Chinese Nationalist troops to Korea. He also wanted authorization to blockade the Chinese coast. He felt that if Washington was not prepared to grant those demands, then the United States should abandon Korea at once. The JCS notified MacArthur that he would have to manage with the men he already had. As for the Chinese Nationalists, the JCS countered that if Chiang sent men to Korea, the far more efficient and valuable British troops would withdraw from Korea. The JCS told MacArthur to stay in Korea if he could but to prepare to withdraw to Japan if necessary.

4. TRUMAN SUGGESTED THE USE OF ATOMIC BOMB.

General MacArthur announced on November 28, that it was "entirely a different War," with the Chinese intervention. He never anticipated it and had guessed wrong. At this juncture, President Truman observed that UN Forces had been incoherently retreated by the Chinese offensive. He announced a suggestive comment in a press conference that he might consider the use of Atomic bomb in Korean. He said "we are fighting in Korea for defending our national security. We had pledged the justice and maintain a world's peaceful order through the United Nation."

In the meantime, England's Premier 'Atlee', upon hearing this news, hurriedly flew to Washington to meet President Truman. He suggested that they should seek a truce negotiation with the Chinese. He had worried about the future of England's control of Hong Kong in which was in Chinese territory. However, Truman then replied to Atlee that he did not want to acknowledge the defeat of the war. He promised Atlee to notify him in advance when an Atomic bomb would be used. Truman had suggested three times thereafter of possible use of the bomb, whenever he was faced with an unfavorable war situations. The new elected Eisenhower, the successor of President

Truman, also threatened the use of an atomic bomb to induce of truce negotiations.

The deputy Secretary of State, Dean Rusk recollected in his memoir saying that "President Truman did not really want nuclear war on the Korean peninsula. To tell the truth, we had only few atomic bombs at that time. The bomb that hit 'Nagasaki', Japan was the only bomb and the last one we had at the time. We had just possessed the nuclear weapon for a strategic purpose. It was not seriously considered to use it for the Korean War."

When the United States warned to possible use of Atomic bomb, Mao declared, "The Atom bomb is a paper tiger. We have the spiritual atom bomb. Weapon decide nothing, Man decides everything."

5. THE CHOSIN BATTLE AND THE HUNGNAM WITHDRAWAL OPERATION

When the United Nations forces resumed their offensive on November 14, 1950, no one was quite sure what was going on. General Walker's Eighth Army would drive to the west border, and Gen. Almond's X Corps, U.S. I and IX Marines Division on the eastern flank and would move North West, toward the Manchurian border. In northern-eastern Korea it was already winter. Up in the high mountain around the high plateau, the temperature had fallen to thirty or forty degrees below zero, with forty to fifty mile an hour high winds dropping it even further. Engine oil froze, gun breeches froze, and hands and feet froze. It was an especially cold winter with heavy snow in that particular year. Under these conditions that seven Chinese divisions along with two North Korean divisions attacked the US Marines and other troops around the Jangjin (Chosin) reservoirs.

The region of Jangjin and Bujong Plateau (Japanese maps call the "Chosin and Fusen reservoirs") on November 28, after dark, the Chinese, six of their seven divisions, took the offensive against the 1st Marine Division, inflicting heavy casualties. They launched heavy attacks, both frontal and flanking, on the perimeter at Yudam-ri, with three division. There were lesser attacks against the Hagaru base, and on the soldiers of 7th Division east of the reservoir. The Americans held these until December 1, but by then it was obvious that there was not going to be an additional United Nation offensive. General Almond, Commanding General of X Corp, was instructed to pull his Corps out and evacuate. On December 1, the 5th and 7th Marine Regiments pulled out with their wounded and dead on trucks. They headed south, with heavy air support from the Marine Air Wing, kept the Chinese at a distance as much as they could. There was frustration and irritation in Washington. Anger and heartburn in Tokyo, but there was fighting and death in Korea. The Eighth Army was below Pyongyang, and on December 6, General Smith began moving south out of Hagaru. The airstrip had been a blessing; 4,300 wounded had been evacuated, and supplies and ammunition flown in. It took the Marines two days to travel twelve miles down to Koto-ri, by the evening of December 7, Gen, Smith had his division concentrated there. He had about 14,000 men, of whom around 12,000 were Marines; most of the rest were Army, and there were few Royal Marines and ROKs. They had to reach Sinheung-ri, some fifteen miles south and then retreat up to Hungnam harbor. Almost all U.N. troops retreated to Hungnam port. It was now the Navy's turn. As the ground forces fell back in the east and in the west coast, there had to be evacuations. The navy began pulling rear-echelon units out of Inchon. From December 7 to January 5, the Navy took off almost 70,000 personnel, 91,000 North Korean refugees and more than 60,000 tons of supplies, as well as 1,400 vehicles.

By the end of the year, UN forces were on 38th parallel. General Walker, Commander of Eighth US Army, was killed in a traffic accident, and he was replaced by General Ridgway.

The real activity came on the east coast, however, for the whole of X Corps was going out by sea in a Dunkirk-style operation. The order of evacuation was 1st Marines Division, ROKA, 7th Infantry, then 3rd Infantry Regiments. As soon as the Marines had fought their way out into the perimeter, they were trucked to the harbor and loaded aboard the attack transports, LSTs, and even some chartered civilian commercial vessels. By the morning of the 15th, the division sailed from Hungnam. No one was sorry to see the coastline recede, and now they felt much relief. Three days later the ROK army soldiers followed. The last of the soldiers went out on Christmas Eve. While this went on, the cruisers, destroyers, and aircraft carriers provided first gunfire and air support. Then engineers demolition fire (590,000 tons) the harbor and factory installations in Hungnam.

The Chinese launched repeated probes against the defense line, but did not make a concerted effort to interfere with the extraction. One of the biggest problems was refugees once again. Many North Koreans were seizing a last opportunity to vote with their feet. The Navy actually took off 91,000 of them, almost as many civilians as troops. Admiral Doyle was in charge of directing the operation. About 132 Navy vessels together with some chartered commercial vessels joined in the withdrawal operation. It was recorded as the biggest Army withdrawal operation in the history of United States. The Navy took off with 17,000 vehicles, 29,000 fuel drums, 9,000 tons of ammunition, and 350,000 tons of supplies and equipment besides the Army personnel and the North Korean refugees.

Speaking of the North Korean civilian refugees, they were mostly ordinary people. Most of the North Korean civilians were afraid of the American's violent air bombing. They were nervous and became neurotic. At the time, the ROKA soldiers and the U.S. Army encouraged as many as possible North Korean people to evacuate to South Korea. Most people were instigated by the ROK Army soldiers to evacuate to South Korea for few weeks to avoid the bombing if they wanted to survive, and return home in short time later. And they said the U.S. Army would conduct more severe indiscriminate bombing after they retreated and might drop the atomic bomb if the war situation would become unfavorable for the UN forces. The ROK and UN forces would definitely come back in a short time later. They strongly encouraged the people to flee to the South Korea for a short time period to avoid American bombing. Accordingly, many people decided to evacuate to South Korea for the time being, expecting they could return home in a few weeks. At that time people let their old parents and young children live at home, telling them they would come back home in a month at latest. But no one knew at the time that the family separation would be their tragic eternal family separation. In Hungnam port, large civilian crowds gathered and they jammed the port to try to get on the LSTs. But the Navy vessel's spaces were limited. The first priority was to load both U.S. and ROKA personnel, its vehicles, equipments and ammunitions, and then the refugees on the first come and first serve basis, as long as the spaces were available. Therefore, many refugees could not get on board and many family members had been parted, between men and wife, parents, their children, brothers, sisters, and loved ones. They were frantically calling each other, screaming with tears. The port was filled by women and children crying each time the vessels departed the port. Many people were still seeking refuge, but there were no more spaces available. Thousands were simply left behind on the wharf of the port. Many people had to trudge wearily back to their homes. Some killed by themselves by jumping into the cold sea water. As a result, they were now separated from their loved one's and families not knowing each other for 62 years. The refugees are now called the "Yisan Kajok" (Separated family) in Korean. In fact, this is the tragic legacy left behind by the Korean War. One of the Korean's popular ballad songs titled "Be Strong! my sister Kumsun!" became very popular song among the Korean people. This is the song singing about the tragic scene of family separations at the cold windy Hungnam port in late December of 1950.

American historian 'Malkasan' wrote in his "Koran War" as follows: [At the time, the ROK and U.S. Army encouraged the North Korean people to evacuate to South Korea as many as possible. I think it was based on the mere humanitarian point of view, but also it could design for the political propaganda efforts to show the world people that most of the North Koreans hated their Communist control and fled to the South Korea.]

6. MACARTHUR WANTS TO EXPAND THE WAR.

Secretary of State Dean Acheson remarked that the Chinese intervention had moved the United States closer to a general war. On December 16, Truman declared a state of national emergency. Truman and Acheson were angered over how badly MacArthur had misjudged the capacity and willingness of China to enter the war. Yet the administration remained convinced that the Soviet Union had incited the Chinese to enter the war, and the CIA warned that the Soviets would give the Chinese maximum military support.

The United State's European allies were even more dismayed by the sudden turn of events in Korea. Having been concerned that MacArthur wanted to expand the war in Korea into major Asian war, they now feared that the Chinese intervention might give the general the opportunity he wanted. When President Truman refused at a press conference to eliminate the possibility of use the atomic bomb against the Chinese, the Europeans responded with shock and outrage. Under the pressure from both public opinion and the conservative opposition in Britain, British Prime Minister Clement Attlee flew to Washington making clear Europe's opposition to the use of nuclear weapons. He also made clear Britain's strong opposition to an all-out war with China, which he pointed out, would threaten British interest in Hongkong, Singapore, and Malaya. Attlee failed to gain what he wanted from Truman, a pledge not to use atomic weapons against China. There was growing support in the United States to use the Atomic bomb if that would bring an end to the war. But the worldwide reaction to the president's press conference was so strong that Truman felt that he could not let Attlee return home empty handed. He told the prime minister, therefore, that the United States was not actively considering the use of Atomic weapons in Asia. He promised not to employ the nuclear option without first consulting the British. Meanwhile the Chinese offensive continued. The Chinese and North Korean Army recaptured Seoul on January 4, 1951, and then proceeded to take other major South Korean towns, including the important railway center of Wonju in the east. Not until January 24, when UN forces had withdrawn to defensive positions roughly along the 37th parallel, did the Chinese stop their attack. By that time, the Eighth Army had retreated more than three hundred miles.

The rout of the Eighth Army placed UNC general headquarters in a state of total panic. MacArthur dispatched a series of frantic reports to Washington warning of the impending annihilation of the UNC. Despite the risk of further escalation, he called for direct military action against China. The use of atomic weapons was not excluded in his demand. Despite MacArthur's reports, escalating the war appeared very dangerous to the Truman administration and the USA's allies. Seeking total victory against North Korea had already brought China into the conflict. Waging total war against China might cause the Soviet Union to intervene as well. With very weak conventional forces in Europe, the west could not risk a war with the Soviet Union. Even if the Soviet Union would not intervene, the United States and UN Command would be immersed in a wider war in Asia that would demand a huge military commitment. Although General MacArthur proposed air and naval attacks on mainland China and the involvement of Chinese Nationalist forces, none of his demands and proposals was accepted. Washington was not prepared to let the Korean conflict escalate into a large war (World War III). The JCS told MacArthur to stay in Korea if he could but to prepare to withdraw to Japan if necessary.

7. THE WAR OF ATTRITION

In a limited war, the total defeat of the opponent is not a goal. Examples of aims of a limited war are seizing a piece of land, causing the enemy to compromise on a particular issue in negotiations, or simply defending one's own territory. In early December, JCS and State Department discussions regarding fighting a limited war were very tentative. There was a great deal of uncertainty over whether the UNC could actually withstand the Communist attack.

At a press conference on 30 November, Truman stated that "the USA would take any steps necessary to meet the military situation." When asked if this included the use of atomic weapons, he replied: "There has always been active consideration of its use…" Although he had no intention of using atomic weapons, the British Prime Minister, Clement Attlee, immediately flew to Washington for a meeting with Truman. He and Truman agreed on the need to fight a limited war and hold the UNC position in Korea as long as possible. The goal of liberating North Korea was abandoned. In the Truman-Attlee communiqué of 8 December, the two leaders called for negotiations with the communists.

The JCS issued MacArthur a strategic directive on 29 December 1950. It stated that a decisive victory would not be sought in Korea or against the PRC. MacArthur was instructed to hold his position in Korea without risking the safety of his forces. In reply, MacArthur put forth his own strategy of escalation. He called for a blockade of China; air strikes and naval bombardments against China's industry; the reinforcement of the Eighth Army with Chinese Nationalist troops; and diversionary attacks from Taiwan against the Chinese mainland. The JCS rejected MacArthur's request. Truman personally told MacArthur to avoid actions that might cause a general war. Meanwhile the Chinese offensive continued and they recaptured Seoul again on January 4, 1951, and then proceeded further to south, near to the 37th parallel.

8. GENERAL RIDGWAY'S WAR

The US Eighth Army commander Walton Walker was killed on 23 December in a jeep accident. Lieutenant General Matthew Ridgway replaced him. He was renowned airborne commander in the Second World War. He always wore a single grenade on his army uniform. His only orders were to defend his positions, inflict maximum damage on the enemy and maintain major units intact. Arriving in Korea, Ridgway was immediately struck by the low morale and lack of discipline among American troops. He toured the front line and visited nearly every divisional commander. Speaking directly with the men at the front, he was overtaken by their demoralization. He later wrote, "I had discovered that our forces were simply not mentally and spiritually ready for the sort of action I had been planning." The men were prone to retreating. Because units failed to keep contact with the enemy, Eighth Army intelligence had no idea of the opposing enemy strength. Also many soldiers were simply not interested in fighting. Civilian life was much more appealing to them. I personally saw him wearing a grenade on his left chest, he visited Koje-do UNC POW compound for inspection.

Second World War veterans, in particular, did not appreciate being called up again for active military duty in five years. It was the time to regroup and it also Ridgway needed the time to restore the morale and esprit of his forces. Problems extended beyond the enlisted men to the officers. Believing that the system of divided command between the Eighth Army and X Corps was a mistake, and he placed the entire UN force under his command. Rejecting the sense of defeatism that had become pervasive even among his field officers, he instilled a new fighting spirit among the troops. He acted to revitalize the Eighth Army. He demanded that Officers command from the front. Divisional commanders were to be with their forward battalions, and Corps commanders were to be with the regiment 'that was the hottest action.'

He ordered commanders to deploy their units off the road and into the hills. Officers were rebuked for failing to keep contact with the enemy. He forcefully repeated the army slogan: "Find them! Fix them! Fight them! Finish them!". To make the army more 'offensive minded' and certain of their cause, Ridgway issued a general statement to the troops, which said that they were fighting to uphold freedom and fight the slavery of Communism.

In the midst of these reforms, Ridgway instituted attrition as the new operational doctrine of the Eighth Army. He supported fighting a limited war and understood that warfare had changed since the Second World War. He especially opposed the use of atomic weapons.

Instead of annihilating the Communists, he sought to wear down their manpower. To do so, superior UNC firepower was to be exploited to the maximum extend. The hallmark of Ridgway's doctrine of attrition was his directive to his subordinates to maximize enemy casualties while minimizing those of the Eighth Army.

Given the daunting Communist numerical superiority, conserving casualties was absolutely crucial. Not a single company was to be sacrificed. There was to be no fighting simply to hold terrain. Other than fighting the expected Communist attack in forward positions around Seoul, Ridgway intended to withdraw carefully to the Han River.

Ridgway's first use of attrition was successful. Peng Du-huai launched the Third phase Offensive in sub-zero conditions on 31 December 1950. Although Ridgway was forced to abandon Seoul, His withdrawal stretched the Communist supply lines to breaking point, forcing Peng to call off the offensive. On 15 January 1951, he mounted a reconnaissance in force, Operation Wolfhound, followed by a full-brown counteroffensive, Operation Thunderbolt, 10 days later. In Operation Thunderbolt, the I and IX US Corps made a careful and step-by-step advance northwards, with heavy artillery and close-air support. The 25th US Division and the renowned Turkish Brigade pummeled the opposing 50th CPV Army in the first day of fighting. Ridgway observed the progress from the air. Frequently, he appeared at Corps and divisional headquarters, or even on the front line, to guide and observe operations. By 9 February, the Eighth Army was back on the Han river again. The counteroffensive surprised the CPV commanders, who had not expected such a quick UNC recovery. Overconfident Mao ordered another attack, the short-lived and ill-advised Fourth Phase Offensive. On 11 February, Chinese forces, led by Deng Hua, broke through the III ROK Corps and threatened the important road hub of Wonju. Further west, the 23rd RCT (2nd US Division) and the French battalion were encircled at Chipyong-ri. Supplied by air, they fought stubbornly and took the momentum out of the Communist advance. By 20 February, the Communists had been halted at the cost of 17,000 UNC casualties. Communist casualties were probably greater. Because of this defeat, Peng instituted a temporary strategy of withdrawing before UNC attacks in order to conserve his forces before launching another major offensive.

Hoping to bring the Communists to the negotiating table, Ridgway outlined an offensive doctrine for attrition in mid-February. It was based on the limited objective attack. A limited objective attack was a concentrated and carefully prepared set-piece assault meant to kill Communists, not capture ground. Inflicting the maximum damage on the enemy with the minimum loss to the UNC remained the principle behind all operations. Massive use of superior UNC firepower was emphasized. No attacks would be made in unfavorable or risky circumstances. Pursuit of the defeated enemy was to be cautious and coordinated, avoiding the kind of reckless advance that had made the Eighth Army vulnerable in November 1950. This also enabled Ridgway to ensure that his forces always had strong logistical support. In late February and March, Ridgway launched a series of colorfully named limited objective attacks. Due to Peng's new strategy, the CPV generally withdrew and avoided a serious battle. This allowed Ridgway to steadily expand his territorial objectives. UNC units advanced into an empty and devastated Seoul on 14 March. Thereafter, Ridgway and the JCS decided to cross the 38th Parallel in order to secure stronger defensive positions to the immediate north. Subsequently taken became known as the Kansas Line. Sited on strong defensive terrain, it ran along the lower Imjin river in the west to Hwachon and then to the east coast, just north of Taepo-ri. The Communists suffered more than 53,000 casualties in Ridgway's limited objective attacks. Total UNC casualties were probably less than 20,000. By now it was clear that Ridgway had turned the Eighth Army into a highly efficient fighting force.

9. KOREAN WAR COULD BE ENDED IN THREE MONTHS

As you have read in the foregoing articles, UN and ROK forces rolled back the North Korean invaders to north of 38th parallel. ROK

Army and US forces arrived there before September 30, 1950. Then the ROK Army crossed over the 38th Parallel on October 1st and the US forces crossed on next day. If the UN forces had stopped at the 38th parallel, as abide by the initial UN resolution on June 27, the Korean conflict could have ended in three (3) months and the United States could have won the war and claimed a substantial victory over the North Korean army and the International communist expansionism. Military containment would have been tested successfully through the Korean Conflict. The North Korean's invasion of the South Korea would have ended in humiliating defeat, and the Korean Conflict could surely have been ended within three months. Thereby saving the lives of several millions of Korean civilians and military soldiers of both sides, also saved tremendous amount of property damage and military expenses. If reason rather than emotionalism had determined the policy of the U.S. government, the Korean conflict would have ended very shortly after the recapture of Seoul. The North Korean troops had been expelled from South Korea, and Syngman Rhee's South Korean government had been restored to full control over the South Korea again immediately. The United States and the UN had successfully achieved UN resolution of June 27. Should the U.S. forces and ROK army have stopped at the 38th Parallel, the United States could declare a victory over the North Korean army in the Korean Conflict.

However, President Rhee and General MacArthur then had tempted to unify the Korean peninsula under the control of Rhee's government. Soon after the Inchon landing, the N. Korean army ceased to be an effective fighting force. By the end of September, in the words of General MacArthur's report to the UN, "the backbone of the North Korean army had been broken. Their scattered forces were being liquidated or driven north with material losses in equipment and men captured." His next report at the beginning of October was: "More than half of the enemy's combat forces were entrapped in South Korea, and they were no longer a threat. Thousands more were lost in their desperate flight north of the 38th parallel. An average of approximately 3,000 N. Koreans had been captured daily since the end of September." Indeed, had United Nation forces advanced to the narrow waist of Korea (around 39th parallel), along a line running roughly from Wonsan on the east to Pyongyang on the west of the peninsula, the United States could have proclaimed an even greater victory, not only stopping communist aggression but liberating the land previously held by the North Korean communists. Even had Communist China (the People's Republic of China, or PRC) entered the war, UN forces would have been in a much better position militarily to stave off a Chinese offensive. But at this time, both S. Korean president Rhee and General MacArthur were seduced by the prospect of total military victory in Korea, and were reluctant to challenge a certified war hero who was venerated by much of the American public, they deferred to MacArthur, who insisted on liberating all of Korea and achieving Korean unification under the control of South Korea. Between November 1 and 3, Chinese troops attacked the ROK II Corps and the U.S. 1st Cavalry Division, inflicting heavy casualties before withdrawing almost as suddenly as they entered the war. Captured Chinese POWs provided detailed information about Chinese forces in Korea. On November 8, the CIA reported that there were between 30,000 and 40,000 Chinese troops now in Korea and 70,000 more on China's border with Korea. Although Moscow radio warned on November 19 that a Chinese and North Korean counteroffensive was imminent, most diplomats and MacArthur believed that China could not attack without the approval of the Soviet Union, and that Stalin did not want to escalate the war in Korea. MacArthur made an assertion that the war would be over by Christmas. On November 24, the general launched his "Home by Christmas" offensive, but on November 26, on the contrary, he was faced with the Chinese counterattacks and the U.N. forces were forced to retreat.

General MacArthur had mistaken thought that the Chinese Army could not enter the war, as same as Kim Il Sung made a grave mistake that US forces would not intervene in the Korean Civil War. General MacArthur had misjudged the capability and willingness of the Chinese leaders to enter the Korean War.

The Korean War could have ended in three (3) months instead of three years, and one month, if the UN/ROK forces stopped at the 38th parallel when they expelled N. Korean army to north of the 38th parallel in the late September 1950 with the restoration of the status quo ante. The Korean War history revealed that neither sides could achieve the intended goal of Korean unification nor gained any more land, since the Armistice line was established near the 38th parallel, although there was three more years of extended fierce fights. Consequently, the both sides fought wastefully for nothing for three more years. The extended fighting was nothing but a killing millions of human lives and destroyed tremendous amount of property damages, along with the waste of huge amount of war expenditure that could have been saved, if the war had ended within three months instead of three years.

10. GENERAL MACARTHUR SACKED

General MacArthur never accepted the new strategy of attrition. Indeed, his rhetoric became more inflammatory the further north Ridgway marched. But Ridgway's successes undermined MacArthur's arguments. The advance of the Eighth U.S. Army in February and March, solidified consensus in Washington that the strategic objective of the UNC was to bring the Communists to the negotiating table through continued attrition. When Army Chief of Staff, General Lawton Collins and Air Force General Hoyt Vandenberg visited Korea to determine whether the Eighth Army should stay in Korea. They were pleasantly surprised to find that the military situation in Korea was much better than General MacArthur had led Washington to believe. Henceforth, the Pentagon and the White House would maintain direct contact with Ridgeway in Korea rather than following military protocol by going through MacArthur in Japan, who increasingly became figure-head isolated from the realities of the war. Aware of the deliberation in Washington, MacArthur issued a statement to the press on 24 March that escalating the war would quickly cause the PRC's military capability to collapse. By advocating a policy contradictory to the one set out by the JCS and the Truman administration, MacArthur was flouting their authority. Then on 5 April, Congressman Joseph W. Martin, Republican minority leader, read a letter from MacArthur in the US House of Representatives. In the letter, MacArthur approved of the idea of landing Chinese Nationalists on the Chinese mainland, and he agreed fully with Mr. Martin's idea, deplored the priority accorded Europe, announced that "we must win" in Asia, and concluded, "There is no substitute for victory." He ended the letter with an endorsement of total victory. Because of these two incidents, Truman acted to relieve MacArthur. The Joint Chief of Staff (JCS) had unanimously recommended MacArthur's dismissal from his posts in Tokyo so that he and his extreme views would not be factors in the war in Korea. With them was his oldest rival in the military, now the Secretary of Defense, George C, Marshal. MacArthur was born in 1880 and Harry Truman who born in 1884, had been only a reserve artillery captain activated in wartime. Now in April 1951, he was commander in Chief over the much-decorated MacArthur, who on his promotion in 1918 was the youngest brigadier general in the American army. In Japan, MacArthur had been looked upon as a head of state himself. Defeated but nominally reigning Japanese Emperor 'Hirohito', to symbolize his subservience, paid a courtesy call upon the general twice a year. For five years, as an occupation forces commander, he controlled Japan with not much interference from Washington. They wanted the relief orders to be conveyed with tact and courtesy. It happened that Army secretary Frank Pace was then in Tokyo. The State Department could then send the relief orders through its own channels to Ambassador John Muccio in Busan, and he could give them to Pace, who would immediately fly back to Tokyo and deliver them to MacArthur in person. Truman wanted to relieve MacArthur primarily for political reasons, but the Joint Chief of Staff had their own urgent military reasons for replacing him with a more levelheaded commander. They knew that the Communists were building up their forces in North Korea for a powerful new offensive, and they felt that they couldn't trust MacArthur to respond prudently to what might well prove to be the war's greatest crisis so far. (Excerpted from Korean War, by Richard Whelan)

Truman wrote in his memoirs: [Time and again General MacArthur had shown that he was unwilling to accept the policies of the Administration. By his repeated public statement he was...Setting his policy against the President's policy...If allowed him to defy the civil authorities in this manner, I myself would be violating my oath to uphold and defend the constitution. I had no other alternative but to relieve him.]

General Singlaub wrote in his memoir: [A soldier's job, whether he be a buck private or a five star general like MacArthur, is to implement the legitimate orders of duly elected civilian authority. MacArthur defied those orders. He tried to bypass the chain of command through allies in US Congress. His goal, he said, was the defeat of the Communist China. To accomplish this task, he called for air and ground attacks against the Chinese mainland, some of which would employ Nationalist forces from Taiwan. He also campaigned for the destruction of the Chinese airfield in Southern Manchuria. This later tactic made considerable sense. But MacArthur's erratic campaign of press conferences that spring demonstrated he was more interested in personal aggrandizement than strategy. He remained true to character to the very end. He had gambled and he had lost.]

After some thought, Marshall, Acheson, and the JCS all agreed in meetings that MacArthur would have to go. On 11 April, MacArthur was relieved of command of the United Nations Command and Gen Ridgway replaced him. He immediately issued a directive to all of his principal subordinates that no actions were to be taken that risked escalating the conflict. General James Van Fleet, Ridgway's successor as commander of the Eighth Army.

On April 11, MacArthur was hosting a luncheon for the guests from America when General's aide, Col. Sidney Huff, heard the news on a Japanese radio station. He interrupted the meal to whisper to Mrs. MacArthur, who then whispered to her husband. MacArthur didn't receive Bradley's cable until about fifteen minutes after the radio broadcast. That fact outraged many Americans as much as did the actual dismissal. They complained that it was inexcusable to treat so shabbily a man who had served his nation with such distinction. General MacArthur returned home to a hero's welcome in the states. He was lionized, but so was Truman; he was vilified, some unions were for him, some were for Truman. State legislatures and universities debated the pros and cons, commending or condemning one side or the other. There was a parade in Honolulu, another in San Francisco, one in Washington, one in New York. In his most famous appearance, MacArthur spoke before Congress, defending his ideas, in fact repeating many of them, and he closed with the lines of the old army ballad, "Old soldiers never die, they just fade away." He of course did not quite fade away, at least not for a while. There were books, there were public appearances, and there were meetings. There was a Congressional hearing in the Senate, and it went on interminably, from early May until August. It confused and obfuscated the issues and eventually bored everyone. The American public lost most of its interest in him, and, except for a brief revival when he made his abortive bid for the 1952 Republican Presidential nomination, he could truly fade away. (Extract from The Untold Story of the War, by Joseph C. Goulden) Many Koreans appreciate and adore him for his outstanding devotions for the Korean people. Koreans erected his bronze statue on the highest hill side of Inchon and named the hill as "MacArthur's Park".

11. MAO AND VAN FLEET LOST THEIR SONS.

Dedicate their sons: The Chinese president Mao Tse-tung and General Van Fleet, who lost their sons during the Korean War.

Chinese Chairman Mao sent his most beloved son An-ing Mao to the Korean War together with Peoples' Volunteer Army (PVA) to fight against the UN forces. Mao An-Ing, who served as a Russian interpreter in the Chinese Army Supporting Command, was killed in action by a US Air attack on November 25, 1950. He was twenty eight (28) years old at the time.

Due to President Mao's sickness, An-Ing Mao's death was not immediately reported to him, but rather Mao's wife, Jin Quing was informed of his death through a letter written by Premier Zhou Eun-Lai on January 2, in the following year. An-Ing's body is now buried in the cemetery of Chinese People's Voluntary Army in DaeYu Dong, Hoechang-kun, North Pyongyang Province, North Korea.

Mao instructed to persons concerned not to give An-Ing special treatment because he was his son. He further directed to bury his son in North Korean territory together with all other Chinese soldiers. And An-Ing's body was buried there along side his bronze bust statue. Chinese government delegates visiting North Korea often pay their reverence to his tomb. In October 2010, Chinese premier Wonja-bao paid a courtesy visit and said "Comrade Mao, now our country became one of the powerful country in the world since you died at Korean War."

General Van Fleet, the replacement of General Ridgeway and the Commanding General of the Eighth US Army, also sent his son, James A. Van Fleet Jr., First Lt., US Air Force Bomber pilot, to the Korean War. From Goonsan Air Force Base, South Korea, he set forth on a night bombing mission deep in North Korean territory and was unfortunately shot down by an enemy MIG-15 on April 4, 1952.

Though he graduated from West Point Academy, James Jr. chose the branch of Air Force instead because of his exceptional desire to become an air force pilot. James Jr. fought in the Korean War to protect the freedom of Korea as a combat pilot while his father served as the Commanding general of Eighth US Army. As General Van Fleet stared at the Northern skies, his face was filled with sorrow and his eyes were moist almost with tears. His beloved son, whom he was so proud of, never returned from the cold soil of North Korea and his remains were never found up to the present time.

Later on, Gen. Van Fleet privately requested to the Communist negotiators through the UN negotiator to find out the whereabouts of his son during a meeting of POW issues at Panmunjom.

The bombing mission for Lt. Van Fleet Jr. was in Mulgae-ri village region, adjacent to Pyongyang near the jurisdiction of 3rd Unit area under the Chinese Rear Service Command. Despite a thorough search and investigation of the suspected bomber crashed site by North Korean and the Chinese Army, they reported an unsuccessful result to the U.S. delegates at Panmunjom.

Gen. van Fleet was very disappointed with the missing report, and through his life time, Gen Van Fleet could never forget the Korean skies with the loss of his beloved son on April 4, 1952. Therefore, now it is time for Korean people to comfort them. The United States Army repulsed the North Korean invasion and protected South Korea with tremendous source of manpower and materials consumed during the Korean conflict.

One hundred forty two U.S. Army general's sons participated in the Korean War, and 35 participants were killed or injured among those 142.

Lt. Colonel John Eisenhower was amongst those were injured. He was the son of General Dwight Eisenhower who later became the president of the United States.

President Eisenhower sent his beloved son Colonel John Eisenhower to the battlefield of Korean War. He was a brave, valiant soldier and rendered distinguished services to defend democratic South Korea. He became a brilliant Army general later. His father, President Dwight D. Eisenhower concluded the armistice of Korean War in July, 1953, and he rendered remarkable services to the cause of World peace. General Eisenhower won the World War II over the Germany and was a War hero of the World War II.

Other soldiers with well-known father generals sons include; Capt. Sam Walker, the son of Gen, Walton H. Walker, Commanding General of 8th US Army; Capt. Mark Bill Clark, the son of General Mark Wayne Clark, Commanding General of UN Forces and Lt.Col. Harris, the son of Major Gen. Harris, the Commanding General of US Marine Corp.

Especially, Capt. Sam Walker usually respected and adored his father very much. But he had to have a bereavement in his father's death in sorrow and many Americans also sympathized his sudden death. Lt. Col. Harris was killed while commanding the brutal battle at Chang-Jin (Chosin) Reservoir.

The Korean War has been a difficult war for the US Army to deal with because of entirely different circumstances and different enemy. The US soldiers had to fight three years of long and tiresome war, since they started the battle from Juk-mi-Ryung, near Osan, Korea. During the three years of the war, the United States suffered the loss of many talented military officers.

Lt. Gen. Walton H. Walker, the Commanding General of the 8th US Army was a highest ranking officer victimized in the Korean War. He conducted and led the defensive operations of the UN forces and ROK Army near the 38th parallel, after retreated by the Communist Chinese offensive.

On December 23, 1950, unfortunately, he was killed in an automobile accident on the northbound road toward Uijongbu, while on his way to attend an award ceremony held at the British 27th Brigade.

Furthermore, Maj. Gen. Bryant Moore was killed in a helicopter crash while commanding the IX US Army Corps during the Korean War, and Maj. Gen. William Dean, Commanding General of the 24th Infantry Division (which was the first American ground combat division), was captured by the North Korean soldiers while retreating from Taejon to Okchon Korea. He remained in a North Korean POW camp for three years until the final repatriation.

Nevertheless, they were proud of fighting the Korean War. They also have great pride, self-confidence and marveled when they see the miraculous development of the Korean economy owing to their own sacrifices and blood sheds. The Korean people should appreciate and pay sincere respects to their meritorious service and sacrificed devotions. The United States had successfully defended South Korea from the North Korean's armed aggression with tremendous source of manpower and materials consumed during the Korean War.

CHAPTER IV

ARMISTICE TALK

1. ARMISTICE TALK PROPOSAL.

Although not nearly as costly for the United States in terms of casualties as World War II, the Korean War nevertheless took its toll of dead, wounded, and missing in action. By the time the war ended in July 1953, U.S. casualties numbered over 157,000; Korea suffered more than 1.3 million casualties, including 415,000 deaths. Other UN casualties amounted to more than 16,000, including 3,100 dead. Communist casualties were estimated at more than 1.4 million. The draft had interfered with the careers of more than 1.5 million American youth who had fought in Korea. The war consumed about 12% of gross domestic production, including 11 percent of all steel produced, 17 percent of all copper, and 24 percent of total aluminum production. As a result of the war also led to an increase in the cost of living for an American family of 12 percent. By the end of the conflict, few Americans thought the Korean War had been worth the human and material toll it took.

The Truman administration, pressured by both the U.S. Congress and by European allies, took the initiative for a negotiated settlement in Korea, and began secret talks with the Chinese government through an intermediary. However, the Chinese proposal for a simultaneous withdrawal of U.N. forces and Chinese troops from Korea created a roadblock in the truce talks. The deadlock was broken when Soviet Deputy Foreign Minister Jacob Malik indicated that the Soviets wanted peace. As early as March 1951, when UN forces were driving the communists once more out of most of South Korea, President Truman had planned to announce that the UNC was ready to enter into armistice talks. The president Truman was under great pressure from America's European allies to launch a peace initiative. But MacArthur had purposefully undermined the peace initiative by issuing a statement effectively portraying the enemy as being militarily defeated.

With the war having reached a military stalemate by June, however, and still under great pressure both at home and abroad to end the conflict, the White House decided to try again to get armistice talks started. Using quiet diplomacy, the State Department let the Soviet Union know that it desired to arrange an armistice or cease-fire. After some delay, during which the United States hinted that it might accept the 38th parallel as the armistice line. Moscow responded in somewhat ambiguous language that negotiation might be possible. China also indicated that it was ready to start the peace process. In response, the administration ordered Ridgway (UNC Commander) to announce that he was prepared to appoint a representative to meet with the communists to begin armistice negotiations. After a short delay over where the talks should begin, both sides agreed to start negotiations at the North Korean city of Kae-song, near the demarcation line between UN and communist forces.

The talks, which began on July 10, 1951, stretched over two years. During this time, the negotiation meeting place was moved to Panmunjom, a small village about five miles east of Kae-sung. On a number of occasions, the negotiations were broken off by the UN and/or Chinese negotiators because of lack of progress or over alleged violations of the neutral zone where the negotiations were taking place. Yet although the bargaining was hard, most of the issues that separated the two sides were settled expeditiously. These included such questions as the demarcation of the armistice line, the renovation or rehabilitation of airfields destroyed as a result of the war, the regular rotation of forces on both sides, and the number of ports of entry for bringing replacement of supplies and personnel.

2. REPATRIATION OF POWS

Korean War might have been ended as early as 1951, two years before an argument was finally reached, if both side agreed to all for all compulsory return of all POWs at the end of the Korean War.

Indeed, one of the troublesome issues that held up a peace agreement was the issue of the repatriation of prisoners-of-war (POWs). Another issue was the establishment of a truce line. The Communists stubbornly insisted that all POWs should be repatriated on all for all exchange, as provided by the article 118 of the Geneva Convention of 1949, which called for quick and compulsory repatriation of all POWs at the end of a war; it did not provide for POWs who did not want to be repatriated. United States announced very early in the armistice that it would abide by provision of Geneva Convention, as did North and South Korea. The UN negotiators at Panmunjom also believe that the fastest way to return UN prisoners home was to agree to an all-for-all-exchange and that the voluntary repatriation would violate the Geneva Convention.

Except for the issue of POW's repatriation, an armistice ending the Korean War might have been achieved as early as 1951, approximately two years before an argument was finally reached. Indeed, after 1951, it was the only issue holding back the signing of a truce agreement.

At the time armistice negotiation began in 1951, no one expected the repatriation of POWs would be much of a complicated problem. They thought was a very easy issue to solve if there was an exchange all-for-all repatriation in the first place. Nevertheless, the issue delayed armistice agreement almost two more years.

During the first and second year, UN forces captured large number of Chinese and North Korean troops, and some American officials began to argue against the "forced repatriation", claiming that the prisoners return to China and North Korea against their will especially for the POW leaders of the anti-communist compounds in the UN POW camps. And therefore some POWs in UN Camps, especially the POW leaders, did not want to return home because of possible retaliations.

Perhaps with this in mind, the US Army's Chief of Psychological warfare General Robert A. Mclure, proposed to General Lawton Collins, Chief of Staff, that Chinese POWs who were former Nationalists army be allowed to go to Formosa (Taiwan). Collins approved the idea, maintaining that this would not be a violation of the Geneva Convention because even Beijing considered Taiwan is a part of China.

Nevertheless, the majority view in Washington was that, at the time of an armistice, all Chinese and North Koreans should be returned home. To do otherwise, it was argued, would not only violate the Geneva Convention, but it also might put in jeopardy the swift return of UN POWs held by the Chinese and North Koreans. The Joint Chief of Staff had gone back and force on the POW issue, at one time favoring the forced repatriation of prisoners to get American POWs returned as quickly as possible, and at another time ordering General Mathew Ridgway to prepare a proposal for the return of POWs based on voluntary repatriation, but then reversing course again and favoring the prompt repatriation of all prisoners on the basis of the Geneva Convention.

However, the Truman administration was just as determined that no prisoner should be forced to return against his will, as they saw more than 30,000 anti-communists POWs in the Koje-do UN Camps. For the Chinese, it was also one of the important problems that they could make no concession. As a result, the war dragged on for two more years. Not until 1953, following a breakdown of negotiations that lasted from October 1952 to April 1953. A complex formula was agreed upon by both sides according to which POWs not wanting to be repatriated would be given a period of time to change their minds and then their cases could be turned over to a Neutral Nations Repatriation Commission, which would help relocate them. In the end, only 628 of the Communists non-repatriates elected to go home and only 10 of the UNC non-repatriates chose to return home, 86 chose India and 51 died at panmunjom. The rest were eventually released the following January.

The Communists attempted to reestablish the 38th parallel as a line of truce, whereas U.N. forces proposed to make the truce line with existing battle line at the time of the truce agreement. These two issues encountered obstacles of the negotiation and the truce talks were suspended between August and October 1951. Meanwhile, the fighting continued with each side attempting to capture more territory and to occupy better strategic positions, which demanded heavy casualties both side. (I wrote more detailed information in the article of Prisoners of War Issue, Part II). It is believed that all those losses were wastefully occurred because of the extended POW repatriation arguments at the truce meeting.

3. CONCLUSION OF ARMISTICE

Talks resumed in later October 1951, at a new place named Panmunjom, an obscure small village located in between Seoul and Kaesong. Before the Korean War, Panmunjom was a small farming village, but it has become the meeting place of the Korean War armistice Commission and the truce village of Panmunjom was put on the Korean map. However, the negotiations reached an impasse as soon as they met. Thereupon, General Mark Clark, the new U.N. commander who replaced General Ridgeway, ordered massive air attacks against targets in North Korea, including Pyongyang. These air attacks of May, July, and August did not bring the Communists to accept the proposals made by the U.N. Command. The United States presidential candidates, General Dwight Eisenhower, said in his campaign speech that "he would go to Korea himself and end the war." The death of Stalin in March 1953 and the unyielding stand of U.N. forces brought Kim Il-sung to end the war he could not win. The South Korean President Rhee opposed the armistice and wanted to continue the fight against the North Korean forces until the unification of Korean peninsula. On June 18, 1953, he arbitrarily released of some 25,000 anti-communists prisoners-of-war who did not wish to return to North Korea and this incident almost wrecked the truce talks. The communist strongly demanded to re-intern all of the released anti-communist POWs. However, Kim Il-sung knew that he could not continue the war. The communist forces attacked only ROK army bases in front line in an attempt to retaliate the Rhee's release of anti-communist POWs. Difficult negotiations with the Communists at the truce village of Panmunjom, conducted by Admiral C. Turner Joy and General Kim Il, North Korean Chief negotiator, brought about the Korean armistice on July 27, 1953. Some 89,000 Communist prisoners of war, including 6,700 Chinese were repatriated to their homelands, while about 30,000 North Korean and 14,700 Chinese POWs, chosen not to go back to their countries.

Meanwhile, Chinese troops withdrew from North Korea completely by the year of 1958. The Korean War caused 157,530 American casualties, including 33,625 deaths, 14,000 casualties of other U.N. forces, and 257,000 South Korean soldiers who were either killed or wounded. Some 244,000 South Korean citizens were killed, over 229,000 were wounded, and 303,000 were listed as missing. Some 129,000 South Koreans were massacred by both sides. Over 84,000 South Koreans went to the North while 200,000 South Korean youths were forced to join the North Korean military (named Liberation Warrior). Among those who were known to have been kidnapped to the north were such prominent nationalist leaders as Kim Kyu-shik, An Chae-hong, Cho So-ang, and Yi Kwang-su. Pyongyang, the North Korean capital, was completely destroyed and entire industrial facilities and hydroelectric plants in the north were either destroyed or badly damaged. The casualties on the part of the North Korea and Chinese forces were estimated at 500,000 and 900,000, respectively. Civilian casualties were not reported by the North Korean regime but presumed much more than South Koreans.

When the Korean armistice was ready to be concluded, the South Korean government refused to sign the truce document with the North Koreans and Chinese. The war which Kim Il-sung launched to unify the peninsula did not bring about his intended object, like the

UN forces and South Korea. The Korea still remained to be divided along with new truce line-4 km wide demilitarized zone (DMZ) which crosses the peninsula, near the 38ᵗʰ parallel. North Korea lost a considerable amount of its mountainous eastern territory, but it gained a small but more economically valuable coastal region of the west central area of the peninsula, including the city of Kaesong. But North Korea was badly damaged during the war. The destruction of cities and industries in the north was much more severe and extensive than those in the South Korea.

No one likes to dwell on his own failure. Some American public perceived the Korean War as a failure-is no exception Americans tend to regard the Korean War as an embarrassment best forgotten, as "the first war we lost." General Mark W. Clark lamenting "that he had gained the unenviable distinction of being the first United States Army Commander in history to sign an Armistice without victory." To this date, a Military Armistice Commission (MAC) and a Neutral Nations Supervisory Commission (NNSC) continue to supervise the truce.

At the Panmunjom, the negotiators had agreed to hold within thirty days of the armistice a political conference to discuss Korean unification and other related matters. But the meeting held in Geneva, did not begin until April 1954. It then became quickly deadlocked over the supervision and conduct of election that were supposed to result in unification. No agreement was ever reached, and Korea still remains a divided nation North and South remain the same as before the war. Technically speaking, Korea is still under a war status unless a peace treaty signed. The Korean armistice should be recorded as a world's longest armistice truce in the war history.

It seems to be the North Korea wanted Peace treaty with the United States to formally end the War; it was a long standing demand of Pyongyang. However, it must be on the stipulation that North Korea should abandon the nuclear weapons first. All other concerned countries should support and guarantee the nuclear free zone and the peace treaty on the Korean peninsula.

4. THE GAIN AND LOSS OF THE WAR PARTICIPANT COUNTRIES

The Korean conflict was a first major military conflict of the Cold War between the super powers. Korea was, rather a turning point in post world war II history with momentous repercussions worldwide. It provided stimulus that transformed NATO from a weak alliance into a powerful force for the defense of Western Europe. It gave the United States undisputed leadership of the UN. The war gave the Truman administration justification it needed for quadrupling the American military budget within two years, thereby triggering the endless and exorbitant arms race. The United States then rehabilitated and re-armed Japan and West Germany.

In a sense, the Korean War was a World war miniature, in which military forces from seventeen anticommunist nations including South Korea faced the North Koreans and the Chinese Communists. Korea became a pawn in a power play between the United States and the Soviet Union. Like the old Korean proverb Korean peninsular was once more caught between two big whales. Korea was politically trapped between two super powers.

a) North Korea (People's Republic of Korea)

The North Korea started the Korean War by attacking South Korea. North Korea thought they could capture South Korea in a month or two and could achieve the Korean unification. The North Korea had mis-judged that American forces would never interfere in a Korean civil war because the US Army did not interfere the Chinese civil war. Furthermore, the US Secretary of State, Acheson declared that the Korea was out of the U.S. defense line in Asia. They assumed that it would take at least two or three months for American forces to enter the war. North Korea could occupy entire South Korea within a month or two before the American forces entered the conflict. In spite of Kim's expectations, the U.S. Army entered right after the conflict and started to destroy almost all the North Korean cities, industrial complexes, rail ways, bridges, dams, airfields, power plants and many private dwellings, by U.S. Air forces bombings.

The North Korean Army lost about 400,000 casualties, 150,000., prisoners-of-war and sustained more than a million civilian deaths. North Korean had also lost about two million refugees who fled to South Korea. The North Korean Communists gave a bad impression of Communism to the rest of the world. The Korean War was the substantial cause of the discord and differences between China and Soviet Union after the war and thus contributing to the weakness of World's Communism Movements. North Korea remained primitive and dictatorial, with growing ties to China rather than to Soviet Union. After the end of the Korean War, the United States adopted a general policy of military containment, diplomatic isolation. They imposed economic sanctions against North Korea. In order to prevent another war, Washington signed a mutual security treaty with Seoul in 1954. Furthermore, to implement its anti-communist containment policy in Asia, the U.S. signed a series of bilateral and multilateral security treaties with South Korea, Japan, the Philippines, Thailand, and New Zealand. However, the U.S. led coalition with Japan and Korea faced a counter-alliance between North Korea, the Soviet Union and China. In the 30-year Treaty of Friendship, alliance, and mutual assistance signed in February 1950, the Soviet Union and China agreed to use "necessary means" to prevent the rival of Japanese imperialism. This Sino-Soviet treaty served as model for North Korea's mutual defense treaties with the Soviet Union and China that were signed in 1961.

Three days after the outbreak of the Korean War, the U.S. Congress approved legalization to ban all economic trade with N. Korea. Over the next five decades, the U.S. legal sanctions against commercial and financial transactions steadily expanded.

Until first part of 1980, following the Korean War, the centrally directed economy of North Korea had been developed more rapid and had larger in per capita income and had grown more rapidly than the economy of South Korea. However, with the absence of rational and strategic economic planning, together with the collapse of communism and the United States constant isolation policy made their advantages reached limits and disappeared. Now North Koran economy was completely devastated.

North Korea was hard pressed politically and economically for about 60 years. They were unable to halt the deterioration of its economy or adequately feed its people. North Korea has been slipping badly in virtually every indicator since the Soviet Union and its European satellite countries collapsed in 1990. Furthermore, North Korea had two consecutive years of big floods and droughts in a row 1995~96 causing most of the rice paddies were smashed and destroyed. As a result, millions people died of famine. The problem of chronic food shortage and poor economic situations were continuously persist the problems of North Korea. The North Korea's national fortune has declined and deserted because of continuing shortage of food and misgovernment.

The Korean Conflict awoke the Americans who had spiritually been slacken up with the rapture of World War II victory, and they have concentrated on the worldwide spread of Communism. Therefore, it might safe to say that the Korean war contributed some extent to the demise of World's Communism, and therefore, it is believed that North Korea itself is the most looser in the Korean War.

b) South Korea (Republic of Korea)

American President Truman made his prompt decision to repulse the North Korean invasion. He saved South Korea from falling into the Communist block. This allowed South Korea eventually to become one of Asia's major economic and industrial powers. It's citizens to enjoy one of the continent's highest standards of living. Despite all the adversities, Koreans had achieved so called "Miracles of Han River." Although the South Koreans were to be governed over 40 years by authoritarian leaders and military dictators who greatly restricted democratic political processes. They could escape from falling under the control of the far more totalitarian dictator regime of North Korea. With communist aggression contained, the Americans and United Nations saved South Korea for democracy and capitalism.

The U.S.-Korean Security treaty pact was concluded and the United States assured to render both military and economy aid to Korea to pacify President Rhee who furiously opposed the armistice agreement. With America's military assistance, the South Korean Army was considerably modernized and strengthened. Despite suffering tremendous personnel casualties and property damages, for decades, South Koreans had developed their economy and industrialized, then finally became the world's Number 10th economic power after rising from one of the poorest countries in the world. Both Koreans underwent many years of slow recuperation from the devastation of the war, the ruination matching the worst suffered by any peoples in World War II.

For more than two decades, the South Korea developed phenomenal economic growth which surpassed the economy of North Korea. Some economic commentators call it a "little Japan", or "another Japan." South Korea has been officially recognized as an industrialized country since 1996 when the country jointed the OECD (Organization for Economic Cooperation and Development.). Now the country plays an increasingly important role in the world economy.

South Koreans are grateful to the assistance and devotions of United States and other countries participated in the Korean War.

c) United Sates

After World War II, most Americans were rapturous and enjoyed the victory of the war. But the Korean War, in some ways, started to awaken American people to concentrate on the worldwide expansion of the Communism. Therefore, the Korean War remains one of the most of events in recent American history. As one writer has remarked, "in many ways Korea did for the Cold War what Pearl Harbor had done for World War II". Prior to the Korean War, the only American political or military commitment outside the western Hemisphere had been the North Atlantic Treaty (NATO). By 1955, the United States had about 450 military bases in thirty six countries. They were linked by political and military pacts with some twenty countries outside Latin America. Also, the U.S. foreign aid program, appropriately named "the Mutual security program," no longer supported economic and social reconstruction but gave military support for recipient countries. Consequently, the Communist menace most importantly was now perceived in Washington in broad global terms rather than in terms of Europe alone, as had largely been the case prior to 1950.

Indeed, as European politics stabilized and the Communist thread diminished over the next ten years, the United States became increasingly concerned with events in Southeast Asia. Ironically, two Democratic presidents, John F Kennedy and Lyndon B. Johnson, came to share the view of Gen. Douglas MacArthur had promulgated during the Korean War. The battlefield of the Cold War would be Asia rather than Europe. The result was the Vietnam tragedy of the 1960s and 1970s.

Yet, the Korean Conflict had not been fought in vain, as the United States and many South Koreans were concerned. Although Washington had failed to achieve its objective, the political unification of Korea, after the Inchon landing in September 16, 1950. In spite of sacrificing a lot of human lives and huge amounts of war expenditure, the United States also benefited from the Korean War many ways. In the first place, although it was no decisive victory, the United States had won over Communism and saved the Republic of Korea.

Even though some argue that it was a stalemate, the Korean War was a successful military venture because it helped contain the spread of communism in the world. America's success in the Korean War was crucial because without it, communism would have been more wide spread throughout the world. Therefore, the Korean War proved itself a success for the United States through the containment of communism in Korea and the world.

The conflict provided assurances of Japan's allegiance to American, while emerging from America's military occupation, Japan could look to United States for political and military support.

The war also jump-started the Japanese economy. This was the beginning process of turning Japan into an economic model for the East Asia nations to emulate, including South Korea. The United States achieved its post-World War II policy for the Far East, based on it's economically strong ties with Japan. In contrast, Russian's lackluster support for China emerged as a strong rival to the Soviet Union within the communist bloc. Especially among Third World countries, which admired and identified with China's successful resistance.

The "police action," As President Harry Truman described, at the outset of the Korean War was a turning point in postwar history, with momentous repercussions worldwide. It provided the stimulus that transformed NATO from a weak alliance into a powerful force for the defense of Western Europe. The Korean War greatly strengthened the special relationship between the United States and Britain. It also provided the motive for fostering the integration of white and black troops within the US Army.

Also as important as any consequence of the Korean Conflict, both President Truman and Eisenhower had considered the use of nuclear weapon on several occasions. Yet the very existence of atomic weapons dictated a limited war in Korea. United States had a security treaty pact with Japan in 1953 and also similar treaty with Australia, New Zealand and Philippines. All these rapid changes of the United States foreign policies were mainly because of the Korean War. Looking on the bright side of the Korean War, it is not too much to say that the United States had gained, in a way, some political benefits in the cold war. Most of all, United States defended South Korea successfully. They showed the word it's strong will to defend the democratic countries from the communist expansion. That was the powerful success for the United States.

d) China (People's Republic of China)

In the Korean War, New born China paid a high price with the tremendous loss of army personnel and properties within a year after the Chinese Communist government established. Despite the inferiority of modern weapons and equipment of the Chinese Army compared to the U.S. Army, the Chinese had successfully repelled the attacks of the U.N. forces which were composed of seventeen countries. Red China remained an isolated and backward giant. China were then alienated from the Soviet Union in many spheres of mutual interest.

Through battles against the World's strongest American forces equipped with most advanced modern weapons and Air Forces support, the poor equipped Chinese Army might acquire much experiences and learned a lot in modern warfare. Therefore, China started to increase the modernization of its Army steadily since the Korean War.

Because of the Korean War, China could not join the United Nations for twenty years because of the Korean War. They also lost the chance to unify with Formosa. Instead paid a high price for the Korean Conflict, China did obtain a secure position of leadership in the third world countries. Today, China has made economic development successfully and became a world number two economic power. Today, any country in a world simply can not under estimate China's vast territory and the world's most populous country.

e) Soviet Union

The Soviet Union had lost much with the Korean Conflict that Stalin approved. The world's community was suspecting that the Soviet Union instigated North Korea's invasion of South Korea and they criticized the Soviet Union for it. After the Korean War the Soviet Union's influence over the North Korea was much diminished in every field. The North Korean invasion proved to be one of the

Soviet leader's most serious mistakes. After the Stalin's death, the new Soviet leaders commenced degradation on Stalin's work achievements. Chinese leaders including Chairman Mao and North Korean Kim Il-sung disliked it and challenged them. Consequently, the Soviet's new leaders, in turn, got angry about the discontents. The two countries relations became extremely strained. At that time the Soviet Union unilaterally took action to pull all their technicians and advisors out of China. Consequently, most Chinese construction projects were all stopped and discontinued. Also the Soviets suddenly demanded payment for the arms aid which they supplied to Chinese Army during the Korean War. At the time, China was under severe financial and social difficulties. Russians emotionally kept asking China to pay back the arm's loan.

The Chinese public knew that Chairman Mao was very irritated. Mao said "pay back all the Soviet Union's debts, even if we would all starved to death, we would never talk again with the Russians for 100 years." He clearly announced the breach of friendship and parted their relationship with the Soviet Union. The two countries were hostile to each other since then, it caused the decline of the World's Communism movement considerably. Therefore, it might be said that all their discord and hostilities were largely based on the Korean Conflict. China emerged as a strong rival to Soviet Union within the Communist bloc and especially among Third World countries, which admired and identified with China's successful resistance to what they viewed as "Western imperialism." It is, therefore, the biggest loser of the Korean conflict undoubtedly was Soviet Union, the supporter of the Korean conflict.

f) Japan

Needless to say, it was Japan most benefited from the Korean conflict. After World War II, the Japanese economy was mostly destroyed and gloomy. It was virtually on the verge of bankruptcy. During the Korean War, Japan played a important role for the U.S./

UN forces as a safe rear base and supply route. It was an important opportunity to make the post war Japanese economy rise from bankruptcy. Japan was America's privileged sanctuary. As a rear base, a staging area safe from Communist attack, the American war planes took off freely from air bases in Japan to attack targets in North Korea. United States Army employed many Japanese laborers to build airfields in South Korea and unloaded military supplies in Korean ports. Also many Japanese ships were contracted for carrying UN troops to Inchon amphibious landing. American military procurement orders to Japanese industry and trade during were the decisive factors in the resurgence of Japanese economy.

Unlike Germany and Korea, Japan was not divided into two parts by the United States and the Soviet Union. They were just luckily occupied only by the American forces at the time. Toyota Corporation was then almost in bankruptcy. But they were quickly revived again with the production of war supplies ordered by the United States Army. About 90% of the purchase orders were military arms. Most Japanese industries were in full operations. They were busy to meet the US Army's procurement orders. During the Korean War, Japan's GDP growth showed 10-12% increase each year. Today, Japan has become the No. #2, world's economic power next to the United States, because of the Korean War. On September 8, 1951, influenced by the Korean War, Japan concluded a peace treaty with the United States. For the security of Far Eastern Asia, the United States needed Japan to cope against the Soviet Union, China and North Korea. Thus it could definitely be said that Japan was the most beneficial country out of the Korean War.

5. CONSEQUENCES OF THE KOREAN WAR

The Korean War was a turning point in post world war II history with momentous repercussions worldwide. It provided stimulus that transformed NATO into a powerful force for the defense of Western Europe. It gave the United States undisputed leadership of the UN.

The war gave the Truman administration the justification it needed for quadrupling the American military budget within two years. That triggered the endless and exorbitant arms race. Korean Conflict was a first major military conflict in the era of the Cold War. The United States then started to rehabilitate and rearm Japan and West Germany. The North Korean invasion proved to be one of Kim Il-sung and the Soviet leader's most serious mistakes. The United States repelled the North Korean invasion and saved South Korea with it's tremendous manpower and materials consumed during the Korean conflict.

The Korean War was a World's War in which military forces from seventeen anti-Communist nations fought against North Korean and Chinese Communists. The figure rises if we discard the then-convenient fiction of Soviet Union noninvolvement and also count those UN members who sent Medical unit and ships to Korea. In addition, we must take into account those non-belligerent nations, such as Japan, West Germany, and some other countries. Korea was to become by the accident of history and geography, a pawn in a great power play between the United States and the Soviet Union. Korea was manipulated by both sides for purposes wholly extraneous to the peninsula and the Koreans themselves became expendable.

North Korea's ambition to achieve the military unification of Korean peninsula failed, and the war almost developed to World war. The war also caused enormous amounts of property damage and casualties during three (3) years and one month of fighting. There is no accurate statistics of casualties and property damages. All the figures are more or less varied in almost every report. The Statistics prepared by Korean ministry of Defense are as follows;

More that 58,808 South Korean forces died, 178,632 wounded, 82,318 POWs and total of 319,759 casualties. 36,991 UN soldiers died, 115,648 wounded, 6,944 POWs, total of 159,583. For the U.S. Army 33,629 died, Missing in action 9,000, total of 150,000.

North Korean and Chinese forces suffered approximately a total of 1.4 million casualties over the same period. (By U.S. statistics reported to UN). The Chinese War Museum located in Dandung in Manchuria shows that the Chinese casualties were 360,000, including 170,000 dead. It is believed this figures are considered too small. There were approximately 350,000 South Korean civilians dead, 220,000 wounded and about 290,000 missing. There were 594,190 houses destroyed. There were about 1.5 million North Korean casualties during the same period.

The loss of military equipment: 1,992 UN Aircrafts, 777 US tanks. 2,186 MIG-15 Soviet Jet fighters and 1,178 Soviet tanks.

The war also caused enormous social dislocation. Several millions of Korean families were separated throughout Korea. Countless orphans, widows, and severely injured veterans were left to pick up the pieces of a shattered society. Most experts believe that the North Korea suffered much more manpower and economic damages compared to South Korea by the severe U.S. bombings. At the end of the Korean War, the U.S. adopted a general policy of military containment, diplomatic isolation, and economic sanctions against North Korea. In order to have South Korean president Rhee to accept the Armistice agreement, the United States signed a mutual security treaty with South Korea in 1953. To implement its anti-communist containment policy in Asia, the U.S. signed a series of bilateral and multilateral security treaties with South Korea, Japan. However, the U.S. led coalition with Japan and South Korea faced a counter-alliance between North Korea and the Soviet Union and China.

In the 30 year Treaty of Friendship, Alliance and Mutual Assistance signed in February 1950, Soviet Union and China agreed to use "necessary means" to prevent the revival of Japanese imperialism. This sino-Soviet treaty served as a model of North Korea's mutual defense treaties with Soviet Union and China that were signed in 1961. These treaties by two rival camps fully integrated the Korean peninsula into the Cold War bipolar system. For over half century following the Korean War, the nature of the economic linkages between the U.S. and North Korea were nonexistent.

North Korea is a society governed by an absolute ruling ideology called "Juche" (self reliance). It is a concept of autonomy and self-sufficiency that leads to the belief that Korea should be free from any foreign intervention. North Korean's economy prominently applies ideology, which means the economy is socialized and centrally planned. The relations between the North Korea and it's allies, China and Russia, were much strained when the two countries opened their diplomatic relations with South Korea in 1990. Kim Jong Il and his government are autocratic and isolated from the World society.

Following Kim Il-sung's death in 1994, who had controlled for almost 46 years, North Korea was hard pressed politically and economically, unable to halt the deterioration of its economy or adequately feed its people. North Korea has been slipping badly by virtually every indicator since the Soviet Union and its European satellite countries collapsed in 1990.

Since the late 1980s, the relations among the two Koreas and pacific powers transformed from confrontation to cooperation. The four Pacific powers—China, Russia and the U.S. and Japan—significantly expanded the scope of their cooperation in military, diplomatic, and economic fields. However, the relationship between South and North Korea was severely strained since 2007, and the cooperation turned into the confrontations. The late South Korean conservative President Lee had denied to recognize the South-North bilateral agreements made by between two his predecessors and the North Korean leader in 2002 and 2006 respectively. President Lee announced it right after his inauguration ceremony and the tension has started since then. The confrontation has escalated since the sinking of the South Korean Navy patrol ship, Chon An, and artillery attack on the Yonpyong Island.

Both sides claimed a Victory: Post the Korean War, North Korean Kim Il-sung insisted at the mass rally in Pyongyang that North Korean army won the war because they had repelled the South Korean army invasion. But contrary to this, South Korean president Syng-man Rhee also proclaimed the victory at the mass rally held in the commemoration of the Korean War which they could successfully stop the North Korean invasion. On September 28, 1950, Seoul had been re-captured and restored and the North Korean army had retreated north of the 38th parallel.

If the UN Command had been ordered to stop at the 38th parallel, the United States could declare a substantial victory over the North Korean army. However, to tell the truth, the United States Army won the North Korean Army but lost to the Chinese voluntary Army. Neither side totally won Korean War. The war ended in a stalemate. It might be able to say that the war was broken even.

After three years of fierce battles that claimed several millions of human lives and enormous amount of property loss, which resulted in establishing the D.M.Z (Demilitarized Zone) near the old 38th parallel. Neither side gained any intended Korean unification but there were only pain and suffering of the Korean people and many other nations. But United States Army had successfully defended South Korea from the North Korean aggression. Therefore, most South Koreans should be grateful to American people and the Truman administration for their devotions and valuable contributions. The 1953 armistice agreement signed by the United States and North Korea and ended the Korean Conflict. In 1992, 2004 and 2007, North-South bilateral agreements on reconciliation, non-aggression and cooperation, agreed, signed by two summits. Since the new conservative South Korean government took the office, the two Korea's relations were very strained. They went back to the confrontations rather than cooperation and reconciliation. Korea is still technically remained in a state of war because their three year conflict ended in a truce. No peace treaty has been signed yet up to the present time. North Korea has developed nuclear weapon secretly during the time and now the six countries talk is underway to deter the North Korean from their nuclear programs. The North Korea should abandon it's nuclear weapon for the peace of Korean peninsula and the rest of the world. The Korean peninsula should be defined the free nuclear zone, under the stipulation of signing the Peace treaty between concerned countries; such as South and North Korea, United States and China.

The Korean War armistice is now 60 years. It is known as world's longest truce in the history of World War. For the peaceful Korean peninsula, the current uneasy armistice should be replaced with a permanent Peace Treaty

On the occasion of 63rd anniversary of Korean War, I solemnly pray their Souls of all soldiers and civilians who were killed in the Korean War may rest in peace in Heaven.

PART III

KOJE-DO UN POW CAMP

CHAPTER I

DRAFTED TO NORTH KOREAN ARMY

1. THE OUTBREAK OF KOREAN CONFLICT

It was a rainy Sunday on June 25, 1950. When I woke up in the morning, I heard Pyongyang radio broadcasted that the South Korean army launched an all-out attack to North Korea across the 38th parallel and advanced 4 to 6 Km into the North Korean territory. At this time, most Korean people believed the news and took their word for it. On the other hand, anti-communist people including myself were implicitly pleased inward with the South Korean army invasion and wished to achieve unification under the control of the South Korean government.

However, at the noon time news, the radio announced that the North Korean Peoples Army started to repel the South Korean army's invasion and now was advancing Southward across the 38th parallel. Three days later the radio news announced that the North Korean army liberated Seoul, the capital city of Korea. I was so shocked and astonished with the news and could hardly believe it. When I lived in the North Korea, I heard covertly from my friends that there was no comparison between the North Korean and the South Korean army that was armed and equipped with most advanced American weapons and military equipment supplied by the United States.

After they captured Seoul, the North Korean forces suddenly stopped it's offensive and wasted 3~4 days in Seoul, and then started to advance again to South towards Daegu and Busan. Pyongyang radio broadcasted the one-sided victory of the news in the triumphant mood along with their army marching songs. North Koreans were in a joy mood of achieving their long cherished unification in their way, socialistic communism. However, it was revealed some time later that it was not the omen of Korean unification but was just the beginning of three years of the most tragic and bloody battles of the Korean War.

Despite the North Korean's insistence that the South Korean Army started to invade the North first, it was later revealed the North invaded the South Korea. Until recently, Western scholars writing on the Korean conflict did not have access to the archives and other records of the People's Republic of China (PRC) and the Soviet Union. Thanks to the end of the Cold War, a growing exchange of historical information between Beijing, Moscow, and Washington. These records have become increasingly available to historians. The materials from Russia and China still have to be studied with considerable caution because they remain incomplete and biased. They do, however, provide essential information on the following questions upon which historians could only previously speculate. What role did Moscow and Beijing play in helping N. Korean leader Kim Il Sung invade South Korea on June 25, 1950. Why did the PRC enter the war in late October 1950? And why did the PRC and N. Korea agree to an Armistice on July 27, 1953?

With respect to the first question, it now seems clear as shown by the Soviet secret letters that the Soviet Union and the PRC played a reluctant at first but, nevertheless, significant role in Kim Il-sung's decision to invade South Korea. Without their assents, as we all knew, North Korea's attack on the South would have been almost impossible.

After the division of Korea at the 38th parallel, most Koreans, both North and South, fervently wanted the independence and unified one Korea. A nationalist South Koreans committed to the unification as well as a Communist North Koreans. Since there was no visible demarcation line at the 38th parallel line, it was a common practice that both side's security forces frequently exchanged armed clashes to get the better positions even before the Korean conflict. The Korean War was destined to break out at any time by either side, because there were two different ideological governments in the North and South Korea respectively. Both sides wanted to unify the Korean peninsula in their way and control. One was pro-American South Korean government and the other was a pro-Soviet North Korean regime.

2. DRAFTED TO NORTH KOREAN ARMY

When the outbreak of the Korean War, I was a student of the Medical College. In mid-August, 1950, School authority called all the students to the college auditorium. The chairman of student union made the following speeches in the meeting: "Our valiant People's Army had now liberated 90 percent of the South Korea except Daegu and Busan. Now, it is almost the time to achieve our long cherished unification of fatherland, which has been our nation's highest and heartiest desire. Under this circumstance, we should temporarily stop our studies and we all must voluntarily enlist in the people's army in order to meet the demands of the great feat of Korean unification."

After his short speech, he distributed the Army enlistment application forms to every one of us and asked us to join the army. In this atmosphere, no one could dare to refuse it and we all had to sign the application form. We all knew that if anybody might oppose his demand, he would later have to confess his wrong doing of "self-critique" in front of the Union meeting. We all hated it. I should say that it was a kind of forced enlistment, in the name of "voluntary enlistment." We all formally became the enlisted army volunteers.

Frankly speaking, we were actually conscripted into military service rather than volunteers. Until that time, we never expected they would call us to join the army, because we were helping to treat the wounded soldiers at the army evacuation hospital in the city.

After we finished signing the applications, they kept us inside the school auditorium and we were not allowed to go back home. We had even no chance to let our parents know of our army enlistment. At about five o'clock in the afternoon, they escorted us straight to the Hamheung railway station where we waited for the night train bound for Pyongyang. At that time the US Air raids were so severe that all trains were operated in night only to evade US air force attacks. That was the moment of my life that determined my destiny and I was to be separated from my family and never saw them again for the rest of my life.

3. FINAL FAREWELL TO MY MOTHER.

We arrived at Hamheung railroad station around 5 pm in the afternoon, escorted by the North Korean Army officer. To avoid the US bombers strikes, we decided to wait for nightfall to take the night train. I was just settling in one corner of the station. When I was looking around, a familiar figure suddenly appeared before me. It was my mother. At the time, there was no telephone installed in each private households. I had no way to let my parents to know about my Army enlistment. She should not have known where I was. Yet, somehow my mother heard the rumor and finally located me. She had walked a long distance to see her son one last time before he goes off to the battle fields. Although I was glad to see her, I rudely blurted out in a thick country dialect, "Mother, why did you come all the way out here when I'll be back home in a month or two. Don't worry about me and go back home!" It was a blunt greeting from a foolish son who had little understanding of an anxious mother whose son is about to go to war. Without a response, my mother only blankly stared at me, her eyes full of worry and sorrow. Looking back, mother must have felt great anguish and deep sadness. Only mothers who have sent their sons off to war could truly understand my mother's anxious feeling at that time. Somehow oblivious to her pain or sorrow, I didn't pay close attention to her.

To this day, 63 years later, I can still recall her sad, blank stare, now piercing to my heart. She had a quiet way about her and even then, in silence she held my hand tightly and bid me farewell. I then tried to reassure her not to worry. She could not erase the sad and concerned expression from her face as though she had some ominous premonition about her son's future. Usually my mother was the type of person who hardly showed her feelings, but I saw tears welling up in her eyes. In silence, we stood there for awhile. Afterwards, she straightened up and wiped her tears. Then she took out a bundle of rice cakes she had prepared for me and said, "eat them when you get hungry. Always be careful and come back home safely and healthy. I wonder when I could see you again." I could feel somewhat her motherly love for me. It was a tearful moment; yet I was indifferent. I was indifferent to my mother's tears, I was indifferent to the fact that I was about to go off to a war, I was indifferent to our separation. I was indifferent because I firmly believed that I will return home in a couple of months. Holding her small hands, I promised her, "Why worry so much when I will be back home in two or three months. Mom, I will promise you that I'll be back home at longest within three months." It was a promise I knew I could keep as we all heard that the North Korean army was already advancing near Daegu and Busan of South Korea, so everyone was expecting this war to be a swift victory for the North. In reality, however, the North Korean army was then greatly struggling against the counter attack of the U.S. and South Korean army at the Busan perimeter. I realized much later that the North Korean Army was on the verge of a long retreat. Obviously back in Pyongyang, we did not receive this disastrous news which they never wanted us to know of it. There was another reason that I responded the way I did to my mother. Being a country boy, I had never been on a long train trip and had never been to Pyongyang in my life. Like a boy going on a school field trip, I was actually a little bit excited to have the train trip to

Pyongyang for a first time. In my foolish excitement, I couldn't really understand or sense my mother's heartache. I just tried to get her to stop worrying about me. I could only tell her not to worry about me. Then, mother finally spoke to me in a low and weak voice, "OK, in three months…I will see you in three months. Be back home safe. I know you could keep your promise, I will wait for you." Then I saw her tears flowing in her eyes. Once again, I just stayed there in silence. I could never realize then the sorrow of separation with my mother, as I did not know the moment was our eternal farewell. I was indifferent with a serene state of my mind. After she calmed down, she took out a white handkerchief from her waist pocket and placed it in my hand, "Training will be hard, and you will sweat a lot. Use this handkerchief to wipe your sweat off." Bit embarrassed, I shoved the handkerchief back into her hand and said "mom, I don't need it". Yet, mother was insistent. She squeezed the hanky into my pant pocket and remarked, "You will need it more than I do." I was then obliged to accept it. My mother must had foresight for my destiny. It is not until later that I would come to realize how this small, frail mother's last act of love towards her son, would save my life later. This handkerchief was to be a fateful, lifesaving instrument for me in the fierce battlefield that I was supposed to face inevitable death. But I could not have known that or ever imagine it at the time. Mother, I just want to let you know that I was the only one who survived in that fierce battle field and all my medical college class mates died beside me. But, mother, you and all mighty God saved my life.

Dearest Mother! I want to tell you now after all these years, the handkerchief you handed to me at the Hamheung rail way station has saved my life. Dearest mother, somehow you must have known. And, perhaps the heavenly maker must have felt pity and saved my life because of you. Dearest mother, you gave me life twice. All I can say is, thank you. When I said good bye to you at the station, I never imagined that it would be our final separation. Even more so, I never imagined the kind of dark disaster and hardship that would lie before me. Mother, this foolish son had come to realize long later after my life had become a nightmare, the fact that you were shedding tears knowing that our parting moment would be our final farewell. From that moment of our final farewell, I have become an undutiful, disobedient, ungrateful, insolent son to you who gave me life and raised me with love. Mother, I have been grieving all these years without being able to see you once more. I regret for not being able to show my love to you who loved me dearly and unconditionally. The ancient proverb saying, "when a child finally understands the merits of his parents, the parents are already passed away." refers to me. Although I am an 82-years-old man, I am still a child in mourning of lost parents. When you said goodbye to me, I should have seen your pain and sorrow. I should have treated you more kind, and more affectionate. I should have wiped your tears with my hands, and shared the sorrow of our parting. Please forgive this foolish son. And now I must live the rest of my life grieving. When I was a child, I know I was the hope of my parents. I was more dear to both you and father above all my siblings. At the age of three, I started to learn thousand Chinese characters. At the age of four, when I read and understood meaning of thousand Chinese characters, your joy was beyond words. I still remember your proud smile as you always called me in front of your friends to read the thousand characters. I tried not to disappoint you in my studies during my school years, never missing a top spot for academic honors since elementary to university. But now, my guilt and anguish is even greater as I disappointed you and your hope for me. One of the Korean popular song titled "This un-filial son is weeping", is the lyrics of this song refers to me. I pound my chest in regret and sorrow but it's too late now, I just lament it.

The Korean Conflict prohibited me from becoming a medical doctor and it gave me nothing but a pain and anguish. Moreover, I learned later that all the anti-communist POWs who had refused to repatriate to the North Korea were named as the title of reactionary to the North Korean regime and they issued the death notification to their parents. I think my parents should also received the notification that I was killed in the battle field. I can't imagine the kind of grief and pain my parents must have suffered upon receiving that notification. For your pain and agony you received for me, I cannot repay them forever.

Sorry mom. I could not keep my promise I made to you then that I would return in 3 months, Dear mother, please pardon me for my undutiful behaviors. You are not here though, but you are always with me in my heart. Mother, father, may you rest in peace in Heaven.!

4. ADMISSION TO N. KOREAN ARMY OFFICERS SCHOOL.

I and 120 of my classmates left the Hamheung railway station for Pyongyang, leaving my poor crying mother behind. The train went so slowly all night that we barely arrived at Pyongyang by morning, but luckily there was no US air raid. It was the first time I had ever been in Pyongyang; traffic was very light. There weren't many pedestrian on the streets even on summer days.

We were directed to one of the girl's high school where we spent all day long taking routine physical exams required to enter the N. Korean Army 1st Military Officers' School. All my classmates passed the entrance test except one of my friends named M.C. Kim. He failed the test because of his poor eye sight. He was then assigned to the regular army. As soon as he assigned the unit, he was appointed as an Army officer because the unit needed an officer to control the soldiers, as he was a college student. At that time, there were very few universities or colleges both in the South and the North Korea. The army unit needed an officer to control soldiers as the UN forces crossed the 38th parallel and advanced toward Pyongyang. He was later captured by UN forces and held in the officers' camp at Koje-do, UN Camp. He was also released as an anti-communist POW by Korean President Rhee. He joined the South Korean army, where he retired as a ROK Army Captain. Like me, many ex-POWs who were college student became ROK Army officer. This was possible because all Koreans are one nation and share same language, customs, and have been one nation for several thousand years. He and I are only two survivors among 120 medical students who were all killed at the battlefield at Pyongyang outskirts that I will describe later in this book. Mr. Kim was a lucky person to evade inevitable death because he failed to enter the Army officer's school.

Upon completion of the physical examination at the girl's High School, we were escorted to the First Peoples' Army Officers School located at Sadong, in Pyongyang. While we were in the school, we were completely isolated from the outside and just put our hearts and soul into the military training, such as military tactics, use of various weapons and practice of shooting training for two months. But they never appointed us as officers. I became to know much later that they had no chance to appoint us as officers because the North Korean leaders had already fled and emptied Pyongyang on October 12, 1950, prior to the US Army launching an attack to Pyongyang.

In the early part of October, they hurriedly formed a Pyongyang Defense unit which was composed of three infantry battalion to defend Pyongyang. This defensive unit was equipped only with rifles, grenades and a few machine guns. It didn't compare to the huge power of advancing US forces. We were assigned in the 3rd battalion. At that time, almost all the North Korean forces were sent to the South Korean battle fields at the start of the war to achieve an early victory of the war. There were not many North Korean forces in the rear. On October 15, our unit was ordered to march to Joonghwa town which was located about 15 miles south of Pyongyang. We left the School at about 1:00 am marching south in a pitch dark night. We were all tired and I was falling asleep while I was marching, which was my first experience in my life.

As soon as we arrived at a hill, back of the town of Joonghwa, we were ordered to dig a small individual trenches. The next day, while resting on the hill, I saw a group of Army officers passed us heading hastily towards Pyongyang. Among the group, I found a friend of mine who was my high school class mate whose rank was Lt. Colonel. He also recognized me at once and shook hands exchanging the greetings. I was very pleased to see him. I hadn't seen him for a long time. He offered me a cigarette and also handed me an apple to eat. Then he talked to me in whisper to my ear quickly that "I want to let you know the American forces are advancing up to Sariwon now and that's why we officers are retreating." He then hurriedly left me to join his group. The meeting was only a couple of minutes. Now, for the first time, I've come to know that the UN forces were advancing towards our unit. When we were in high school students together, he had voluntary enlisted the army and became an Lt. Colonel. Even though he was a pro-communist and I was an anti-communist, I felt his warm heart of his friendship. Now that I know UN forces advanced up to only ten to fifteen miles before us, for the first time, I realized that the war situation reversed unfavorably for the North Korean army.

The next day, the U.S. Air strikes continued almost all day long on Hukkyo town which was located about 14 miles from us. I could hear the sounds of the raid almost all day long. I observed thousands of low morale soldiers who were desperately retreating disorderly from the front line towards north to Pyongyang. They looked nothing more than a disorderly crowd without a military chain of command and discipline. In the dawn, our battalion was also ordered to retreat and we all ran desperately towards Pyongyang in the darkness on the rice paddy fields. The roads and rice fields were crowded by thousands of retreating North Korean army soldiers. There were no army disciplines and the chain of commands. They were nothing but a rabble and disorderly crowds rather than an organized and disciplined army. When we reached the outskirts of Pyongyang, the dawn started to break.

5. THE UN FORCES CAPTURES PYONGYANG

It was early morning of October 19, 1950, when we reached the4 outskirts of Pyongyang. At this time, the two US L-19 reconnaissance planes suddenly appeared in the sky above us. They did a reconnaissance flight over us at a very low altitude. It was a cloudy morning then a rainy day. Sometime later, as soon as the U.S. reconnaissance L-19s disappeared, a score of U.S. fighters jet planes suddenly appeared in the sky above us and started to strafe and machine-gunning, along with artillery fire and tank guns. At this time thousands of the retreating

North Korean soldiers including myself were lying their face down on the ground trying to avoid the jet fighters air raids. There was a flat rice paddy without any trees and no place to hide. Thousands of North Korean soldiers were immediately killed at this place by these fierce joint attacks. The North Korean soldiers had no chance to fight back because of these sudden attacks both from the air and the land. The retreating North Korean army then had no fighting power and morale. UN forces at that time attacked Pyongyang with all concentrated fire powers along with all kinds of possible air and ground power. The US Far East Air Force bombers then launched a strategic bombing against Pyongyang which targeted virtually every possible industrial, transportation, or military facilities of considerable size. The raids also devastated the countless nonmilitary structures and even civilian dwellings indiscriminately.

With the support of such aerial attacks, Eighth US Army advanced with several hundreds tanks of 1st Cavalry division, and the 1st ROK Division, entered Pyongyang and could easily capture Pyongyang without facing any North Koreans armed resistances. On the October 24th, MacArthur ordered his commanders to advance as quickly as possible with all forces available, so that operations could be completed before the onset of winter. The next day they could keep advancing north towards the border of China and North Korea, without having any strong armed resistance of the stampeding North Korean forces. North Korean government leaders had already left the Pyongyang and fled to North on October 12, 1950. There was no chain of command and the country was in a state of anarchy. North Korean Army was almost completely destroyed and not capable of any kind of armed resistance against UN forces. They fled in disorderly retreat and US forces advanced without facing any strong North Korean army's military resistance.

I surrendered to the US Army soldiers at the scene and was captured as a prisoner-of-war at the outskirts of Pyongyang and narrowly escaped from my inevitable death. I am going to describe this in the next chapter in detail.

6. SURRENDER TO THE U.S. ARMY

The sounds of fighter planes' massive air raids, tank machine gun fire, and artillery shell blasts surrounded me, ripping out my ear drums and numbing my head. I lost my mind and was flurried. As myself, my classmate Kang and other my medical collage classmates along with many other soldiers, hunched down instinctively on a sloped embankment of a ditch to avoid strafing. Our lives were like a candle light before strong wind. It appeared as my life hung by a hair. I was terrified at the sight. I did not know what to do next. I was hardly breathing. At this time, one of fighter started strafing us from very low altitude and I instantly looked up the fighter jet. As I remember I could see the pilot's face momentarily. He shot machine gun at us and killed all the soldiers around me but missed me. I could hear the machine gun's bullets noise lodged into the ground next to me and it sounded like a large hailstones dropping. I had no chance and couldn't even try to escape the strafing, but luckily the shower of strafing bullets just missed me and all mighty God allowed me to live. Then, I saw the fighter was making a circle and I intuitively realized he was coming back for us again. I shouted "Let's get out of here!" to my friend Kang lying down next to me pulling his back-pack. I then ran immediately about 30~40 feet on the sloped embankment and jump into a puddle (hole) created by a bomb-shell. There were three soldiers were already hiding in it. As soon as I jumped into the crater, the same fighter pilot machine-gunned us and killed three other soldiers beside me inside the puddle. Their blood squirted out of their wounds, some blood squirted out on my uniform and face. The pilot didn't kill me this time either. I couldn't believe how I could have survived again. Until that time, I didn't notice the US Army soldiers and tanks passing by me on the Seoul-Pyongyang main supply highway on the top of the embankment that I hid in. Neither the machine gunners on the tank nor the black soldiers marching beside the tanks noticed me hiding inside the puddle on the embankment. I was now completely trapped in the mortal circumstances to meet with inevitable death. I was hovering between life and death at the time. But I never lost my conscious and kept calm at the time. During my high school days, as I described before, I've watched a Hollywood movie and was impressed by American soldiers. As I remembered the movie titled was "The Bridge of Spree River" in Berlin, Germany, where both American and Soviet soldiers were embracing each other celebrating the war victory over the Germany. Since then, I became to be very friendly towards the United State and the US Army soldiers with the influence of that movie. United States is the democratic new country, a different kind of nation that the world has never seen. I saw the American GIs in the movie were more cleaner and gentlemen-like compare to the Soviet soldiers who I had seen them every day in the North Korea. My friend Kang and I had promised together that we would surrender to U.S. army soldiers rather than to fight if we were ever to be in a situation that we had to take a stand. We both made a firm promise to each other at Joongwha even before we started to retreat to Pyongyang.

In the midst of the chaos and critical situation, a flash of thought crossed my mind. My mother's handkerchief! I had always kept my mother's white handkerchief in my pocket. If there ever were time to surrender, it had to be now. Without any hesitation, I took out the white handkerchief and tied it up the barrel of the gun I held, and then I stuck my head out of the puddle. I could see the row of several tanks with machine guns continuously firing and soldiers passing by on the highway above my embankment. The sky was still filled with the awful sound of fighter planes, napalm blasts, heavy artillery and tank fires. But I was determined to live. I firmly believed and trusted the American soldiers were gentle and would save my life when I surrender. I did not want at all to fight against the American soldiers. Then I began to wave my little white surrender flag as hard as I could. I know this was a cowardly action for a soldier to do but this was the only way I could survive to avoid meaningless death. I continued to wave the white surrender flag and then peered out of the hole. At this time a black soldier saw me about 20 yards away. He aimed his gun straight at me and he gave me a hand signal to come out. As I was about to come out of the ditch, the tank gunner started to turn his machine gun towards me to shoot me. Loads of machine gun bullets flew right by my ears, head and body. There were bullets showering all around my head and body. I could hear the bullets noises around my ears. Startling me, I ran back into the crater right away. The gunner might have thought I was running out of the ditch to attack him rather than surrender because I forgot to put my hands-up on my head. As matter of fact, I didn't even know how to surrender. I couldn't even come to think of "hands-up" in that noisy, critical situation. No wonder the tank machine gunner took me as an attacker rather than a surrender. I forgot to raise my hands high up on the head, as I had no such experience before in my life. The machine gun bullets "whizzed" by my head, ears, arms, legs, and sides, and tore my uniform in several places. One of those bullets struck me on the left thigh but it wasn't deep enough to cause any major injury, it was a just minor scratch. Blood came out but I didn't even noticed then. It was a complete miracle that I did not get killed this time too. It was undoubtedly a miracle that I can not explain other than all mighty God protected me and saved my life. But I did not realize it at that time because I wasn't a Christian.

As I ran into back the ditch, the machine gunner on the tank continued to shoot at me. The bullets stuck into the dirt wall of opposite side of the puddle. Looking back, I still don't know how I was able to evade all the shower of bullets. I think all those bullets rather simply just evaded me. I was able to be survived out of sheer luck. I had miraculously survived from the jaws of death. All I can say that it was a mere miracle. I then waved hard the surrender flag out of the ditch again and again. Then the shooting stopped and I peered out once again. This time, several black soldiers saw me and gave me their hand-signals to come out and then I started to come out the ditch. As soon as I came out of the ditch, the black soldiers quickly gave me their hand signals to raise my hands above my head. And I did so as quickly as I could. I observed then that all the black soldiers were on the front line, walking by the tanks when the US forces advanced towards Pyongyang.

Now the distance between us was just about 20 yards. I could clearly see the numerous barrels aimed straight at me. If any one of those barrels had fired me, I should have been gone. Everyone was killed but me I was the sole survivor in that area, so they could kill me at any time if they wanted to. However, they let me live. I still thank those black soldiers for letting me live. I placed my hands high on my head as I was instructed by the black solders and walked toward them. And as I walked up the embankment, I glanced at a place where my friend 'Kang' had been lied down before with me. When I saw him, I was so shocked and astonished. He was lied down in the same position as I had left him. There was no evidence of bleeding. His face was pale white and no motion at all. I realized then he was gone. I felt my body shiver, my mouth half opened in shock. Around him there were numerous bodies of dead soldiers. There was nothing I could do for him as I was walking towards the black soldiers with my two hands raised high up on my head. At the time, the situation did not even allow me to attend and deplore the death of my close sworn friend. I just had to pass him by. Only a few minutes ago, we were alive together and promised firmly each other that we would surrender to US soldiers when the time would have come. He was my closest friend and class mate, but now we are eternally separated by death. The life and death was a paper thin difference between us. I could never see him again, never to share our friendship, never to console each other about the miserable Korean War.

When we were lying down side by side, he must have been struck by one of those many strafing bullets that had narrowly passed me. Now I can still feel the same cold shiver I felt 63 years ago and still clearly remember the hellish memories of that moment. I believe my life was spared by some heavenly father's help. There is no other way to explain as to how I could possibly have survived. Fortunately, I have survived to have a hairs breath and a narrow escape from the jaws of death. All I can say is that it was a miracle. The miracle that I can not explain and I did not know why and how it happened for me but nevertheless it had happened. I have survived from the three attempts to be killed at the battlefield. The cruelty, brutality, and atrocity of war are beyond my descriptions. All I can say is the War is a hell on Earth. Many young lives were mercilessly killed without their faults. Perhaps my life was spared by all mighty God to relay the atrocities of war and the bitter experiences of the POW's life for the future generations to remember. Moreover, the miserable war should never ever happen again on the Korean peninsula.

I approached the black soldier who found me and gave me his hand signal. I stepped in front of him. He started to search my body and found about 20 submachine gun bullets inside my pants pocket. He then shouted at me. "God Damn" then he slapped me once in my face. Then I realized that I was so bewildered that I didn't even know I had the heavy bullets in my pocket. I was so disoriented and no time to think of it at that time. The black soldier then hand gestured me to go to opposite direction of their marching line. While I walked the opposite direction of the advancing U.S. soldiers, I took a glance at the both side of rice fields and I saw thousands of North Korean soldier's dead bodies that were scattered around on the vast rice paddies. I have never seen so many dead bodies in my life, not even in the war movies. To my great astonishment and disappointment was that all of my medical collage school peers got killed at the scene as I found out later. I was the sole survivor among my peers. I observed smoke was still rising out of the dead bodies with Napalm bombing's blasts. Those North Korean soldiers who retreated from the 38th parallel to this place on their way to Pyongyang were all killed. There were only about 10~12 survivors (POWs) including me at the scene. Several thousands of retreating NK soldiers killed almost instantaneously in that early morning attack on October 19, 1950 at the southern outskirts of Pyongyang. At that time, several thousand North Korean soldiers were lying down on the ground to avoid the US Air forces raids, then the US forces three dimensional attacks started. Then the North Koreans had no chance to fight back. The US air power was a decisive factor in the Korean War. Air power, as epitomized by the strategic bomber, was able to attack, paralyze, and destroy the North Korean army, industries, rail roads, communications, the populated cities, the political structures and were mostly destroyed. All were vulnerable to the US air assaults. In the evening, American soldiers took us to one of the Elementary schools play ground located in the suburbs of Pyongyang. They made us to sit on the cold outside rainy ground. It was cold winter weather and was raining all night long. It was such a cold rainy night that we were all shivering with cold. We embraced each other to keep warm our body temperatures. US soldiers made us to sit on the cold school ground for five days without any food or water and we all almost starved to death. Most of the wounded prisoners already died there. We were not given any food or water for the next five days. One day, they took us to Dae-dong River running in Pyongyang and we were forced to do a hard labor work building a pontoon bridge on the river. Without food and water over five (5) days, we were almost starved and had no energy at all to do the labor work. Whether the American soldiers knew of this or not, they kicked and beat us hard with the butt of their rifle mercilessly for not moving fast enough. G.I.s yelled out "Huba, Huba!" and brutally kicked and hit hard with their fists and gunstock. Every time they hit, weak POWs fell on the ground feebly. I have never heard and seen such a slavery working conditions in my life. It was even more brutal than the slave works in the movie. I was so disappointed and stunned seeing the brutal acts and behaviors of American soldiers at the time. It was quite contrary to my prior concept that American GIs were generous and gentlemanly. I was much discouraged and lamented and the bitter experience rankled in my heart at the time. I then began to resent and contempt those who started this bitter, miserable Korean War.

CHAPTER II

1. MOVE TO PYONGYANG PRISON

Before I start to write my POW's life, I think I have to describe now the fact that U.S. Army soldiers handling POWs with very rough treatment in the early stages of the war, but they treated POWs much better later in the Koje-do POW camps. I fully understand their situation that they had to concentrate and immerse in the fighting. I think the US Army authority did not have enough time to take care of POWs. However, it was the fact that some US Army soldier treated POWs with inhumane treatment. They should not assault POWs brutally.

After five days of starvation and forced labor, we were all transported to Pyongyang prison and there they gave us a rice ball first time to barely keep us alive. I observed there were thousands of POWs in the Pyongyang Prison, collected from many different places. So many prisoners crowded in each small prison cell and so it was even hard to find room to sit. More than twenty people were thrown into each small prison cell. Although it was overly crowded, it was warmer and felt much better than freezing field ground of the elementary school. In the prison, one of the ROK Army officers appointed me as a leader of four prison cells to control them. I was free to go outside of the prison cell to supervise and control the crew to deliver the cooked rice from the mess hall to each cell. It was more comfortable and convenient that the ROK Army soldiers controlled us rather than US Army soldiers because they speak the same Korean language. Moreover, they never assaulted us and treated us better than US soldiers.

I had a hard time to select and appoint the rice ball delivery crew members because everybody wanted to do that job so that they could even temporarily get out of the crowded prison cell and get some fresh air. Anyway, they supplied us a rice meal along with water the first time in 5~6 days and we could barely keep our lives alive. In the meantime, we didn't know anything about the warfare situation. We didn't even know the Chinese communist army entered the Korean War. In the first part of December, we were instructed to move further south by cargo train but we didn't know our destination.

The last night we were scheduled to move from the prison, there was a big fire broken out one of the prison buildings across ours and a lot of POWs were suffocated and burned to death by the fire because they were locked in the prison cells and no body unlocked the doors and rescued them. It was a miserable sight of a fire disaster. I heard one of the prisoners was whispering to other prisoner about the fire. He said somebody might set the fire on purpose. He further stated that the prisoners had no matches or lighter to set the fire and he suspected somebody to set fire.

The next day we were moved to the Pyongyang textile factory whose building roof has been blown off by the US air raids. We all sat on the cold concrete floor for three days without any food or water, waiting for a train to transport us to Inchon port. It was a severe cold winter in December and we had to fight against both cold and hunger. Our physical condition rapidly deteriorated and we all became weak, sick POWs died one by one. I've lost a lot of weight during the time. When I touched my bony body, I felt sad and missed my mother. My ears were numb and could hardly hear. I felt at that time that human beings are very weak animals that can easily be devastated, and they became miserable both mentally and physically with starvation and the cold weather. After three days waiting, we were transported by cargo train to Inchon port. Two days later we were put on board of Japanese cargo ship that was carrying black coal. All the ships crew members were Japanese. When I asked them about our destination, they replied "they didn't know either." I then suspected they might take us to one of islands of Japan or any other foreign country.

2. JAPANESE HELLISH CARGO SHIP

We were transported to Inchon port city about 40 miles west of Seoul and we were almost dead with severe cold weather and starvations.

The Japanese ship was a coal freighter and they put us in a large hold which was almost the height of a three story building. It was too hard for the weak and sick POWs to climb down on the steel ladder into the hold. Black coal dust filled the ships cargo room, and many weak POWs fell off the ladder, suffered serious injuries and some were even died. They overloaded thousands of POWs in one ship's hold and it was so jammed, crowded that it was even hard to find a place to sit. As the time went by, the air of the dark hold room became so contaminated and hot, produced by thousands POWs breath and body heat. We were hard to breathe and every body in the room was almost suffocated for the lack of oxygen. There was no food and no water during three days trip to Busan, and everybody was hungry, thirsty and completely exhausted. I observed a POW near me, held his own urine in his hand and drank it. I could simply imagine how badly thirsty he was. It was really a hellish atmosphere in the small jammed ship hold. We were almost dead. The second day of the voyage, the Japanese ship crew tried to drop down steel drum can containing steamed rice from the deck to feed the POWs down in the hold. The starved POWs raced to jump on the rice drum can to get the cooked rice before other people to get. During the disturbances many weak POWs were crushed down to death by the strong prisoners stepped foot on and pressed on their bodies. This kind of practice had repeatedly occurred every time the cooked rice drum cans came down from the deck. Because of those disturbances, most of other POWs could not get the food for three days and many other prisoners were almost starved to death again. There was no leader to control the prisoners in the ship hold and it was a hell itself. I might guess almost a hundred POWs were killed by these incidents. Furthermore, I saw many people even sat on the dead bodies because the room was so small and jammed with thousands POWs. It was even hard to find a place to sit down. We were all almost dead than alive. In other words, most prisoners became almost living corpses. We were scarcely kept alive in the hellish ship hold. I would like to call this cargo ship "a hellish ship" and that Japanese ship deserved to be called a "Hellish ship on earth". I thought even the Hell might be a better place than the Japanese black cargo ship. The old adage says that war is hell, certainly applied to us and the Korean War. After three days voyage most POWs were completely exhausted inside the black steel ship's hold and became nearly dead. Many dead bodies were left in the ship's hold. I have no idea how many POWs died in the ship hold, but it is not an exaggeration if I said about a hundred.

Somehow we finally arrived at the Busan in the dark evening night and the GIs made us sit down on the cold and windy wharf of the Busan port. It was so cold, as we have just got out of the hot ship's hold in which was the stifling heat, and we could hardly stand the cold wind which pierced to our bones. No wonder we felt so cold because we all wore summer uniforms and some POWs even wore only underwear. American soldiers often took POWs uniforms off when they do the body search at the time of catching POWs. With such a cold, it seemed to me that Busan was the coldest place in the Korean peninsula. Busan is located at far south of the Korean peninsula and it has warmest weather on the Korean peninsula.

3. BUSAN POW CAMPS

a) Seomyon Compound:

We all walked to the Seomyon POW camp through the streets of Busan City in the dark late evening. I could see no pedestrians or cars traffic on the quiet streets. I instantly realized that this city was Busan, Korea, rather than a foreign country when I saw the store signs written in Korean letters, and I felt somewhat relieved. The warm dim lights reflected on the private house windows made me feel so warm. I felt such kind of warmth for the first time in my life, since my body was so cold. It seemed to me at that time that the inside the house room must be a homey and a happy cozy paradise. How lucky and happy the people inside the room were! I felt envy of them at that time.

One way or another, we arrived at Busan Seomyon POW camp and were assigned to each tent. It was much warmer inside the tent compared to outside in cold weather and we were all some-what relieved and felt more comfortable for the first time for a long time. During a couple of months, we have been lived in the hellish living condition and we all lost a lot of weight with the starvation and cold weather, reducing us to an almost skeleton body with miserable features. Moreover, the Japanese coal ship made our faces painted black with black coal dust.

There were many POWs in the Busan POW camps collected from all over the battle-fields. After Three days, we arrived at the Camp, we were forced taken to the Suyong air port located at the outskirts of Busan. There we delivered the gravel and sand bags for the airfield construction. At the work site, the GIs kicked and hit POWs hard with sticks and gun butts, yelling "haba! haba!, (Quick, Quick!)" to make the POWs move faster. I saw the same slave labors are enforcing here at the airfield the same as the one we had at Pyongyang Daedong River. Worst of all, one of the GIs threatened and pretended to stab a POW's face with his rifles bayonet. It was really a hard time for the feeble, hungry POWs to lead their lives under the slavery working condition with cold weather and starvations. I hate to describe this kind of brutality stories committed by American G.I.s but I have to write down because it was a true story that I have witnessed.

Under these adversities and unsanitary conditions, most weak POWs were exposed to the utmost danger of contagious diseases, such as influenza, amoebic dysentery and other epidemics. It was a good hotbed of infectious diseases for the feeble POWs living under the unhealthy living conditions. I witnessed approximately 50 to 100 POWs died everyday in our compound with various kinds of the epidemic disease mainly with amoebic dysentery. There were scores of POW compounds in the Busan area and it must have amounted to a large number of total deaths including all other compounds. I have no idea how many prisoners died all other compounds in Busan area at the time. But I presume the total number of fatalities should be much more than I thought. As far as what I know about dysentery, it is not a life threatening fatal disease in normal physical conditions and social life, but it was so contagious and spread so rapid among the weak POWs who suffered from starvation and cold. It was a fatal disease for the weak POWs. I was so surprised to see that they died so fast and easily. They have been through all kinds of adversities since they were captured as POWs, but they died so easily and miserably suffered from the epidemic diseases. Their poor corpses were just wrapped up by their own dirty blankets and were thrown onto a truck to leave their bitter life without receiving anybody's sympathy or condolences. And I thought the war was a hell that mankind could make on this living planet. I then really felt the grimness of war and the bitterness of the POW life pierced my heart.

b) Busan Koje-ri POW Compound;

The compound authority moved us to the new Busan Kojeri Compound which was established on a wider scope and more extensive than the Seomyon compound where we almost became a living corpse. Since we became POWs, we were never given the chance to wash our faces smeared with coal, cut our hair, or even brush our teeth. The miserable POWs life made us to be skeleton men that no one could identify as human beings. If Busan citizens saw us at that time, they must think that all the North Korean army soldiers looked like barbarians and we were different people than Korean.

A large number of POWs were interned in each Kojeri compound and they were organized the same as the Army organization; such as battalions, companies and platoons. Each compound interned of about six thousand and all POW leaders were assigned on each level of units. Those leaders were mostly the dropouts of the ROK Army soldiers and some are South Koreans who were impressed and voluntary enlisted to the North Korean Army when they occupied Seoul.

In Busan Camps, there were many former ROK Army soldiers POWs who were captured by the North Korean Army. They were impressed and voluntarily enlisted the North Korean Army, and later recaptured by the UNC forces. In the Busan POW compounds, those former ROK Army POWs took over the most compound's leaderships. They controlled POWs very brutally, beating with club and bat, all the same as the South Korean army did. The North Korean people's army never beat their soldiers or abuse them. Therefore, we all got angry for their acts of mistreating and despising other prisoners although we are all the same POWs status. Since these ex-ROK soldiers professed themselves to be anti-Communist and were usually favored by the ROK guards, they were able to win supervisory positions. Those leaders can eat more food than other regular POWs and also exempted from the hard labor work.

I am going to introduce a funny story about the toilet facility in the compound.

Prisoners had to stand in long line waiting for toilet because of shortage of toilet facilities. To make the temporary toilet, they dug big hole on the ground and put a long wooden ladder on it. Scores of people had to sit down at the same time on the same wooden ladder (toilet) by the order of the bathroom POW guard. He then order sternly "take your pants off, and start!", and after 4-5 minutes later he orders loudly "Stop and get up now!" At this time, regardless of what is your present situation, you must stop and get up right away. Otherwise you would get a hard blow by the stick of the guard relentlessly. The order of the toilet guard seemed to be more strict and fearful to POWs than the order of the Ruler of the Hell.

The cold winter weather mercilessly attacked us who mostly wore North Korean Army's summer uniforms and the devil of death threatened to kill us. I could see the dim lights of Christmas decorations far away from the city and I could hear the sound of church bell ring. But it did not give us any solace and comfort at all, in that we all were in an atmosphere of sorrow and grief with cold and hunger. All the prisoners seemed to live with dangers the same as the 'candlelight in front of hard wind'. With these adverse living and working conditions, our lives were exposed in danger of death. Even on Christmas day, we got up early in the morning and had to go to work at Busan port in the cold winter weather in January. They unload the US Army supplies from the ships and load it on truck under the slavery working conditions. We all had to fight against hunger and the cold weather that severely threatened our lives constantly. As we didn't have any eating utensils, we had to receive a ball of rice with our dirty blanket and eat it with dirty fingers. I heard somebody complaining that his life was worse than a dog's life; even a dog has enough food and his own dish.

First of all, Water was the major problem to get, as there was no water supply line or facilities. We had to pick up dirty, filthy water to cook steamed rice, from a streamlet running from upper village where the villagers washed their clothes and other things early in the morning. The water was really dirty and contaminated. Accordingly, the rice boiled with that filthy water smelled terribly bad, but we had to eat such an unsanitary bad rice to survive. But still all the hungry POWs had to eat without any complaint. When you are really hungry, there is no time to complaint. We had no other choices but to eat the bad smell, unsanitary cooked rice for our survival.

In the cold early morning, we must have a head count before we headed for the Busan port wharf to do the work transporting C-rations and other military supplies. American GI guards yelled "huba! Huba!" and hit hard with his rope on the back of POWs who worked slow and idle. There were also same slavery forced work here as the same as Pyongyang and Suyong air field. One day, one of the G.I. found a hungry POW eating a can of C-ration and then the guard gave him two more cans and forced him to eat. The guard yelled and ordered him "You hungry? You chop!, chop!", "You no chop, chop? I hit you!". As he could not eat them all, the GI hit him hard on his back with his tent rope. The GI gave him so called 'eating torture' I should say it.

Then I thought POWs should be treated humanely according to the 1949 Geneva Convention. I am writing this true story because I want to let Korean people to know the tragedy of War and we must prevent another Korean War at any cost. I think more former POWs who experienced the Koje-do POW camp's life must write down more true stories, good and bad, for recording in the Korean War history. I think I am the one of person who God allowed me to survive and let me write the miserable POW's life to record in the Korean War History and let the Korean people know about the miserable Korean War that claimed several millions' human lives, bitter agonies and tremendous amount of property damages. The second Korean War must be prevented at any cost.

In January 1951, good thing that we started to supply clothes (US Army uniform), cap, shoes, a rice bowl and spoon for a first time. Thank God! Now we have at least necessities to protect us from cold weather and eat normally. Our bodies were so much dirty that the new uniforms were too good for our dirty bodies. Thanks to the U.S. Army authorities supplying us the uniforms and utensils.

A little later they sprayed D.D.T. for disinfection of our dirty bodies to kill parasitic insects and it helped greatly to get rid of worms. It had contributed much to reduce the contagious diseases in the POW camps. All the D.D.T. spray crew members were N. Korean female POWs. They all wear clean U.S. Army uniform and looked very cute and pretty to the eyes of all male POWs. Those girls looked like the most beautiful and sexiest girls in the world to the eyes of male inmates. Even an ugly looking girl seemed to be the most beautiful girl in the world to their eyes. It was quite reasonable that all the females looked very pretty to their eyes because they see only the same ugly male POWs every day in the compound.

Now we were getting better treatment by the UN authorities. We were much relieved, comfortable and felt much better than before. Now we found our lives worth living and our health conditions were improving gradually every day in the Koje-do POW compounds. It seemed to be over the miserable hell's life anymore.

c) Call from Camp Headquarters;

One day, I had a call from the Compound Headquarters and I attended the call. Inside the quon-set hut, about ten POWs were there waiting for their call with the worried faces. I was also waiting for my turn in the waiting room. While later, I then heard a painful scream coming from the next room. The interrogator speaks Korean language instead of English and I heard sometime he beat his prisoner with his club during the interrogation. I then noticed why other people waiting here showed a worried faces with a gloomy mood. I never heard of such kind of torture scream in my life and started to somewhat worry about myself a little bit why they called me here. Questions continued to strike my mind, but I could never come up with an answer because I never did any wrong doing against the U.S. Army soldiers. I suspected that somebody might have devised a plot against me so that he could evade the blame of his own wrong doings or probably somebody might have tried to entrap me with some false accusation and incrimination. I had firmly believed that I have done nothing to be ashamed of myself. I was just a college student and not a communist or any politician. I was forced to be drafted by the North Korean army, simply because I was born and lived in North Korea. I had never fought against UN forces at anytime at all. I never shot even one bullet towards the UN forces. I am pretty sure I never did anything wrong. I then tried to calm myself down. By and By, it was my turn to enter the investigation room. There were several investigation teams in the room and each team consisted of an interrogator and an interpreter. My investigator was an American GI wearing an army uniform without any army insignia of rank, and a Korean interpreter was sitting beside him.

As soon as the American interrogator saw me, he stared at me for a while, and he abruptly asked me "YOU! We know you were one of the North Korean army officers, weren't you?" He yelled at me with a loud and overbearing voice. I answered distinctly "No" to him, and he yelled at me again with coercive tone of voice. "I know you are one of the North Koran Army officers and you should confess and admit it now!" I answered "I'm absolutely not, you misunderstood me and you are wrong." He continued "We know that all the university or college students of North Koreans are Army officers and you also must be one of the Officer because you were one of the Medical college student. Furthermore, you have trained at a North Korean Army military Officer's School; therefore, you were definitely one of the N. Korean Army officers. Don't lie to me and confess it right now" Now I understood the reason why they called me in this room and why they thought I was one of the N. Korean Army officers. Now all my questions that I had it before entering this room were solved and cleared to me. I told him then "I am going to tell you all about the truth and actual fact why I could not become an officer. It was true that I was drafted and forced to enter the Army officer's school in late August, 1950. Just before our graduation, on or about October 12 1950, all the North Korean government officials, army high rank commanders had hurriedly retreated from Pyongyang to north towards the Korean-Chinese border, just before the UN forces captured Pyongyang on October 19, 1950. They had no time to appoint us as an officer and that's why I remained as a military cadet and a private soldier." I told him the truth as it was, and it took me a while to convince my interrogator.

Finally he was convinced and started to understand me with my sincere explanation that I was not one of the North Korean army officers. It was the true fact that I was not a North Korean army officer. Quite unexpectedly, he asked me then whether I have learned English. I answered "yes". I have learned the English for three years in my middle and high school days. I managed to answer his question in English. Although, I spoke very poor English at the time, but he looked to be little surprised to learn that I spoke in English and he started to show his interest in me. He might think I could speak good English. He then showed a friendly feeling toward me and he asked me whether I could write English letters too. I answered precisely

"Yes I can". He looked to be pleased to find out the prisoner who can speak and write English. He then told me that the Compound authority badly needed a person who could translate the Korean letter into English. He then said he would find out the translator position for me and he would let me know later.

4. BECOME POW LEADER

A couple of days later, I started to work for translation job at the Compound head-quarters. My job was to translate all the POWs name, date of birth and their army unit written Korean letters into English, which was a very easy job for me. From now on, I don't have to work hard labor job on the cold wharf of Busan port. My life has suddenly changed from the painful hell to joyful paradise and I was in a good pleasant mood. I then greatly appreciated my parents who gave me a collage education. As the proverb says that "turning a misfortune into a blessing when you are patient!". I have learned and experienced that a person lived with patience should have eventually changed an adversity into a prosperity. I then realized for a first time that the importance of English language. The English language made my life much easier and more convenient. Since then, I was exempted from the hard labor job and later I became one of the POW leaders all the way until the time I was released by the South Korean president Rhee on June 18, 1953. As I always worked for the Compound headquarters, working with Sgt. Coon, the compound NCO In-charge, my English knowledge was much improved. Sgt. Coon liked me very much and we had a good relationship and became a good friend of mine. He was my first American friend.

Sometime later I got recovered completely my body weight and physical condition. I was looking good compare to other POWs and always wear clean brand new US Army uniform.

At the early stage of my POW's life, as I mentioned earlier, I had a hard time and I had experienced that the human beings are not more than an animal when they are hungry and cold. However, even in those adverse days I was spiritually so strong and was not infected any contagious diseases that killed many prisoners of war in the compound. Since then, my life has been changed favorably and was much better than before until I was released.

5. MOVE TO KOJE-DO POW COMPOUND

With the amphibious landing at Inchon and the re-capture of Seoul by the Eighth US Army, the North Korean Army began to fall back. Large numbers of North Korean soldiers were taken prisoner in the swift maneuver and sent to the rear. Prisoner's number rose to over 130,000 in November, 1950. And the Busan temporary POW camps were not enough facilities to receive those POWs.

December, 1950, UN forces started to retreat with the Chinese army offense up to 38th parallel and retreated further to south and lost Seoul again on January 4, 1952. The UN Command decided to isolate and move the rapidly increasing number of POWs to Koje-do, an island off the southern coast of Korea, near Busan. We arrived at the north coast island in early part of April, 1951. Koje-do is the second largest island in Korean peninsula next to the Cheju Island. It is 399 square Kilometers, was a poor sleepy island. Koje-do is today the modern city connected to the mainland with bridge. It is home for big ship-building industries of Samsung and Daewoo ship yards, sports, fishing and booming tourism. Its population was then probably less than 2,000, but it was a home for 100,000 civilian refugees from North Korea plus about 170,000 North Korea and Chinese POWs interned in 28 compounds and were much crowded.

Unlike the Busan temporary compounds, Koje-do compounds were established to a much large scale and had better facilities in all its aspects. American GIs treated prisoners much better than before and they did not beat or curse POWs as they did before. Food and clothes supplies were still insufficient, but it was far better than before. Consequently, most POWs were much recovered from their poor health conditions. On Koje-do there were little or no natural water resources on the island. Construction began in January on the first enclosure of UNC prisoner of War Camp Number #1 and by the end of the month over 50,000 POWs were moved from Busan to Koje-do. The POWs had to build dams and store rain water to serve all the population.

6. EXODUS FROM THE RED 76TH COMPOUND

My colleagues and I were moved to new Koje-do camps quite later after all other POWs moved to Koje-island. We were the last POWs moved to Koje-do Compound. But, unfortunately, we were assigned to the 76th compound that was later found one of the most violent communist POW camps on Koje-do. They arrived here much earlier than us and they already took over the compound leadership and all the supervisory positions. When they saw us they were scared and worried about that we might chase them out and deprive their leadership. They already knew that we were a group of leaders at Busan POW camps. Therefore, they confined us immediately in one tent and guarded us 24 hours putting two watch dogs on each side of the tent entrance doors. Our tent was located at far south corner of the compound just beside the barbed wire security fence.

One sunny afternoon, After we were detained inside tent for five days, I was looking at the rice paddy and hills outside of the compound. Just then, I saw Sgt Coon was walking on the road just outside of the fence. What a coincidence! It was purely by chance that I saw him. I then called him "Hi, Sgt Coon!" and he heard and saw me. He then answered with his loud voice, "Hey, Tony, stay there, I was looking for you too. Don't move and stay there until I come to get you!" and then he hurriedly left there. He used to call me 'Tony' in American name when we worked together at the Busan Compound headquarters. He was then the NCOIC, in charge of the compound.

My colleagues and I, we all cheered with joy at the time. We all prepared and ready to go with Sgt Coon. We wanted anxiously to leave out of the 76th compound where we were confined. I've learned later, this compound became a leader of most violent communist compounds and abducted General Dodd, the Camp Commander on May 17, 1952. They rioted and made demonstration many times against compound authority and for the compulsory repatriation instead of the voluntary. They killed many anti-communist POWs in their compound through the name of "People's court" (Kangaroo court) relentlessly. If I was kept in that compound, I know I am the No #1, target to be killed by them. When I was captured at the battled field, I was confronted with many life perils but every time I faced it, I was lucky to avoid the dangers miraculously.

Sometime later, Sgt. Coon came to me and told us "Let's go!". He had already stopped at the compound headquarters and got the permission to take us with him. At this time, about a hundred POWs in other tents also wanted to get out of the compound with us and follow us. Sgt Coon also accepted them and took all of us to his 83rd Compound where he was in charge of the compound. Because of Sgt. Coon's help, I and hundred other non-communist POWs could escape from the 76th communist compound and we saved our lives. Thanks to Sgt. Coon! We all escaped from the 76th compound that was a main communist center that the central committee of the communist organization called "Liberation alliance" was formed and their headquarter was located in the compound. They supervised and controlled all the communist's compounds in Koje-do and conducted and controlled a lot of riots and demonstrations against the UNC.

7. MOVE TO 83RD COMPOUND

With Sgt. Coon's favor, I and other hundred anti-communist POWs got out of the 76th compound. He saved our lives, and took us to the 83rd Compound where he was in charge of the Camp. The 83rd compound was a relatively new established one and had less number of prisoners compared with other compounds. All POW's supervisory positions of compound headquarters were filled already, but each battalion's supervisory positions were still available at the time. Sgt.

Coon wanted me to be a 1st Battalion commander, but I refused his proposal at first. But he kept asking me and I accepted the position finally. He then asked me to recommend my friends to be assigned for three other Battalion commanders. He accepted my colleagues who I recommended him without any objection.

At the time the compound leader was Lee, K.S. who was a student of Seoul National University and was very intelligent man with a good personality. We all worked for the administration field and controlled the POWs in our compound. All the POWs were organized in the military system. I also, as a battalion commander, tried to treat prisoners good and fair with all my efforts. At that time, the UN authority did not directly control the POWs and let the POW supervisors to control all POWs instead, as same as the self governing system. To US Army MPs guard the main gate of the compound only and the ROK army security forces only performed the sentry guard duty outside the security fences. They are not allowed to enter the camps. We had our own POW security guards inside the compound. The POW security guards (police) treated ordinary prisoners very brutally and frequently they tortured them at night, both the same in the communists and the anti-communist compounds alike. They interrogated and tortured POWs to find out their ideological opponents.

At the Ponmunjom truce village, there were lengthy arguments on the issue of the POWs repatriation. The communists insisted the compulsory repatriation and the UN forces the voluntary one. This argument, in turn, provoked the bloody fights between POWs, right and left, in the Koje-do POW camps.

Our compound was an anti-communist compound, but we could hear almost every night a painful scream produced by tortured POWs out of the POW security office tent. They tortured relentlessly the POWs who wanted to repatriate to the North, in the name of "anti-communism", and endeavor all means to prevent POWs from repatriating to the North. In the communist POW camps, to the contrary, they tried to find out the person who refused to go back to North Korea and they did the same thing. Some of the POWs were deformed and even killed as a result of such tortures. In some anti-communist compound they encouraged and enticed the prisoners to tattoo the letter of ["anti-communism, ROK, South Korean flag]" on their arms and breast to prevent to return to North Korea. With these tattoos of anti-communism slogans, they could not go back to North Korea because they did tattoo the anti-North Korean slogans on their body. They knew that they would get severe punishment for it, and that made those tattooed POWs could not go back to their native places.

On the contrary, the pro-communist compounds endeavored to make more POWs repatriate to North Korea and if they found any stragglers, they beaten and tortured the same way as they did in the anti-communist compounds. Under those fear and duress atmosphere, it was some true that such unjust practice affected adversely and reduced the true meaning of voluntary repatriation. I think, in this matter, the POW security guards of both compounds are responsible for it and qualified to be blamed for their malignant acts. While truce negotiators debated long time on the POW repatriation issue, the ideological struggle between communist and anti-communist POWs had brutally struggled and killed each other in the UNC compounds. These terrible wanton killing occurred because of the repatriation argument, either compulsory and/or voluntary, in the Panmunjom truce meeting. There was no such a precedent in the history of the prisoner of war.

The outbreak of dissension and the demonstrations, the riots were mainly cause of the lengthy POW repatriation argument on the compulsory and voluntary repatriation issue at the truce meeting. At this juncture, the prisoner's supervisors, especially POW's security guards realized that their future was at stake. They started to fear of retaliations when they should return to the North Korea. It is known that the repatriation refusal first started from the former Chinese Nationalist soldiers who later joined into Mao's communist voluntary army. They wanted to repatriate to Taiwan instead of mainland China. The North Korean POWs supervisors and the security guards also started to refuse to return to North Korea because they worried about the retaliation and punishment for their atrocities they committed to the regular POWs.

CHAPTER III

THE TRUCE MEETING AND POW CAMPS

1. OUTSET OF THE TRUCE CONFERENCE

The UN forces were able to stand up and recovered from the Chinese onslaught as soon as they entered the Korean War in November 1950. It can be attributed in large measure to the sheer tenacity, and military brilliance of General Ridgway, who took over command of the Eighth Army at a critical juncture in the war and remodeled UN forces into an effective fighting team. In the end his cautious turnaround gained momentum when the officers and men saw that the enemy was vulnerable and overextended and the victory could be won. That seems like a fair assessment of what took place under General Ridgway's command. Enjoying enormous initial success, the Chinese army engaged in their own efforts at "roll back'" driving UN forces well below the 38th parallel. However, China's lack of technology and sophisticated military equipment limited what China could achieve on the battlefield. What followed as a result were two years of largely military stalemate as the focus of the war shifted from the battlefield to the negotiating table.

George Kennan, formerly of the State Department's Policy Planning Staff, was the foremost Russian expert in American government. With Acheson's approval, the State Department suggested that Kennan approach Yakov Malik, the Soviet UN ambassador, with a message roughly as follows: "The United States and the USSR are on a collision course over Korea," something the American felt neither power wanted. Both countries seemed to be drawn further along by the Chinese. Would it not make better sense for all concerned if an armistice and cease-fire were sought in Korea, perhaps along the line of the present troop dispositions?

The Soviets were as eager as the Americans for peace, as revealed by a prompt reply. Less than a week later, on June 5, 1951, Malik called Kennan to his office. He told him the Soviet government wanted a peaceful solution in Korea, because the soviets had no direct involvement in the war. Any approaches should be made to the Chinese and the North Koreans. Malik proposed at the UN general meeting on the Korean armistice on June 23, 1951. The American ambassador "Alan Kirk" in Moscow visited "Andrei Gromyko", the deputy foreign minister on June 27. He confirmed Malik's UN proposal to stop fighting and accept a settlement at the 38th parallel.

On June 28, 1951, Rusk outlined in a JCS-State meeting a recommendation that Ridgway broadcast an invitation to enemy commanders to attend a conference. Ridgway's statement, broadcast at eight o'clock in the morning of June 29, 1951, Korean time, was carefully honed:

"As Commander in Chief of the United Nations Command, I have been instructed to communicate to you the following: I am informed that you may wish a meeting to discuss an armistice providing for the cessation of hostilities and all acts of armed forces in Korea, with adequate guarantees for the maintenance of such armistice. Upon the receipt of word from you that such a meeting is desired, I shall be prepared to name my representative. I would also at that time suggest a date at which he could meet your representative. I propose that such a meeting could take place aboard a Danish hospital ship in Wonsan harbor."

The communists replied in short order. On July 2, 1951, Peking Radio acknowledged Ridgway's message and continued: "...we are authorized to tell you what we agree to suspend military activities and our delegates will meet with you to hold peace negotiations. We suggest that such talks be held at Kaesong, on the 38th parallel. If you agree to this, our delegates will be prepared to meet your delegates between July 10 and 15, 1951." The message was signed by Kim

Il Sung, as commander in chief of the Korean People's Army, and General Peng the-huai, commander in chief of the Chinese People's Volunteers. Kaesong in western Korea lies a few miles south of the 38th parallel. In July 1951 it was under control of the communist, with the nearest Eighth Army units ten miles away. On July 10, 1951 both the UN and Communist negotiating team had a historical first meeting at Kaesong.

UN representative Joy said bluntly that the UN delegates intended to discuss military matters pertaining to Korea, and nothing else, either political or economic. So far as the UN was concerned, the fighting would continue until agreement was reached on an armistice, and the armistice commission at work. He then presented a nine-point agenda drawn up by the UN delegates.

1. Adoption of the agenda;
2. Location of and authority for the International Committee of the Red Cross to visit POW camps;
3. Limitation of discussion to purely military matters related to Korea only;
4. Cessation of hostilities acts of armed forces in Korea under conditions that would assure against resumption of hostilities and acts of armed forces in Korea;
5. Agreement on a demilitarized zone across Korea;
6. Composition, authority and functions of a military armistice commission.
7. Agreement of the principle of inspection within Korea by a military inspection team;
8. Composition and functions of these teams; and
9. Arrangements pertaining to prisoners of war.

North Korean General Nam Il countered with a proposed return to the June 1950 status quo, with both sides withdrawing to the 38th parallel and all "foreign troops" leaving Korea. He wanted an immediate cease fire and the establishment of a twenty-kilometer demilitarized zone along the 38th parallel. Once this was done, POWs would be exchanged and peace would be at hand.

To Joy, the Communists proposals were overly simplistic. He wished a formal agenda, in which disputed points were laid out one by one for discussion and resolution. Removing "foreign troops" from Korea was a political matter. The United States would not abrogate its right to keep armed forces in a friendly nation by invitation. (Extracted from Korea, The untold story of the War, by Joseph C. Goulden)

2. THE REPATRIATION OF POW ISSUE;

In the Armistice meeting, the main agenda No #1: Drawing a demarcation line and No #2: Establishment of the Neutral Nations Supervisory Commission for the armistice, were agreed without having much problems. However, except for the issue of repatriating the prisoners of war, an armistice ending the Korean War might have been achieved as early as 1951, two years before an agreement was finally reached. Indeed after 1951, it was the only issue holding back the signing of a truce agreement. The irony was that at the time armistice negotiation began in July 1951, no one anticipated that the repatriation of POWs would be that much of a problem if they would repatriate all for all exchange. Although it seemed to be a simple matter to solve at first, it was much harder and complicated matter which delayed armistice almost two more years.

The problem, in a perhaps too concise nutshell, was which prisoners should be released after an armistice, and to whom and under what circumstances. The international law was very specific: Article 118 of the Geneva Convention of 1949 (which the United States signed immediately but did not ratify until mid-1950) stated flatly: "Prisoners of War shall be repatriated without delay after the cessation of hostilities."

At first, the Truman administration thought about compulsory repatriation of POWs, as mandated by the Geneva conventions, so that the American and other UN POWs could return home as quickly as possible. But later the American policy changed when they received the report that about 10,000 former Taiwanese Chinese did not want to return to mainland China, and about 30,000 North Korean POWs also refused to go back to North Korea. Especially, if the POW leaders of the anti-communists compounds were forced to be repatriated to China and North Korea against their will, they might be executed. This was the basis of changing the Truman administration policy and started to insist on voluntary repatriation.

Neutral agency to interview all POWs on both sides to determine their destinations. But for the communist side, it would not only be great loss of armed personnel but also big loss to international communism movements. North Korean General Nam Il, the chief communist delegator, furiously opposed the voluntary repatriation and strongly insisted on the compulsory repatriation as mandated by the Geneva convention. Nam Il blamed the UN delegation that the Americans forced the POWs not to go back their homeland. And that argument continued for more than a year. In the meantime, the conflict dragged on for two (2) more years, which caused twice more number of casualties for both sides than the number of the anti-communist POWs

The U.S. Army chief of psychological warfare, General Robert A. McClure, proposed to General Collins that Chinese POWs who were former Nationalists be allowed to go to Formosa. General Collins approved the idea, maintaining that this would not be a violation of the Geneva Convention because even Beijing considered Formosa is a part of China.

Nevertheless, the majority view in Washington was that, at the time of an armistice, all Chinese and North Koreans should be swiftly returned their home. To do otherwise, it was argued, would not only violate the Geneva Convention it might also put in jeopardy the swift return of UN POWs held by the Chinese and North Koreans. The Joint Chief of Staff had gone back and forth on the POW issue. The UN negotiators at Panmunjom also believed that the fastest way to return UN prisoners home was to agree to an all-for-all exchange and that voluntary repatriation would violate the Geneva Convention.

President Truman felt it would be morally wrong to force POWs to be repatriated against their will. "He did not want to send back those prisoners who cooperated with us". Complicating matters were the small number of UN POWs the communists claimed to be holding, the imbalance between that number and the number of prisoners held by the UN Command. The growing opinion of public commentators and administration officials, including the president, was that the communists could not be trusted to return all UN POWs even on the basis of forced repatriation, that involuntary repatriation would benefit the enemy because of the imbalance in the number of prisoners held by both sides. That forced repatriation would send more POWs over to the enemy. This became a significant moral and propaganda issue when Truman came out firmly in favor of voluntary repatriation of POWs as "the right thing to do." Besides the humanitarian factor, this position, as the Truman administration interpreted it, would be a tremendous propaganda boost for the West if the Prisoners held in UN camps did not want to return to their homelands North Korea. The UN negotiators at Panmunjom were instructed in January to insist on the voluntary repatriation of POWs. Against their better judgment, the UN negotiators carried out their orders by proposing the establishment of a neutral agency to interview all POWs on both sides to determine their destinations. But for the communist side, it would not only be great loss of armed personnel but also big loss to international communism movements. North Korean General Nam Il, chief negotiator, furiously opposed the voluntary repatriation and strongly insisted on the compulsory repatriation as mandated by the Geneva convention and the argument continued for more than a year. In the mean time, the conflict dragged on for two more years. Meanwhile China lost an estimated 800,000 men, and the North Korean suffered the loss of about 400,000 personnel. The ROK Army and UN forces also lost numerous their men proportionally.

In order to find out the statistics of both repatriated and non repatriated prisoners, the UNC screened POWs. It showed that more than about 10,000 Chinese and 30,000 North Korean prisoners did not want to go back to their homeland. This was the basis of changing the Truman administration policy and started to insist on voluntary repatriation. Both communists and UNC delegations were surprised with this unanticipated repatriation number. This number made the communist negotiators at Panmunjom more ill-tempered and rude than ever in dealing with Admiral Joy and his UNC delegation. Nam Il blamed UN delegations that the Americans forced the POWs not to repatriate their homelands through a placation. He stopped the meeting for two more weeks. At Panmunjom the truce delegates were still hammering away at each other. The problem became even more acute when the results of the latest "final screening of prisoners" became known. Initially the Americans had suggested to the Communists that of the 170,000 or so captives they held, as POWs or civilian detainees, probably about 116,000 would choose to go home to live under Communism. Of the other 54,000, most were in the civilian classification (UNC considers South Koreans drafted or volunteered N. Korean army). It therefore came as a serious shock, and ironically an embarrassment to both sides, when the tally revealed that of the 170,000 total, a mere 70,000 were willing to go home to the Communism. When that figure was calmly delivered across the table at Panmunjom, it was met with the stunned silence, followed by a request for an immediate recess. To the Communists, such a massive rejection was, of course a shock, and a grave setback to their attempts to propagandize the rest of the world about the glories of their system.

The UN Chief negotiator Joy, like a surprising number of the UNC senior commanders, believed the Truman administration had made a serious mistake in insisting on voluntary repatriation. He felt that the decision put the welfare of anti-communists prisoners above that of UNC prisoners in enemy hands. "Since we were not allowed to achieve victory," Joy remarked later, "I want the war halted as quickly as possible." Voluntary repatriation cost us over a year and a half of war, and caused our United Nations Command prisoners in Communist camps an additional year and half of captivity. The United Nations Command suffered at least 50,000 casualties in the continuing Korean War while we argued to protect a lesser number of anti-communist POWs who did not wish to return to Communism." From late April 1952, voluntary repatriation was the only major issue not settled at Panmunjom. Interestingly, the JCS (Joint Chief of Staff) remained divided on the POW issue. Once Joy felt that the UNC truce team had committed itself in negotiations to voluntary repatriation, he did not oppose it publicly for fear of causing his delegation to lose face or appear divided.

In February 1952, Alexis Johnson and General John E. Hull, deputy assistant secretary of state for Far Eastern affairs and Army vice chief of staff, respectively, put forth a plan to solve the problem by simply releasing anti-communist POWs who did not want repatriation. Joy and Ridgway vigorously opposed the Johnson-Hull plan, arguing that it would mean abandoning voluntary repatriation, to which they were committed by this time in the negotiations, and it would endanger the lives of the UNC POWs in communist prisons. Joy remarked: "I condemned the idea vehemently pointing out how such an action would jeopardize the return of our own POWs held by the Communists.

I claimed that it would be a breach of faith on our part which would wreck the conference. He told Generals Hickey and Wright of the Far East Command that he was so opposed to the Johnson-Hull plan that "If I was directed to carry it out, I would ask to be relieved." Eventually the plan was discarded without Joy having to make more threats. (Extracted from the Korean Conflict, by Burton Kaufman)

The United States had decided that it would keep fighting rather than force men to return against their will to live under the Communist system. Chinese prisoners were in separate compounds. Most prisoners were former Chang's National army soldiers who they later joined the Communist Chinese army. In the beginning, twenty three Taiwanese army specialists were dispatched and allowed to enter the Chinese compounds with the approval of UNC. They pacified and induced the POWs to go to Taiwan instead of mainland China.

In a mean time, some Korean army intelligence officers, attached to the U.S. Army intelligence Office such as C.I.C., started to take some action to support voluntary repatriation, which I am going to describe later.

3. SGT COON'S SURPRISE OFFER

As I described before SFC Coon was my first American friend and he was my benefactor who saved my life and others by rescuing us from the communist 76th compound. At the Panmunjom Truce conference there was furious disputes and arguments over the POWs repatriation agenda.

At that time, in the Panmunjom truce meeting, two sides were having a heated argument on the POW's repatriation issue. He then really worried about my future after repatriating to North Korea. He did not want me to be repatriated to communist North Korea and wanted me to live in the free world. I still remember and appreciate his warm heart that he wanted me to have better civilian life. I appreciate his favor from the bottom of my heart. I will forever remember his warm friendship. Since I have been living in the United States, I've tried to locate him but I failed. Last year, I have requested Mr. Rick Harne of Military Police Regimental Association, at Fort Leonard Wood, Missouri the search of Sgt. Coon's whereabouts. He said he could not locate him. Several years ago, I have also requested Mr. Andy Watson of US Army Military Police, historian at Ft. Leonardwood, Missouri, for his whereabouts, but he could not locate him either. I was very frustrated and lamented to hear the sad news. I hope he is still alive, healthy and happy somewhere under the blue sky of the United States.

4. YI, BECAME THE C.I.C INFORMANT

U.S. army C.I.C. office, stationed outside of the POW compounds, randomly called POWs to obtain some sort of information and interrogation. Yi, Kwan-soon who was one of the POWs in 83rd compound was summoned by the C.I.C. office to be interrogated by one of the ROK Army Intelligent officer, first lieutenant Kim, Son Ho. While he was being interrogated, Yi told the Lt. Kim that he was not a communist but an anti-communist. He was a member of the North Korean Democratic Party which he said the party was anti-communism. He then showed Lt. Kim the party member's I.D. card that he always kept with him. He then wanted to work for Lt Kim's private informants inside the compound. He further stated that if Lt. Kim trusted him and let him be his informant, he would collect all the necessary information that Lt. Kim wanted. Especially, he would find out the communist POWs and for their movements inside the compound. He would like to perform all the instruction of Lt. Kim. Although Lt. Kim did not fully trust him at that time but he gave him a permission to do so, if he so desired. Lt. Kim stated later that Yi worked hard as his honest informant and collected much information for him. In the mean time, with the background of C.I.C Lt. Kim, Yi started to collect the colleagues who were all born in Pyongyang with his same native place. At first, he got about ten (10) strong and healthy colleagues and then he gradually expanded his club ring secretly in the 83rd Compound to perform the anti-communist Coup de'tat later.

5. YI'S ANTI-COMMUNIST COUP D'ÉTAT (ROD COUP)

One late night (date unknown), Yi and his colleagues armed with rods, clubs and baseball bats, invaded surprise attack the 83rd compound POW's headquarters and all the battalion offices (except my office). They arrested 48 POW leaders, including leader of 83rd compound and three battalion commanders except myself. He tortured and transferred them to other compound. Then he took compound leader's job and Chief security guard job. At the time, a hot debate on POW repatriation agenda was being engaged in the truce meeting.

The former leader was South Korean and a good Seoul University student. He was handsome, very intelligent and had a very warm hearted man. He came to my office several times and I talked with him about our college life. He never spoke about any politics or any kind of communist like remarks or did any pro-communist actions in the compound. The 83rd compound was very calm and quiet compound until Yi Kwan-soon carried out his so called "stick Coup d'etat." They carried out another anti-communist coup d'état to other compounds started from the neighboring 82nd compound and later several more other compounds, in the same manner, in an attempt to prevent POWs from repatriating to North Korea.

One thing I don't understand was why Sgt. Coon, in charge of the Compound accepted Yi as a new compound leader without any opposition. I presumed Sgt. Coon might have received some sort of instruction from his senior officer in advance about the rod coup. Some days later, Yi had organized the "Korean Youth Anti-communism Association" in our compound first and expanded gradually into all other anti-communist compounds. We, the anti-communist compounds POWs, made demonstrations almost everyday to support the voluntary and oppose the compulsory repatriation which the communists' negotiators stubbornly insisted at the Panmunjom negotiating table. On the contrary, the communist compounds had demonstrated and rioted furiously for supporting "all for all" compulsory repatriation and to oppose the voluntary one.

6. CONCILIATION OF POWS

a) North Korea's Appeasement:

There were five different compounds for the UN forces prisoners of war in North Korea, all were along with the riverside of the Amrok (Yalue) river. The Chinese army supervised and controlled all the compounds, taking over from the North Korean Army. According to the repatriated American POWs, they were terribly treated early stages of the war with the hunger and cold, when they were retreating, the same as the POWs of the UN Forces Compounds. However, much latter, the communists endeavored to treat the American prisoners better than before because of the Geneva Convention. The communists allowed them to write letters to their families back in the United States and supplied them five to six packs of cigarettes each month and allowed them to have various kinds of sports activities. They also allowed having Christian worship with clerics and Reverends. There was yet no evidence or testimony of hard labor or tortures inflicted on their prisoners in the communist's compounds.

When both sides started to argue on the POW's repatriation issue at the truce meeting, the Chinese started to pacify the UN forces POWs. Some GIs were assimilated by their placation and they announced the communiqué in the radio that they criticized the United States meddling into Korean domestic matter, and twenty three American POWs refused to repatriate back to United States. To one's astonishment, about thirty eight US air forces pilots had disclosed that they dropped biological bombs. Among them, Colonel Frank Schwable confessed it. He was the chief of staff of the 1st Marine Corps. They returned to the United States after the armistice agreement in 1953, but they all insisted and denied their confessions, in order to avoid their military trial. They insisted that they confessed it under the threat and duress.

Speaking of the ROK army prisoners, former ROK army second Lieutenant Cho, Chang Ho returned back to South Korea through Ponmunjom and made the following statement in his book: [One of the North Koran army Intelligence Officer usually gave us "study class". He called us "liberated hero (fighter)"in the study class instead of "friend, comrade" that they usually call us in the compound's daily life. In fact, we were somewhat interesting in what the communism theory looked like, but on the other hand we were frightened about their placation. A North Korean army captain introduced himself he was an Army intelligence officer. Unexpectedly, his placation was quite simple and short. All he said was "I understand you all were hungry in this cold POW camps. If you voluntary join the People's Army to serve for the unification of father land and the people, you would eat good meal with meat and rice and you would not be hungry any more" "It was neither the tone of compulsory nor the instigation for joining the North Koran Army. However, surprisingly many prisoners voluntarily joined the North Korean Army. After the class, we all gathered together and discussed the matter about joining their army. The majority opinion of the prisoners wanted to join the North Korean army and most of the prisoners voluntarily enlisted the North Korean Army", Cho stated.

b) UN's Conciliation

The CI & E (Civilian Information & Education) was established for each POW compound by the UNC. They educated prisoners on the contradictoriness of Communism and superiority of the Democratic capitalistic system. Most teachers were the university students of both North and South Korea. They tried to educate prisoners to be friendly towards the United States, South Korea and oppose the North Korea communism. A tent church was established in each compound. Korean civilian Christian ministers and some catholic fathers performed worship and church services to prisoners. They also attempted to instill the superiority of the Democratic system and the contradictory of communism. Father Chang Tae-Ik, who was a ROK army catholic chaplain, stated on Korean MBC television that "I taught them bible but also taught them an anti-communist education as I was instructed to do so. And therefore, I was welcomed by the anti-communist compounds but received unfriendly treatment by the communist POW camps. When I showed at the communist compounds, they ridiculed me and yelled at me "Here comes a black crow again!. Sometimes they threw rocks at me."

With the UNC's approval twenty three Taiwanese military specialists were assigned to Chinese compounds from the beginning. They educated and pacified Chinese prisoners who were mostly former Chang's nationalist army soldiers to return to Taiwan instead of the mainland China.

7. WOMEN POW COMPOUND;

There was a women compound in Koje-do POW Compound. I have no idea how many inmates were in there, as I don't have the statistical records about it, but there should also be many female POWs. They were mostly North Korean army medical corps. They also worked here as nurses at the POW dispensaries and a hospital. Once or twice a year, those girls came over to each male compound to give vaccination and spray DDT on the male prisoner's body. At this time, most male prisoners were captivated by the female beauty. They felt a secret love with unrequited affection and suffered alone by themselves. As they made contact and associated with ugly male POWs everyday in their compound, it is quite natural that any girl, even ugly looking girl, was easily affectionate to them. Those even ugly girls began to look like very beautiful girl in the world. Most male prisoners feel one-sided secret love for those girls and crazy about those girl's charming and sexy bodies, but it was just a pie in the sky. But, at the same time, I could also realize that those girls also seemed to be yearning and fantasized for the male sex. I felt it by their mental attitudes and facial expressions.

Surprisingly, there were many babies and pregnant girls in the woman's compound. I hesitated to write down the story but I have to do it, because this story is based on true fact. Many babies were born in the woman POW camp and I should call these babies as "Koje-do POW compound babies" and their native born places are "the Koje-do Woman POW camp." Most mothers of the baby's mothers work for the POW's hospital or dispensaries, where-in they work as nurses and other jobs together with many male workers including POWs, GIs, ROK Army soldiers and some civilians. They work with them in the hospital almost every day. Therefore, the girls had relatively easy chance to contact with those people and so it is believed that babies might be born between them. Today, all those babies are mostly age of 60 years old now. I believe it was also one of the sad stories about the Korean War. My heart was gloomy and heavy when I witnessed that event.

CHAPTER IV

INTERESTING STORIES IN POW CAMPS

There were about 6,000 prisoners interned in each compound at the UN POW Camps in the Koje-Island. I believe there should be many more interesting stories and episodes in each respective compound. It was completely impossible for me to know all the stories of every 28 compounds. Therefore, the stories in this book should be only fragmentary, due to the limited range of my memories.

The prisoners in Koje-do UNC POW camps were composed of many different kind of inmates. There were mostly North Korean Army, Chinese voluntary army, South Korean's voluntary enlisting to the N. Korean Army, partisan guerillas, former South Korean Army POWs captured by North Korean Army and later joined the North Korean army, some ROK Army soldiers who dropped out their unit formation while retreating. There were also unknown numbers of Korean civilians interned in the POW camps.

a) Grandfather and his Grandson;

There were about 200 senior inmates in the 82nd Camp. They were all civilians. Among them, the oldest person was sixty seven year old grandfather and youngest one was a ten year old. They are grandfather and grandson. In December 1950, when UN forces were retreating with the Chinese offensive, all the family members of the grandfather were War refugees and evacuating from their native place, towards South. When they have reached up to Pyongtaek, South Korea, an

US air force jet fighter attacked the US Army truck transporting a bunch of prisoners of war. At this time, many prisoners escaped from the truck taking advantage of the US air raid. After the jet fighter had gone, the GI guards of the truck worried about the loss of the POWs. As they worried about their duty responsibility, the GIs started to pick up any civilians near by on their truck to fill the figure of the escaped North Korean POWs.

The boy's parents along with other Korean civilians escaped from the scene, but the young boy and the grandfather were picked up by the GI guards on the truck along with some other Korean civilians. They were later transported them into the Busan POW camp and became prisoners of war against their will. Because of the language barrier they could not explain or protest at the time of the incidence. Although they protested to compound authority several times but their complaints were not accepted. Compound headquarters stated that they had no authority to erase their names, since once their names were already listed on the POW list. hey had to be confined in the camp along with other prisoners, in place of the North Korean POWs who had escaped at Pyongtaek, during the US air strikes. All of the mentioned civilian elders in the compound were not soldiers but they were all civilian refugees. During the Korean War time, there were a lot of misunderstandings between Koreans and American GIs mainly because of the language barrier and cultural differences. During the War time, there was not much social order and there were many social absurdities.

In this compound, there interned not only the young boy and senior elders, but also there were three (3) ROK Army soldiers captured. They fell off their retreated unit formations and wandered from place to place when their unit fled in disorder from the Chinese army offensive in December 1950. While they are retreating, they happened to find the US Army trucks passing by and got on the truck. They found the US Army truck was hauling a full load of North Korean POWs. It was too late when they got on the truck. They automatically became the status of the prisoner of war. Because of language barrier, they then could not explain their identities to the American soldiers. They appealed their mistreatment later to the Camp authority complaining through the ROK Army officer but they did not accept it. Once your name was on the POW's list, no one could erase or eliminate their names. Believe it or not, many ROK army dropouts soldiers became POW and interned in the UN POW Camps, the above stories are full truth,

b) Woman Company commander;

Shorty Kim Young-kil, was a messenger boy of our Battalion headquarters. He was a cute, pleasant young boy and everybody liked him. He was 18 years old and we called him "shorty". He delivers Battalion headquarters messages to all Company headquarters along with other assigned duties. He was under age to be enlisted in the Army. However, due to the shortage of North Korean army personnel, he was forced to be drafted. One day he told me his story about when he was captured as POW by ROK army soldiers. He was 17 years old when he was drafted into the North Korean People's army (NKPA). As soon as he was drafted, he was sent directly to the fierce battle field of Daebu-dong front battlefield which was one of the most decisive battles in Korean War history. He was assigned as a messenger for the Company commander. The Company commander was uniquely a woman officer and her rank was Captain. At the time, the North Korean forces were big disadvantages in the battle-field under severe attacks by the UN forces at the Rak-dong river front line. Their supply line was completely destroyed, cut-off by the UN forces' successful Inchon landing and by the US air forces fierce bombings along with the enforced artillery attacks.

The Daebu-dong battle was a fierce seesaw fight between ROK army and North Korean forces. Both forces took turns advances and retreats, several times. There was an interesting story about the Dabu-dong battle field that General MacArthur once threatened through General Walker to General Chong Il-kwon, the Chief of Staff, ROK army, that all the US forces would have to retreat out of Korea, if the

South Korean forces lost the Daebu-dong battle defeated by the North Korean forces. And you can easily imagine how fierce the battle was. Kim continued to state that he could not even raise his head because of the continuing fierce artillery strikes of both US and ROKA forces. He and his woman commander were hiding inside a trench. They had a scarce chance to escape from their death. His company had received a crushing attack. There were more personnel killed than survivors by the UN force's furious fire attacks. At one point, when the artillery attacks ended, the battle front was quiet, then Kim came out of the trench. At that time he heard a loud voice "Hands up!" on his back. He obeyed immediately. When he looked back he found several ROK army soldiers had pointed their rifles at him. Kim was starved for a couple of days and physically very weak at the battle field. The ROK soldiers started to interrogate Kim. Kim was trembling with fear. They asked Kim "Are there any other soldiers in here?" He then answered pointing toward the trench, "Yes, my Company Commander was in the trench." Then one of the soldiers shot a couple of blank shots and shouted "come out, now!" And then the woman officer came out of the trench. Her sudden appearance made all the soldiers astonished to see a woman officer unexpectedly. "Isn't this a girl?" One of the soldiers shouted with curiosity. His rank was Staff sergeant. "Was your Company commander this Woman Officer?" Kim replied "yes". It was quite natural the ROK soldiers were surprised by the appearance of North Korean Army Woman officer. The ROK Army had no Women Officers at that time.

At this time the ROK Army soldiers tempted to play mischief on her as a plaything. The Staff Sergeant asked Kim "how many times did you have a fun with this girl?" Kim remained silent. Another soldier asked him again, "tell me frankly how many times did you sleep with this girl?" They all spoke in a blunt Kyongsan (Busan) provincial local Korean dialect. They asked Kim with the dirty language in front of the lady officer. When Kim replied that he did not do anything, two soldiers hit him hard on his back with the M-1 rifle butt. He fell to the ground. Watching this miserable, touching sight, the woman officer couldn't stand it anymore. She told Kim to tell the soldiers that we did it just one time. She tried to help Kim to avoid hitting and torture. "What? One time? You are lying." They hit him even harder this time, then continued to beat him. Consequently, he had falsely confessed that he did sleep with her three times. Kim thought they would kill him. He was so afraid he trembled at the time and he had to lied to them. Fortunately, one of American Army officers unexpectedly showed up and saved them from their distress. The officer picked up Kim and the woman officer with his jeep and left the scene. The US officer later turned both prisoners into UN POW camp in Busan.

The young Kim Yong-kil has later been released as an anti-communist POWs when Korean president Rhee released all the anti-communist POWs on June 18, 1953. He was also drafted the ROK Army along with all other released anti-communist POWs. After 10 years of South Korean Army service, he was discharged as Sergeant Fist Class. One of the summer in 1956, when he still served in the ROK army, he had a special annual leave from his unit. He then happened to meet his former lady Company commander on the ulchi-ro street in Seoul. She also refused to go back to North Korea and was released in the South Korea. And Kim observed at the time she had a baby on her back. They had a good reunion meeting and enjoyed a long conversation about the painful past memories of the fierce Daebu-dong battle-field where they were almost killed.

c) Volunteer Soldier and His Horse;

Kim Hak-Kyun, south Korean, a student of Seoul University was drafted to the Voluntary North Korean Army, when Seoul was captured and under the control of North Korean army. At the time, many young South Koreans volunteered to join the North Korean Army with the glamour of occupied forces in Seoul. But Kim, tried hard to evade enlisting but all his efforts were in vain. He was forced to be enlisted in the N. Korean People's Army. He was captured at Korang-po battle by the advanced UN forces. I was very interested in Kim's past sad story. Kim's parents were rich and his family members had a good life. He owned a horse to ride at his leisure time. When the North Korean Army occupied Seoul, they also commandeered his horse to pull a horse carriage delivering the army supplies. Kim, did not know his horse was also requisitioned by the North Korean army after his conscription. Both Kim and his horse were drafted together by the North Korean army. When the North Korean forces were retreating, Kim was also retreating north along with his unit. When he passed through Sari-won, he happened to meet a poor bony horse pulling a heavy carriage loaded with heavy army supplies. The horse was very weary and scraggy. When the horse approached nearer to him, the poor horse finally recognized his old master and started to cry horse sound to get Kim's attention. Kim then went closer to the horse and he finally recognized the poor horse was his own horse.

As soon as he confronted his beloved horse, he embraced his horse's neck, he wept so much with sadness and sorrow. Although the horse could not express its emotion, his horse too had tears in eyes, seeing his owner's miserable appearance. It seemed the horse took pity on his miserable looking master who was used to ride on his back with great joy and dignity. No body paid attention at that time to the scene of their pitiful reunion, the other soldiers paid their attention to retreat toward north. The reunion with his beloved horse came to an end in a short time later when the US air fighter strafed the area. Everything was scattered away, he also parted with his horse again. He shed tears of remorse, thinking about his poor horse. He blamed and resented the painful Korean War. It seemed to me that his sad story was the same story of the novel or a war movie story. His sad story made me swallowing my tears. After a few days we separated when the UN authority segregated the South Korean from North Korean. I have no idea where he lives now. I still remember his sad story which makes me deeply saddened when I recall it.

d) *The Civil Service Agent Choi;*

Choi's Excesses: The later part of autumn, the slacken Panmunjom truce meeting started to make much progress. Both sides had exchanged the POW lists. At this time the UN side found unexpectedly, the more numbers of missing persons (MIA) than the actual number of American POWs. Choi, the Korean civil service official hired by 8th US army CIC, was a fat person. He impersonated a high ranking official. He often came in POW compound trying to get information about missing American GIs (MIA) and possible mass slaughter of American soldiers committed by North Korean soldiers. He asked POW Security guards to find out the said information. As a result, almost every night many POWs were randomly called to the POW's Security office, where they received an interrogation. Most of the time they were tortured with clubs, baseball bats and pick-ax shafts to force them to confess that they killed American GIs, even though they had never fought against US forces. If they denied of killing the GIs, they received severe torture until they made false confessions that they killed the UN soldiers. they all received injuries from the tortures. They all had to crawl about on hands and knees to get out the security office with the relentless tortures. About 300 POWs were interrogated and tortured in 82nd compound only, all for Choi's excessive loyalty to the UNC, and for his personal aspirations for fame.

Many tortured people were forced to make false confession that they killed ten or more GIs, in order to avoid the brutal torture. When they denied killing of GIs they get more severe tortures until they made false confessions. As a result, those false statements swelled and inflated to the total figure counted up to almost 3,000, just in the 82nd compound. It would amount to almost 12,000 Missing UN forces personnel out of four anti-communist compounds, not including 20 more compounds. The number could increase to more than 70,000 Missing In Actions soldiers, which showed false figures. It was quite reasonable that the figure was completely fabricated. The UN authority, of course, never trusted these wrong figures and finally started to mistrust Choi's working ability. The UN authority finally believed the estimation of about 9,000 US soldiers Missing-in-Action.

Every night we could hear the painful cries and screams of tortured POWs came out of the POW Security guard office. That made all other ordinary prisoners tremble with fear. One night, in the deep of dawn, the US Army MP patrols heard the painful screams came out of the POW Security office tent. An MP Officer along with a couple of his MPs entered the compound and went into the security office tent where they witnessed the scene of savage torture committed by the POW's security guards. At this time the MP Officer was taken aback and startled at the sight of tortured scene. He shouted "God damn, Stop it!" He then found a bloody prisoner lying on the floor moaning in pain. He was taking tortures on his naked body and blood was spread on his body and the floor. The US MP Officer surprised when he personally witnessed the miserable scene of torture. "Oh! My God!" he grieved. When the other two MPs tried to raise him up, he became unconscious. MPs then confiscated the tools used in torture, and they arrested Security chief Yu, Chi Hun at the scene, then took him out of the compound in his MP jeep. Yu was arrested and reassigned to 81st Compound right after that incident. After Yu was arrested the notorious torture interrogation to find out the missing GIs was ended. All the tortured prisoners had all returned to North Korea when the repatriation was carried out at Panmunjom. They all became more radical communist soldiers because of the barbarous tortures inflicted on them. I think they undoubtedly returned to North Korea bearing grudges against Choi. Choi was entirely responsible for it. Consequently, the fat Choi was not faithful to the UN authority. He was more harmful than beneficial to the interest of US Army and the South Korean government. Choi had instructed POW's security guards to find out the MIA of US Army soldiers by all means for his personal gain. The POW's security guards, the perpetrator of Choi's order, executed his order by means of threat and tortures which was brutal violation of the human rights.

The civil officer Choi was later exposed that he was a faithful cat's paw for the Japanese imperialist during the period of Japanese occupation of Korea. He worked for the Japanese Army military police detachment as a Korean informant pawn agent. He collected information and apprehended many Korean resistants, patriots who fought against Japanese imperialist in Manchuria for the Korean liberation and independence. He was one of the notorious traitors who used to royal to the Japanese imperialist.

2. A STORY OF ROKA DROP-OUT POW

One of the Korean Army drop-out soldiers, Mr. Lee was also interned in our Compound. He was frost-bitten on his toes received by the severe cold winter in a high mountain near DMZ area. As he was unable to walk, he had to drop-out from his unit and obliged to stay in one of civilian house. During the time, the US army returned back the area. He was picked up by them and transported to Busan POW camps. He told us the following interesting combat fight stories, I rewrite by the courtesy of the person.

a) ROK Army retreated by the Chinese Voluntary Army

It has been observed a couple of days since the Chinese Voluntary Army were approaching to the 38th parallel line in late December, 1950. At the time, UNC authority was closely watching whether or not they would cross the line. However, the Chinese (CVC) started to attack us at 20:00 Hours on 30, December 1950, and they captured our positions and we had to retreat to the rear.

I observed our company commander had sneaked away from the position. He disappeared without giving us any combat order. I thought then, he would come back later and give us his combat order, but he never came back. He was the only high raking Battalion Commander in our unit at that time.

Under the condition, the Master sergeant of our Company loudly ordered us instead of Company commander "Fight back! I'm going to shoot and kill you if you run away!" I was ready for my combat posture at the time. I made up my mind to fight to die for my country. Now is the right time to do that. I hid inside the house's fence and looked through a hole of the fence. I saw 4~5 enemies were on the road outside of the house talking to each other about something. I then started to fire at them with my Carbine rifle and they ran away. I don't know how many enemies died with my fire. I quickly ran into the house, I found that every body had left the house. I was the only one left at the scene. The master sergeant who ordered us to fight back or he would shoot and kill us, also escaped his position and fled the scene.

I then ran into the yard and hid in a crevice between the house and the fence, and looked for the enemy movements. A little later, I observed an enemy soldier approaching towards me and I shot him when he approached close to the fence. He instantly fell down on the ground and I whirled back to hid. I felt extremely good at the time. At this time I observed the guy wriggled trying to grab his riffle. I then came back to him immediately and I gave him two more confirmatory shots. He was my third Chinese soldier who I killed by that time.

A little later, another Chinese soldier was approaching the person I killed. He seemed to help his comrade soldier. I was waiting until he came close to me within one meter distance and I shot him twice, he died immediately. He was the forth enemy soldier I killed so far. After that, I observed that four enemy soldiers were again approaching to me yelling "Hands-up", "Hands-up" repeatedly in Korean language. My mind strained a little bit but I then made up my mind to kill them all and aimed my riffle towards them. I wished I had a grenade. I carefully aimed, shot them and killed one person with my first shot. They started to run away. As I exposed my position to them I ran into the house and hid. Later they came back and threw the grenade toward me and part of the house was destroyed. I then ran away from back yard of the house. They started to shoot at me. But luckily they could not kill me as I ran from the house. I ran about 30 second down the mountain stream and I was safe from their bullets. I always believed I wouldn't die. Strangely, they stopped shooting and never chased me. Perhaps the Chinese army's policy was that they trained to stop chasing and shoot at the enemy who are running away.

At the stream, I happened to meet Lt. Lee. He told me that our Battalion headquarters was captured by the Chinese. Also the 32nd regiment assistant commander Lt. Colonel Ham was caught as Prisoner of War by the Chinese Voluntary army.

Lt. Lee and I were resting under the pine tree on the ridge of the mountain, when we saw the Battalion commander, 2nd company commander and the master sergeant. They were passing by us spiritlessly and we joined them in retreat. All the remnants of defeated troops were retreating followed by Major Choi, the Battalion commander. We were retreating toward south for many days. There was about 500 meter high mountain in front of us where we met a Korean civilian. He told us "comrades!, If you want to survive, climb up this mountain.!" He was probably one of the North Korean guerrillas. One of our soldiers was going to shoot him but the Battalion commander stopped him. At this time, we heard two rifle shots. As soon as we found that was the North Korean remnants of the defeated soldier's shot, about one thousand of our soldiers started to run away down the mountain. At this time, the Battalion commander also sat on the snow and slide down on the slope of the mountain. Then we all followed him sliding down the hill. At the bottom of the mountain, I was much disappointed to see many soldiers were bewildered and at a loss what to do.

Battalion commander then ordered us to form a reconnaissance unit to reconnoiter the enemy's position and movements. I was also included one of ten (10) members of the unit. We went down the valley and waited for reconnaissance of the enemy. It was a dark night. Chinese troops seemed to find our position and started to shoot toward us. I could hear the flying bullets noises. And what is it all about!. At this time all the soldiers waiting at the valley started to run away climbing up back to the mountain hill that we just slid down to the valley sometime ago. At this time, Major Choi loudly shouted and ordered to the disorderly soldiers. "You listen to me. I am Major Choi, Commanding Officer of 1st Battalion, 32nd Regiment. If you want to survive, just follow me." I didn't know before he had such a strong loud voice. He then started to climb up the hill but only few soldiers followed him, but the majority of the soldiers did not follow him. Only about 50 soldiers followed the Commander including me. We were retreating disorderly from the offensive of the Chinese Voluntary Army.

b) Execution of Chinese POW

Our unit retreated 4 days on the snow covered mountainous rough road and retreated just 12 miles in few days. The Battalion commander said that we were too slow for retreating and we are out of food and supplies. Let's go down the mountain and walk on flat wide road boldly in front of the enemy. Let us take a hazardous venture and risk our lives. When we meet and confront with enemies, we would disguise as the North Korean guerrillas, and if our true identities be disclosed by them, we would fight against them until we die gloriously in the battle. At the time we could see the commander's firm resolution on his face. He then started to walk down the hill and we all followed him as he started to walk down the gill we all followed him. We could walk down much faster pace on the plain road than the snowy rough road on the mountain. When we walked down on the road we found five (5) Chinese soldiers were in the hillside. They seemed to be looking for something. The commander ordered "remain calm, don't break the formation line and keep on walking."

One of the officers asked Master sergeant.

"Can you speak Chinese, sergeant?"

He answered "Yes sir, a little bit"

"Then ask them, who are they." "Yes, Sir"

When Master sergeant approached them he asked them who they were. They answered, we were Chinese soldiers. They were much relieved when the master sergeant lied to them that we were North Korean guerrillas. Armed with M2 riffle I followed Sgt Park. I was poised to shoot them anytime. Sgt Park extended his hand to shake hands with them saying: "we are people's guerrillas." They told us the Chinese 00 division's headquarters was stationed behind the mountain for 2~3 days and there were many more troops stationed around the area.

A little later the Battalion commander ordered: "We were going to disarm them, everybody be ready!" We then started to surround them to disarm them. At this time, they started to resist yelling "aiya, Maya!", but it's too late. Thy looked around 16 to 20 years old. We arrested all five at once. Binding their hands tied behind, we interrogated them while marching together. They all were former nationalist soldiers but they were enlisted into the Chinese communist army. They said they were looking for some medical herb and the wild edible greens in the mountain during their break time.

Execution of the Prisoners: Our commander ordered us to execute four (4) prisoners. He wanted to save 16 year old youngest prisoner to show the boy to the Regiment Commanding general as the proof of his war result.

Our Battalion commander ordered to Lt. Lee to execute them. Lt. Lee in turn ordered to Sgt Chu Sung-chan who told myself and Heo Jong Ho to perform the execution. We discussed execution, then decided to stab them with our rifle bayonets instead of shooting them, in order to not be detected by the enemy with the rifle shots sounds.

We took them into the hill side about ten meters, and Sgt. Chu said; this was the right place to execute them. "Let's do it right here." As soon as he said it, he stabbed into the right chest of the two enemies with his bayonet. They fell down feebly without any resistance and the pain made them groan. At this time Sgt. Chu told us to do the same way to other two prisoners. As matter of fact, I then felt an impulse to do the same thing as Sgt. Chu did, and I was just about to do it.

Other two enemy soldiers were frightened at the miserable sight that two their comrades were stabbed and died just before them. They cried saying "maya!" I then approached to one of them taking my bayonet aim at his breast. He was so scared to death taking a couple steps backward and fell down. He was fainted and stooped down on the ground. I then stabbed hard in his back, but my bayonet recoiled, bent and back. I thought then my bayonet probably stabbed right on his spine and made my bayonet recoiled. He then screamed loudly and almost out of breath. I then stabbed hard again in his right side of the back relentlessly. At this time my bayonet went through so smoothly all the way through his chest and I could see the point of the bayonet beyond his shoulder. My rifle bayonet stabbed his chest so easily as if I prick in a pumpkin.

It was a cruel cold-blooded murder but I felt a strange indescribable pleasure at the time. I will call it as a warfare mentality. Of course, I was in an abnormal state of mind at the time.

I told then Private Heo to kill the last prisoner, but Heo refused my offer. So I decided myself to kill the last one. I was approaching him aiming my bayonet at his chest. He was so scared and turned his face, stooped his waist fell down on the ground feebly. I stabbed in his right side chest as hard as I could. Four Chinese soldiers were killed at the same place. I killed six Chinese enemy soldiers so far.

I didn't know why I felt pleasured when I killed them brutally like a savage beast without having any sympathy. Were these brutal murders I committed because I had a brave soldiers' spirit or of the allegiance to my country?

I experienced that human nature is so cruel and brutally unlimited. I didn't know at the time that it is the wanton violation of the international law when you kill the prisoners of war after they surrendered on the battle field. And that is the same murder offense as I commit the murder in civilian life. However, if I want to defend myself, I was a soldier and I must obey the order of my senior officers. I had just performed the order of my senior officers.

Therefore, I must insist that the war is miserable and hopefully it will not occur in this civilized world anymore, especially on the Korean peninsula.

As I discharged from the ROK Army, I often regretted my past brutal acts of war. I sincerely apologized to them by praying for them to take a peaceful rest in the heavens.

CHAPTER V

PRO AND ANTI-COMMUNIST POW CAMPS:

1. PRO-COMMUNIST CAMPS

There were about 170,000 POWs interned in about twenty eight UN POW camps in Koje-do. Each compound accommodated more than 6,000 prisoners. In the truce meeting, both sides struck strictly to their respective proposal that the UN forces proposed a voluntary repatriation and Communists a compulsory one. The negotiations wasted longer than a year and proceeded with difficulty. Accordingly, with this problem, POWs in the Koje-do compound started to divide into two groups, communists and anti-communists (compulsory against voluntary repatriation), and they started deadly fight each other in the compounds. Two groups formed two different ideological organizations respectively named the "Liberated Alliance" for the Communist and "Korean Anti-communist Youth Union" in the anti-communist compounds. They opposed each other, brutally tortured the opponents and killed each other.

Anti-communist compound prisoners supported the voluntary repatriation and the Communists compounds wanted the all-for-all compulsory one. The communist POW camps killed some POWs who had refused to repatriate to North Korea. September 1951, fifteen prisoners were murdered by a self-appointed people's court. Three more were killed when rioting broke out on the 19th in Compound 78. Contrary to this, in the anti-communist POWs camps the prisoners who wanted to repatriate were tortured and some killed. Most of all compounds were Communists, except 6 or 7 anti-communist camps.

The communist compounds including the officer's camp that opposed the voluntary repatriation, supported violently for all for all forced return. Colonel Lee, Hak-koo was known as the leader of Communist compounds. He organized, controlled the demonstrations and riots for the compulsory repatriation.

All the communist compounds raised the North Korean flags high in the air. They hung the portraits of Kim Il-sung and Stalin, singing the North Korean national anthem and the song of Kim Il-sung. Under these circumstances, they all wore the North Korean army uniform remodeled with the US Army uniforms supplied to them. They did everything in a military way and performed the North Korean army close-order drill, almost every day. Seeing their camps, people could easily confuse that it was the North Korean army garrisons in the South Korean territory. They exerted almost every day demonstrations and riots demanding to improve for better treatment and support of the compulsory repatriation. The 66th Compound which was officer's Compound, accommodated about 3,000 Officer inmates. The rumor has it that the communists POWs planned to capture Koje-do first. Then capture Busan with cooperation of Partisan (guerilla) forces in South Korea to disperse the UN forces fighting power from the front battle-fields to rear. A groundless rumor that the Communist prisoners communicated with guerillas. The North Korean channel received a secret order from them through shortwave radio. The rumor was spread out that Communist POWs cooperated with the North Korean forces, they would capture the Koje-Island, later Busan with the captured US army tanks and weapons.

2. CLASH BETWEEN POW AND ROK ARMY SECURITY GUARDS

On March 13, 1952, a second major clash occurred between S. Korean Army guards and Communist prisoners. A group of anti-communist prisoners were marching around 92nd and 95th Communist POW compounds, escorted by 5th Company, 33rd Battalion, ROK

Army military police, commanded by Captain Kang. They were marching and passing by the 92nd compound, shouting loudly the slogan that they were against the compulsory repatriation and down with the communism. At this time, the communists POWs suddenly began to hurled rocks Tat the marching anti-communist POWs. Capt. Kang then ordered his men to fire and the guards began firing into the compound. They killed scores of POWs instantly. Two more were mortally wounded, and injured twenty six. Resentment between ROK and North Korean soldiers flared very easily into angry words, threats, and blows. Part of the tension stemmed from the circumstances that the prisoners get better rations and clothes (all made in USA and Japan) than the ROK Army soldier guards who wore poor Korean made uniforms. The communist delegation at Panmunjom's truce meeting immediately protested the incidence and labeled this as another "barbarous massacre."

3. UNLUCKY N. KOREAN ARMY COLONEL LEE, HAK-KOO

After the successful Inchon landing, UNC forces planned a two-pronged attack to retake Seoul from the North by South Korean army and South west by UNC forces. Anxious to capture Seoul, the US Army attacked from the South west. The fight for Seoul was ferocious. US artillery fire combined with the close Air force support greatly assisted ground forces of the UNC, and destroyed much of the city. Many Korean civilians were killed by the incendiary bombs started by Napalm bombs. At this time the North Korean Army soldiers fanatically fought against the advancing UN forces to defend Seoul, using suicide squads to destroy American tanks. The North Koreans had resisted for 12 days defending Seoul. They were finally defeated when UN Forces recaptured Seoul, and raised the Korean flag at the Capital building on September 27, 1950.

The successful Inchon amphibious landing and recapture of Seoul cut the supply lines of the NKPA. They had to retreat in desperation. In the meantime, at the Nakdong-river defense line both the US and S. Korean Army started to break out from the perimeter on 23 September 1950. They kept advancing all the way to Osan, trapping large numbers of NKPAs. At this time many NKPA soldiers escaped to Taebaek Mountain where they joined with the S. Korean guerrillas. During the time many N. Korean army officers and soldiers frequently surrendered to US Army and ROK forces. Among them, Colonel Lee Hak-koo, the Chief of Staff, 13th NKPA Division. He shot its Commanding general, Major General Hong, Yong-jin, who incompetently killed many of his soldiers in fighting. He still wanted to continue reckless death attacks on the American forces. Under these circumstances, Lee wanted to retreat his forces to save the lives of his men but his Commanding general wanted to resist and kept fighting against the UN forces. Col. Lee insisted that he had to kill his Commanding General to save his men's life. He then surrendered, along with his 150 soldiers, to the US Army. He was the highest ranking NKPA POW. Lee himself insisted that he was a defector but not a POW. After all the interrogation finished, he was taken to General MacArthur's Office in Tokyo. However, it has not been confirmed and it might be just a rumor. He then served to broadcast from US Army L-19 aircraft to N. Korean soldiers on the front line to surrender safely to American soldiers to save their lives. After that he was later put in the Koje-do UN POW Camp.

In the POW Camp, he had eventually changed his mind. He subsequently became a leader of the Communist POW Camps who made a lot of trouble and rioted to oppose the voluntary repatriation proposed by the United States. As I mentioned earlier, In Koje-do POW Camps, among the POWs were divided into two groups, Pro-Communists and Anti-Communists. They were fighting and killing each other. And thus, at the truce conference, the dispute on voluntary repatriation made to spend more than twenty one (21) month delay of signing the cease-fire agreement. The POW repatriation agreement finally signed on June 8, 1953 and agreed to start repatriations on August 5, 1953 at the Panmumjom truth village.

On July 27, 1953, the truce agreement was signed. POWs from both sides started to repatriate from August 5, and ended 6 September 1953 for 33 days. When Lee, Hak-koo returned to N. Korea, he had a warm welcome at first by the North Korean people. It goes without saying that he must be punished later and purged for the violation of military law for killing his Division Commanding general.

4. COMPOUND 62 RIOT (2:18 RIOT)

The POW-atrocity campaign began on February 18, 1952, while both sides were at the height of their dispute over voluntary repatriation. Before this incident, at the Panmunjom the Communist delegates wanted to know how many POWs wanted and refused to repatriate to their home land. They asked to the UN delegates to provide the exact number of non-repatriates. UN delegates then also wanted to know that how many UN forces POWs wanted to refuse to be repatriated. The UN Command also wanted to take this time to segregate two different groups in a small compound of about 500 POWs, to make easy control and also to prevent troubles.

The UN POW Camp authority had almost finished the screening operation for all other compounds except Compound #62. Most prisoners in compound 62 were former South Korean college students. Half of which were indoctrinated by communist ideology, and they strongly insisted "all the prisoners of the compound # 62 wanted to go back to North Korea. Therefore it was unnecessary for the screening or segregation in their compound, it would just waste of time. They insisted that they all opposed the voluntary repatriation."

Despite numerous incidents most internee compounds were screened during January and early February except for the inmates of Compound #62. Here the Communists had firm control and they refused to permit the segregation teams to enter. On Feb 18, 1952, an incident occurred when the US troops entered in force to the compound #62 in preparation for screening. The POWs attempted to block up the U.S. screening team. The purpose of the screening was to identify those who would accept or refuse the repatriation. Between 1,000 and 1500 of the 6,000 inmates in this compound resisted against U.S. troops to enter the Compound. They resisted with compound-made steel tipped poles, knives, barbed wire flails as well as rocks. The Americans immediately began firing. In the melee resulted, one American was killed and 38 wounded. 77 POWs were killed on the spot, 22 died later, and 162 were wounded. As a result of this fight, U.S. troops withdrew from the compound and they could not enforce the screening.

On February 23, 1952, North Korean General Nam Il, the Chief of Red delegation at Panmunjom, protested "the sanguinary incident of barbarously massacre large numbers of our personnel, in violation of the Geneva Convention." The UN delegates rejected the protests on the ground that the Koje-do incident was an internal affair, since it involved civilian internees, not POWs. They were former South Koreans before they were drafted by the North Korean army. The US Army said they were civilian detainees, not Prisoners of War, therefore was an internal matter in South Korea. But obviously that story had holes in it. They were South Korean civilians before they voluntary enlisted in the North Korean Army when the North Korean Army occupied Seoul. This enraged the communists. A new worldwide propaganda campaign was born. General Van Fleet replaced the Camp Commander with Brigadier General Francis T. Dodd, but riots and incidents continued.

Meanwhile, in Washington the question of voluntary repatriation was being debated throughout February. The final decision was President Truman's. As he wrote later in his memoirs, "just as I had always insisted that we could not abandon the South Koreans who had stood by us and freedom, I now refused to agree to any solution that provided for the return against their will of prisoners of war to communist domination." He also later issued a statement, "We will not buy an armistice by turning over human beings for slaughter or slavery."

5. RIOTS AT 76TH, 77TH, 78TH RED COMPOUNDS

At first, those pro-communist compounds protested for the suspension of their heavy labor works, demanded more ration and better treatment in accordance with the Geneva Convention. The protest changed to demonstration and finally it became to a riot. The UN authority had to discontinue the hard labor. They cut down half of their food supplies instead in the way of punishment. The riots were increasing as time went by. Every time the US Army MPs attempted to enter the compound to suppress the demonstration and riot, an armed clash occurred accordingly between the two forces. The U.S. Military Police force started to shoot at random. They threw about ten hand grenades towards the resisting prisoners. Prisoners threw gravel and small pebbles; that was their only weapons, against the advancing the US armed forces. The scene became instantly a battle ground. As a result, there were many prisoner casualties. (Figure is unknown). MPs started to apprehend the key persons of the riot. The POW's superficial and plausible excuse of the demonstration was a demand for better treatment, more rations and the suspension of hard labor. I think their main purpose was to help the North Korean forces, by keeping more American forces into Kojedo UN POW camp. Thus dispersing the U.S. Army manpower from the front battle ground to the rear. A few days later, as may be expected, many additional new American soldiers arrived on Koje-island. They encircled the outside of the Communists compounds and lined up their positions. It seemed like war clouds hung over the Koje-island POW's compounds.

6. POWS SEIZED GENERAL DODD, CAMP COMMANDER

While the both sides were engaged in a heated war of words on the subject of the POW repatriation at the truce meeting, there were fierce demonstrations and riots frequently occurred in Koje-do POW compounds. And also there were sanguinary fighting between two different groups of POWs in the compound; voluntary against compulsory repatriations. Under this situation, the POW leaders of the 76th Compound asked for an interview with General Dodd (Frank T. Dodd). He was newly assigned as Camp Commander. On May 7, 1952, Dodd had gone to the gate of Compound 76 to meet with the leader of Communist prisoners to find out their complaints and grievances. During the meeting, the compound gate opened to let the labor POWs exit. After that some other POWs also came out of the compound and started to besiege, and quickly seized Dodd. They carried him into the compound. Immediately afterward, the prisoners hoisted a sign indicating, "General Dodd would be safe if accede to our demands or Dodd's life would be forfeited, if U.S. troops used force to recapture him." Dodd himself said in his message that did not use force to save his life. Accordingly General Vanfleet, Eighth Army Commander, ordered that no force be used to free General Dodd unless he ordered. General Dodd, UN POW Camp Commander, was now a prisoner of his prisoners. This unprecedented news spread to world wide news and world eyes concentrated on the small island of Koje-do in South Korea. The POWs sent out word demanding:

1. Camp authority should recognize their organization: The liberation Alliance.
2. Installation of Telephone line between compounds.
3. Improve and better prisoner treatments.
4. Allow representatives of other compounds to meet for conferences, and two representatives from each compound are sent to Compound 76 that evening.

The fear was not just for Dodd's life, but that a full-scale attempt at breakout might be imminent, and force might precipitate a pitched battle with severe loss of life. General Van fleet also formally relieved Dodd as Commandant of the Camp. He replaced him with Brigadier General Charles F. Colson, chief of staff of I Corps, who left immediately for Koje-do. Before Colson arrived on May 8, the prisoners made several demands, the main one being that they be allowed to establish a formal association. When Colson arrived, he informed the Red leaders that Dodd no longer was Camp commandant.

Unless he was released US Army troops would enter the compound and free him by force. The prisoners ignored Colson's demand. Meanwhile, Ridgway and Clark flew to Korea. They conferred with Van Fleet and with Admiral Joy. Ridgeway authorized Van Fleet to take to use whatever force required to get Dodd's release. However, VanFleet did not react swiftly or forcefully, out of fear for Dodd's life.

He ordered a tank company of the 3rd Division to move two hundred miles by road from its position in the north and to transship by LST to Koje-do. The 2nd Division's 38th Regiment and a battalion of the 9th Regiment also moved toward Koje-do by LST. On the morning of May 9, General Colson demanded Dodd's release. Six hours later he issued a second demand. The prisoners refused and wanted to talk. Although this refusal should have resulted in an immediate assault on the compound, but Colson decided to wait until the tanks arrived late that night. No attack could be launched until the morning of May 10. In the meantime, Colson authorized the prisoners to hold a meeting from prisoner leaders from other compounds.

In the early afternoon, Van Fleet flew into Koje-do to talk over the situation. Ridgway and Clark had decided to permit no press coverage of the emergency. He informed Colson that the negotiating period with the POWs should end at 10 a.m. on May 10, Colson had all the authority to use all the force he required. Meanwhile, Dodd, who had been supplied with a telephone, asked Colson for an extension until noon on May 10. With Van Fleets order still in his ear, Colson refused. During the night twenty (20) 3rd Division tanks, five equipped with flamethrowers, arrived on Koje-do and moved into position.

Early the next morning, with U.S. troops poised for the expected assault on Compound 76, the prisoners dispatched their latest demand to Colson. Although their English was awkward and not always clear, it constituted a powerful propaganda document. It was obviously phrased for a world audience. The POWs demands were:

1. Immediate ceasing the barbarous behavior, insults, torture, forcible protest with blood writing, threatening, confinement, mass murdering, gun and machine gun shooting, using poison gas, germ weapons experiments, by your command.

2. Immediate stopping the so-called illegal and unreasonable volunteer repatriation of NKPA (North Korean People's Army) and CPVA (Chinese People's Volunteers Army) POW's.
3. Immediate ceasing the forcible screening which thousands of POW's of NKPA and CPVA be re-armed and fallen in slavery, permanently and illegally.
4. Immediate recognition of the POW representative Group (Commission) consisted of NPKA and CPVA POW's and close cooperation to it by your command. This Representative Group will turn in Brig. General Dodd, on your hand after we receive satisfactory declaration to resolve the above items by your command. We will await your warm and sincere answer.

This remarkable POW document gave Colson pause. He had got a disturbing report from his intelligence officer that other compounds were ready to stage a mass breakout as soon as he launched his assault. Afterward, Colson replied to the POW demand. "He denied the UN Command committed the offenses alleged, asserted the matter of voluntary repatriation was being decided at Panmunjom, accepted a POW association and said there would be no more forcible screening of POWs in this compound, nor will any attempt be made at nominal screening." The prisoners continued to haggle with Colson. Around noon Dodd phoned Colson to present the prisoners' case. Dodd argued there had been incidents in the past when prisoners had been killed, whereas Colson's answer denied everything. The problem, Dodd said; was mostly semantics. The communists would not free him until these questions of meaning were cleared up. Then an astonishing thing happened: with the POW leaders sitting beside him, Dodd passed on their demand. He own suggestions to Colson to rewrite his reply in a form acceptable to the communists; Dodd even offered to write in the changes the prisoners considered mandatory. Colson then drafted a reply along lines demanded by the prisoners. Here is the response Colson sent:

1. With reference to your item 1 of that message, I do admit that there has been instances of bloodshed where many PW has been killed and wounded by UN Forces. I can assure in

the future that PW can expect humane treatment in this camp according to the principles of International Law. I do all within my power to eliminate further violence and bloodshed. If such incidents happen in the future, I will be responsible.

2. Reference your item 2 regarding voluntary repatriation of Korean Peoples Army and Chinese Peoples Volunteer Army POWs, that is a matter which is being discussed at Panmunjom. I have no control or influence over the decisions at the peace conference.

3. Regarding your item 3 pertaining to forcible investigation, I can inform you that after General Dodd's release, un-harmed, there will be no more forcible screening or any rearming of PW in this camp, nor will any attempt be made at nominal screening.

4. Reference your item 4, we approve the organization of a PW representative group or commission consisting of Korea Peoples Army and Chinese Peoples Volunteer Army, PW, according to the details agreed to by Gen. Dodd and approved by me."

Having achieved this agreement, next morning they escorted Dodd to the gate, decking with flowers. But Colson had enough, and demanded Dodd's immediate release, and at 9:30 p.m. May 10 Dodd walked out of compound 76 and immediately was taken to a place where he was kept incommunicado.

Historian Hermes summed up the bitter harvest of the affair: "Colson traded Dodd's life for a propaganda weapon that was far more valuable to the communists than the lives of their prisoners of war." Van Fleet tended to discount the effects of Colson's letter, but General Clark and the leadership in Washington recognized its extreme damage at once. For an American general officer, whatever the circumstances, to admit mistreatment, killing and wounding of prisoners, and to promise in the future to give prisoners humane treatment was a political disaster. In Tokyo, Clark denounced the Colson statement as "unadulterated blackmail," and said POWs had been killed only as a result of violence.

In Washington there was talk about repudiating Colson's statement. Truman decided not to use the term, but to do the same thing in other words by having the JCS direct Clark to say Colson's exchange "has no validity whatsoever," as it took place under "duress involving the physical threat to the life of a UN officer." General Van Fleet recommended both officers be reprimanded. He recommended to the JCS both be reduced to the rank of colonel and that Yount be reprimanded. Clark's recommendations went all the way up to the president who approved them. They were carried out. Clark also quickly replaced Colson with Brigadier General Haydon L. Boatner, assistant commander of the 2nd Division. Clark sent in the 187th Airborne RCT and a tank battalion, raising total American forces to 15,000 in Koje-do.

At Panmunjom the Reds made the most of the Dodd affair. North Korean General Nam Il said on May 9: "The endless series of bloody incidents occurring in your prisoner of war camps clearly proves that your so-called screening is only a means of retaining forcibly captured personnel of our side."

The next day he denounced the UN Command for "systematically taking a series of barbaric measures to attain your long-deliberated objective of forcibly retaining our captured personnel."(Excerpted from The first war we lost)

7. SCREENING OF PRO AND ANTI-COMMUNIST POWS

During the debate on the POW repatriation issue at the Panmunjom truce meeting, there were many demonstrations and riots occurred almost every day in Koje-do POW compounds. The communist POWs opposed the segregation plan. They supported the compulsory repatriation. The acceleration of violence could be attributed in large part to the execution of the screening process in the prison camps. Under these circumstances, the segregation interview for the repatriation was enforced by the Commission of Neutral Country. The Commission interviewers asked to POWs as to whether they wanted or not to return to their home land. Answer to this question was simply "Yes" or "No". "Yes" means he wanted to be repatriated and "No" means he refused to go back to their home land. The interview had started from the Anti-Communists Camps (74, 81, 82, and 83ʳᵈ). They put up the tent in front of the main gate of each compound and upon completion of the interview, had the prisoners who wanted to repatriate North Korea to go out left side of the door the other were to go out right side door. U.S. Army trucks were waiting outside of the camps and took the repatriating POWs, transported them to other camps as soon as trucks had full load.

It looked like a simple process, but for POWs, it was a very hard thing for them to make their decision. It was a matter of deciding their fates for the rest of their life. It was not easy decision to make their mind to separate with their families, friends and relatives in their homeland and stay in the South Korea. It needed prisoners to make a courageous decision on which way to go. It was their turning point that they had to choose their destiny. I could see most POWs had anguished and a gloomy states of mind. They could not hide their afflictions their gloomy facial expressions. At the anti-communist compound, there were many POWs accidently answered "No" to the screening official in their bewilderment, contrary to their real minds wanted to go back to their home land. This kind of phenomenon occurred as a result of dreadful state of minds because they used to live in the fear atmosphere in the compound. They used to be terrified by the compound's dread circumstances made by POW security guards. Some prisoners suffered from their obsessions. According to the Korean social morale and tradition, it was quite natural and the right thing that they should go back to their hometown where all the families, friends and relatives who were waiting for them. It is quite reasonable that their families should be considered first and the ideology secondly. Most of the POWs were worried about difference social life of the South Korean. They had no families, friends and relatives, and most of them worried about their future lives in the South Korea.

As for me, I made a firm resolution to remain in South Korea. I decided not to go back to my home-land from the beginning for the following three major reasons; firstly, I am an anti-communist and I'd like to live in a life of the democratic society. I've firmly decided to remain in South Korea with my democratic ideology. Secondly, So far I have been working with POW supervisory positions in the anti-communist POW camp all the way to the end of my POW life. Moreover, I was one of the POW supervisors at the most hearty and radical anti-communist Compound. Therefore, it was almost certain that I should be retaliated if I would return to North Korea. I knew that I would certainly be punished by their law for treason. They would put me in their jail, or at least the black list would always follow me for my background for the rest of my life. Thirdly, my sister's family has been living in Seoul. Basically those three reasons made me to decide to remain in South Korea. Therefore, I refused to repatriate to the North Korea. I am proud that I made the right decision. I am satisfied, happy with my South Korean and now with the American life. I have been living in the United States for 38 years now as a proud American citizen. I had lived in North Korea for 19 years, 25 years in South Korea and 38 years in the United States, which I lived longest years of my entire life. I married in 1958 in Seoul. I'm a father of two sons and two daughters whom they all graduated from universities in the United States. They are all satisfied and having their happy lives as good citizen of the United States of America.

8. AT THE SCENE OF SEGREGATION SITE

The UN forces wanted to segregate POWs between the repatriates and non-repatriates. At the time, all the prisoners did not know about the purpose of the segregation screening plan, they entirely misunderstood it. When we went through the Separation interview, we thought that we could be released right away either to the North or the South Korea. But this was completely wrong, since UNC authority did not inform us the purpose of the segregations. It was later disclosed that the UN Command wanted to find out the statistics of both repatriated and non-repatriated prisoners. It showed that about 10,000 Chinese and 30,000 North Korean prisoners did not want to go back to their homeland. Both Communists and UNC delegations were surprised with this un-anticipated repatriation number. The UN authority also wanted to reduce the compound size of 500 internees instead of 6,000, in an attempt to reduce troubles and to control more effectively by the UN authority.

Most POWs who were tortured previously by the POW security guards wanted to repatriate to their home land. They had even secretly instigated other prisoners to go back to their home land even in the anti-communist compound. The POW security guards made them to become real communists with their merciless tortures. No one could deny that there were a lot threats and intimidations in many Compounds, either Communists or non-communists.

Most of the POWs on the repatriation trucks were rejoiced over their repatriation. They sang the North Korean Army marching song. At the very time, one of the POWs on the truck shouted toward the non-repatriated POWs inside the compound; "Hey, You bastards and traitors! When we return to the father land, we're going to seek revenge on all your families and kill them all, in retaliation for your treasonable acts, you son of bitches!." and retaliated for your treasonable acts, you son of bitches!"

Before non-repatriate POWs heard of this abusive curse, we've even felt a sorrow of parting them after the long prisoner's hard life together. We even blessed their bright prosperous future. But when we heard of such a bad curse, we suddenly became angry and started to pelt them with rocks. As a result, many POWs in the truck sustained injuries. Many were hit in their faces causing severe bleeding. I heard, at that time, some prisoners inside the compound even expressed their joy at seeing the POWs on the trucks with bleeding faces. I saw then a young poor boy after being hit by a stone was bleeding on his face suffering from severe pain. I was in a deep sorrow. I could never forget the boy's bleeding face. I was haunted by the memory of the poor boy for a long time. Right here, I also could see the tragic scene left behind by the Korean War which was caused by division of the Korean peninsula at the 38th parallel. Korea was divided by the United States and Soviet Union at the end of the 2nd World War. At this time somebody ordered them to stop throwing rocks. They did so right away.

When the repatriation trucks were about to leave, some POWs who wanted to remain in South Korea, had suddenly changed their minds and dashed up to the trucks and joined the returning POWs. Among them three of Security guards who had tortured POWs were included. I heard later from a C.I. & E official that they were assaulted and killed by enraged POWs as soon as they arrived at their new compound. The former three security guards were immediately killed by other prisoners who had big grudges against the security guards. It took about 6 hours to finish screening 6,000 prisoners. It seemed roughly to be about 4,500 prisoners wanted to go back to their home land and about 1,500 remained in the camp. It was very small and crowded accommodation for 6,000 prisoners before but now became such a large room for about 1,500 prisoners. The remaining POWs now, longing their dear hometown, felt hollow and felt somewhat lonesome without them.

9. MASSACRE IN THE 83RD COMPOUND

This brutal massacre occurred at the 83rd anti-communist compound, just before the night of segregation interview day. On this occasion, the UN Command intended to separate the POWs between communists and non-communists respectively. However, for the lack of information, all the POWs didn't know the intention of the UN Command at the time and we simply thought that we would be released right after the segregation either to the North or to the South Korea, as I described former chapter. Moreover, we thought the segregation was a final decision to determine our future destinations.

It was a hard decision to make for most of the POWs who had all their families, relatives and friends in North Korea. It appeared almost every one had some kind of anguish of heart. They could not hide their agonized faces. They had no friends and families in South Korea. They would have to start their new life all over again in the unfamiliar capitalistic society of the South Korea. Therefore, their decision needed great courage and firm determination. Nevertheless, all my friends including myself firmly determined to remain in South Korea. The decisions made that night literally would determine our future lives.

Now, I might have to disclose the horrible scene of massacre committed by the "Korean Anti-Communist Youth Organization" led by Lee, Kwan-soon, since I witnessed the terrible scene.

The night before the UNC separation interview day, the above said POW organization distributed a small piece of white blank paper to all the POWs and directed them to write down their name, POW number and his decision of the repatriation, either "North or South." And Lee and his thugs further tricked all POWs that "This is the United Nation Command's order that you have to express your decision. Your decision would be final. It would be a strict confidential and no one could take a peep at your decision papers. We'd deliver those decisions directly to the UNC authority tomorrow morning and they will process your decision accordingly. That's the final decision whether you repatriate to the North or remain in the South Korea."

This scheme was a well kept secret that no one knew of it. Without suspecting anything, all prisoners believed it. They honestly wrote down their decisions on the paper, either North or South. It was later revealed that it was a malignant scheme planned and performed by the 'Korean Anti-Communist Youth Organization' directed by Lee. They want to find out who wanted to repatriate to North Korea and kill them all before the UN Command's segregation interview. At approximately one o'clock am, as they planned the scheme, about 160 POW PGs (Security guards) armed with clubs, baseball bat, steel pipes, knives, and pick axes, started to beat and kill those POWs who wrote down "North" on the small piece of paper last night. I was awaken by a hideous screaming of hundreds of men in the middle of the night, I ran out of the tent to see what was going on. Then I was startled at the sight of the massacre. I witnessed the POW security guards were chasing, beating down and killing many prisoners on the compound playground. The guards beat prisoners with clubs and stabbed them with knives brutally until they died. The bloody steel pipes and axes were striking on the helpless bodies of the screaming victims. Horrifying screams of victims were everywhere on the playground. The horrible screams come out of dying man filled with painful terror. It was hideous scene of massacre that no one could imagine nor describe exactly about the horrible scene. I can hardly describe exactly all the horror of the massacre that I witnessed that night. I was just trembling myself. I just stood absent minded at the time. Even now, the barbarous massacre scene rose again in my mind. I still can hear loud miserable screams of the victims together with the noise of thunderous running footsteps. I just want to leave this horrible scene to your imagination, since I can not find proper words to describe the eye-popping, tragic scene of bloodbath. The air was thick with the bloody scent of the victims. It was a 'hellish' scene itself. I couldn't move; my feet frozen to the ground. I just stood there like a man in a fuzzy and absent minded. "This can't be real!" I cried. But it was real and was happening right before my eyes. It was like a scene of some violent Hollywood movie. My eyes and senses could not comprehend this massive, barbaric violence that was taking place right in front of my eyes. Many people who also witnessed the massacre scene should also agree with me. That night, I was one of the few who actually came outside of the tent and witnessed the massacre scene distinctly while most of other prisoners were inside their tents, peeking outside trembling with fear. This horrible massacre lasted less than one hour. Then everything became suddenly calm. After this horrible terror, the sudden silence was as just as dreadful. No one dared to speak and everybody had a sleepless night. After the long night of hell, morning finally came. I saw about 160 POW's dead corpses scattered around the playground of the compound. It looked like an aftermath of battle-field. That was the second time I saw so many dead bodies scattered around one place. The first one, as I mentioned before, was near Pyongyang battle ground. Many thousands of North Korean soldiers killed and were scattered around on the rice paddies when the UN forces captured Pyongyang. I have no idea how many more prisoners were killed in this way at other anti-communist compounds.

In the morning, "the Neutral Nations Supervisory Commission" arrived our compound to enforce the screening interview. The Panmunjom UN armistice negotiators also arrived here to observe the segregation interview process. When they saw the dreadful scene they were also utterly shocked by the gruesome scene of the bloody dead bodies. The delegates were shocked and remained speechless. While they stood there silently, one ROK Army officer assigned to U.S. Army C.I.C. seemed to be very embarrassed and abruptly yelled out, "Who's done this !, you bastards!" That was the end. Every body was silent for a while. After the ROK officer's shouting, the incident was over, and the massacre became shrouded forever. I then personally saw Admiral Joy, Chief of the UN Armistice negotiators, from the close distance. They came here to observe the segregation interview which was carry out by the Neutral Nations Committee. Even the UN's chief negotiator, Admiral Joy, noted in his diary saying that "the reliable reports he had received of some POWs being "beaten black and blue or killed" after stating their desire to be repatriated to their home land." I think he is very honest man and wrote the true fact in his diary book.

The dead bodies were later loaded in several US Army trucks and carried out of the compound. There is no secret in this bright world and nothing could hide it forever. This barbarous and horrific act of massacre planned and executed by Lee. His culprits should be exposed distinctly and written in the Koje-do POW camp history. Lee and his collaborators should take full responsibility of their premeditated murder of innocent lives. They committed a grave crime to execute in such a barbarous massacre. This dark back side of the Korean War should be disclosed, recorded in the history of the Korean War and POW camp life, since it is big event and a barbarous crime. I don't want to think any Korean government organization was involved in this massacre. However, it might be possible to speculate that some organization probably knew of the information in advance. Because some Organization has been supporting Lee for the time being. I don't think Lee could commit such a hideous crime by himself without any background support.

Lee and his POW security guards who killed many prisoners should regret and suffer from those barbarous killings, if they have a scrape of conscience. I think some of them might get nightmares every night and are tortured by those poor deceased POW's vengeful spirit ghosts. Any one of them involved in the bloodbath should disclose all the hidden stories concerning the massacre. There are many other eye witnesses of that massacre besides myself. This kind of killing was not only in anti-communist compounds, but it presumed to the common practice of the Communist POW compounds also. They occasionally punished and killed their ideological opponents through so-called "People's Court judgment." This kind of incidents, demonstrations and the riots were frequently took place on account of the POW's repatriation matter; compulsory and voluntary.

I think this massacre incident should be recorded in the Koje-do POW camps history. All the historical events and incidents, good or bad, should be honestly recorded in the history book "frankly" as it was. The historic events and incidents should honestly be written with plain truth not influenced by the politics or ideology. I think the people who are responsible for the massacre at the 83rd POW camp, still live somewhere under the blue sky of the South Korea. I hope they could have true repentance for the crime they committed and get down their knees and apologize truthfully for their atrocities to the soul of the people they killed.

10. THE STALEMATE OF THE POW REPATRIATION ISSUE

As a result of the initial POW's screening and segregation, there were about 70,000 POWs wanted to repatriate to North Korea, and this figure made a surprise to both sides of the negotiators. The communists blamed the UN delegations that UN forces used force to influence the POWs not to go back to their homeland, and the communists stubbornly insisted that they would never accept less than 100,000 POWs. At Panmunjom, North Korean Chief Negotiator, Nam Il protested on May 9: "The endless series of bloody incidents occurring in your prisoner of the war camps clearly proves that your so-called screening is only a means of retaining forcibly captured personnel of our side." The next day he denounced the UN Command for "systematically taking a series of barbarous measures to attain your long-deliberated objective of forcibly retaining our captured personnel." Thereby, the truce meeting was stalemated and postponed indefinitely in October, 1952.

In the mean time, Admiral Joy, chief negotiator of UN forces was replaced by Major General William Harris in early June, 1952. More fierce fights continued all over the battle fields and UN fighters attacked with indiscriminate air bombing both front battle lines and rear bases. In opposition to the UN forces attacks, the communists responded with their heavy artillery attacks on the positions of UN and ROK Forces. One day in September 1952, the Chinese and the North Korean artillery units rained more than 45,000 artillery fire shots on the UN forces positions, and one day in the month of October, they showered about 93,000 artillery shots on the UN forces positions.

In July, the screening of POWs and separation process was again carried out. As a result, the repatriation number of POWs increased to 83,000 from 70,000. The communist negotiators then insisted again that they would not accept less than 100,000 prisoners. To tell the truth, from the beginning, there were 23 Taiwanese army pacification work teams dispatched to the Chinese Camps in Koje-do and they were authorized to pacify Chinese POWs to go to Formosa instead of Mainland China. They were authorized to form an anti-communist organization in the Chinese POW compounds. Two thirds of the Chinese prisoners were former Nationalist army soldiers who converted to become Mao's Communist army when they won the Chinese civil war.

Each compound commander was an American GI, but some Chinese camps were managed by Taiwanese military officers. But still outside of the security perimeter fences were guarded and patrolled by the ROK army soldiers.

Gen. Van fleet, Commanding General of Eighth US Army, has later recollected that the ROK forces' fighting power has much increased owing to their intensive training and has been a great help to the UN forces. The number of ROK Army soldiers and the UN forces totaled up to 788,888 men. The number of total Communists forces at that time was almost 800,000 men, including 279,000 men of the North Korean Army and 530,000 men of Chinese Voluntary army. These two big hostile forces fought against each other on the battle-field of the small Korean peninsula, so it was quite natural that the both sides suffered tremendous losses of both manpower and property damages in the war of attrition. As a result, both sides lost much more numbers of their soldiers than those of anti-communist POWs of 30,000, during two more years of the extended fighting especially in the mountainous "Iron Triangle" near the 38th parallel. It is therefore believed that all those losses occurred due to the lengthy arguments of the POW's repatriation talks which was the argument for the voluntary and the compulsory repatriation. Thus the truce meeting arguments looks to be harder than battle-field armed fighting.

11. 76TH RED COMPOUND RIOT

All the Koje-do UNC compounds interned about 170,000 prisoners (both US and South Korean figures) including the most extreme elements. Because each compound located so close to one another, a general prison uprisings were to be possible. It was extremely difficult to prevent the riots and casualties accordingly. Although the prisoners had no weapons but the vast number of prisoners could become a strong, dangerous power to the UN forces. Therefore, UNC planned to disperse the prisoners to about 500-men on a compound in Koje-do, the mainland, and the island of Cheju which is located about eighty miles below the southwest coast of the mainland. When the breakup of the Koje compounds started on June 10, non-communists compounds prisoners were very cooperative and successfully completed the separation operations, but the Communists compounds were very resistant especially at the 76th compound. Resistance centered once again on the 6,000 prisoners in Compound 76th. General Boatner, the camp Commander, was not going to negotiate. Instead he sent paratroopers of the 187th Airborne moved into Compound. Using only concussion grenades, tear gas, bayonets and fists. They drove or dragged the prisoners out of the trenches they had built within the compound. As a half-dozen tanks rolled in, resistance collapsed. Colonel Lee was captured and dragged out of the compound. It was like a battlefield and the resulting violent clash cost the life of one American soldier and 14 GIs wounded. During the two and a half hour battle, 31 prisoners were killed and 139 were wounded. As a result, all other compounds submitted and accepted the dispersion without resistance.

When the 76th compound were cleared, guards found 3,000 spears, 1,000 gasoline grenades, 4,500 knives, a large number of barbed-wire flails, clubs and other weapons. The leaders of Compound 77 and 78 swiftly agreed to do the separations. In compound 77, they found the bodies of sixteen prisoners who had been murdered by a self-appointed people's court. December, 1951, rival fictions-Communist and anti-Communist vied for control of the compounds. A large scale of rock fight between compounds on 18 December was followed by riots and demonstrations. Fourteen death and twenty-four other casualties resulted.

CHAPTER VI

REPATRIATION OF POWS

1. EXCHANGE OF SICK AND WOUNDED POWS

After suspending the truce negotiations, the communist negotiators returned to the bargaining table. But they held fast to the position that nothing short of the return of at least 100,000 POWs would be acceptable to them. In October, after months of negotiations without any progress and after the communist negotiators rejected the UN's latest proposal, General William K. Harris, the new UN Chief negotiator, suspended the talks indefinitely. The US administration decided, instead, to rely on increased military pressure, mainly stepped-up bombing of North Korea, to end the war.

This was the situation when newly elected President Dwight Eisenhower took office January 21, 1953. He also agreed to a statement, made at the Truman administration's behest, backing the White House position on voluntary repatriation and reiterating that there would be no change in that policy once he took office. Eisenhower was determined to take new initiatives to end the war, including the possible use of nuclear weapons. Like President Truman, he remained steadfastly committed to the principle of voluntary repatriation. With neither side offering any new proposals to resolve the POW issue, the truce tent at Panmunjom stayed empty. On April 10, 1953, however, a major breakthrough occurred when the Chinese and North Korean negotiators agreed to a proposal from the International Red Cross in Switzerland made in December and accepted by the UN Commander, Gen. Mark Clark, for an exchange of sick and wounded POWs. Clark agreed to the proposal after conferring with Washington, not because he thought the Chinese and North Koreans would accept it, but because he believed UN acceptance would have a favorable impact on world opinion and also wanted to get UN forces sick POWs repatriated back.

Accordingly, a sick and wounded POW's exchange operation began on April 20 and was concluded on May 3, 1953. The communists handed over to the UN Command 684 POWs of UN forces in exchange for 6,670 POWs held by the United Nations Command, thereby making good to their promise to swap sick and wounded prisoners successfully.

2. ZHOU EN-LAI'S NEW PROPOSAL

Much more to the surprise to the UN negotiators, was the Chinese and the North Koreans both agreed to the exchange of the sick and wounded POWs. They even suggested that the negotiations be resumed at Panmunjom. With growing optimism now that peace might finally be at hand, the UNC reopened negotiations at Panmunjom. Two days later, China's premier, Zhou En-lai, delivered a radio broadcast in which he offered to have all non-repatriates turned over to a neutral state, like India, for 90 days and have them decide their minds, which was their compromised proposal.

On May 7, however, the Chinese and North Koreans made another major concession by no longer insisting that the fate of remaining non-repatriates ultimately be settled at a postwar political conference. They also agreed to a maximum of 120 days for non-repatriates to be retained, the first ninety days of which were to be used to try to persuade them to change their minds.

Why the communists accepted the UN proposal several months after it had first been offered is not entirely clear. But undoubtedly the death in March of Soviet leader Joseph Stalin and the desire of the new regime in Moscow, headed by Gregori Malenkov, to improve relations with the West seemed to be a factor. Pursuing what some political observers called Soviet peace offensive, fearful that the war could escalate into a global conflict, and more confident about its own military capability now that they had their own nuclear arsenal, the Soviets most likely applied pressure on China and North Korea to end the war. The Chinese were also probably anxious to end the conflict, which they could claim as a victory, because they had driven UN forces from the Yalu River back up to south of Seoul and now to a military front approximately the 38th parallel, but which had become stalemated and increasingly costly to them.

As the two sides at Panmunjom drew closer to an agreement on the POW issue, the United States had to deal with the obstinate leader of South Korean President Syngman Rhee, who opposed the armistice and did not want the war to end until Korea had been unified under his leadership. At this time, Koreans were demonstrating in most cities opposing the armistice and wanted unification following President Rhee's desire, by ending the North Korean army. Where-upon the National Security Council (NSC), the governing council of America's national security apparatus, considered an alternative. If Rhee would not go along with the armistice plan, the Central Intelligence Agency would inspire a military coup to topple him from office, to be replaced by a hopefully more amenable military government. If Rhee continued to resist, he would be eliminated.

On June 18, 1953, a month before the armistice agreement was signed, President Rhee sought to undermine the truce talks by releasing 25,000 anti-communists POWs under the UN custody. Rhee's action infuriated the Chinese and North Korean negotiators who demanded to recover all the released POWs immediately and they also wanted to know whether the United States would be able to control the South Korean army, should an armistice be reached. But even though Rhee's action gave the communists justification to suspend negotiations, they did not do so. Instead they launched a retaliation military offensive against South Korean forces as a warning of the military power they could employ against the government in Seoul if it tried to sabotage an armistice agreement. They wanted to kill more numbers of ROK soldiers than the 25,000 anti-communist POWs Rhee had released.

As a result of the battle, both sides sustained much more than 60,000 total casualties.

3. RHEE RELEASED ANTI-COMMUNIST POWS

On June 8, 1953, the repatriation of POWs issue finally came to an agreement by both sides of negotiators at the Panmunjom truce meeting. The South Korean President Rhee could never accept it, because he consistently insisted to release all the anti-communist prisoners who did not want to return to their homeland. However, both side negotiators agreed to the Chinese new proposal that all the anti-communist POWs should be sent to a neutral country, such as India, for 90 days to give them an ample time to make their decisions. Under this circumstances, South Korean president Rhee made up his mind to release arbitrarily all the anti-communists prisoners on June 18, 1953. Rhee had to seek some kind of a bright idea to obtain about 30,000 anti-communist POWs and to obtain US-Korea Defense Pact and military assistance from the United States by interrupting the truce agreement. Rhee's idea was an arbitrary release of the 30,000 anti-communist POWs without getting approval of the UN Command, which startled the world's leaders at the news.

On June 8, 1953, he instructed his Army Provost Marshal, Colonel Won, Yong-dok, to release all the anti-communist prisoners covertly. No one anticipated such a bold action of Rhee. It was also his dangerous life time gamble. At that time, ROK Army military police soldiers were performing all the guard sentry duty outside of all POW compound's security fences and so there were no problems for the President Rhee to release the anti-communist POWs. The ROK Army Provost Marshal then, under the name of President Rhee, ordered his Military Police to release all the anti-communist POWs at once at 1 am, June 18, 1953. At the time, all the anti-communist POWs were separately held in Busan, Masan, Kwangju, Nonsan and Bupyong camps respectively. I was then in the Busan Kaya compound after the segregation and we all were just waiting for the day to be released.

Rhee, opposing the armistice, wanted to take his own chance to unify Korean peninsula by advancing North Korea independently with his own South Korean army, after having all the foreign troops both UN and Chinese forces withdrawn from Korean peninsula. The United States strongly opposed his idea and said it was an unreal and reckless idea. At that time, in our compound, most prisoners were considerably accommodated their POW lives because we had almost enough food, clothes, supplies and medical facilities. We, anti-Communist prisoners, were treated fairly by the UN authority than the Communist POWs. We were used to our long time POW lives. As soon as I woke up every morning, I played basket ball and I became one of the best player of our compound team. We played games with other compounds often and I was the team leader of our team. Whenever I had spare time, I studied English by myself with English text book and performed as an interpreter of our compound. I was one of the leaders of our anti-communist compound. At least twice a week I taught mathematics (math) and physical science to POW students as a part of C.I.& E program.

At about 10 pm, June 17, 1953, we have received following urgent message from the ROK Army Military Police stated as "President Rhee ordered to release all the anti=communist POWs. At one O'clock, June 18, 1953, Korean Army military police would cut the barbed wire of the east side fence to make a hole wide enough to let you to escape from the compound, and go over the Kaya-mountain to get to Busan city. You may enter any Korean houses to change your civilian clothes. After that the Korean police men would guide you and just follow their instructions. Korean people are all waiting for you. You are free now, Don't you worry and fear, this is a President Rhee's order. Good Luck!" Receiving this unexpected message, we had a little doubts and questions at first. Soon we began to trust the Korean government; especially it was the President Rhee's order. We immediately distributed the message to all prisoners of the compound secretly. We told them to make full preparation for escape. We all put shoes on, tied shoe strings tightly and were waiting for the appointed escaping time, 1 am. But we all were very anxious. Finally, the time has come, we went to the designated place. There we found a big hole on the barbed wire fence as they promised. We then went out through the hole and ran fast east towards the Kaya mountain behind Busan. We ran frantically towards the mountain in the pitch-dark night, having a sense of impending danger that US Army MPs might chase us and shoot. None of the thousand men running crowd said anything and it was a mass silent escape, except grand noise produced by thousands of runner's combat boots. The foot-steps of a thousand combat boots felt were a large scale of earthquake sounded. The "thunderous sounds" echoed around the pitch-dark hill side. I can't express right word of the grand noise produced by the running thousands men's' footsteps on the gravel ground. It was a kind of dreadful sound to me. When I furiously climbed up and down the rough mountain in the darkness, I bumped against rocks, scratched by tree branches, and my legs sustained scratches and abrasions. But I never felt any pain or fatigue in my adrenaline filled body. I was fully soaked with sweat. I realized that man produces a supernatural power when faced with extreme tensions and emergency situations. Fortunately, all the POWs of Busan area compounds escaped successfully and safely at that dark night. I heard later, many other area including Non-san and Bupyong compounds, were detected by American MPs, they completely failed. Many POWs were shot to death by US Military Police guards when they tried to escape from those anti-communist compounds.

I climbed down the mountain near East Daesin-dong, Busan, there were many village houses. The first house I entered was located at the mid-slope of the mountain. The house entrance door was already wide opened for me. I entered the house without hesitation. The man and his wife warmly welcomed me with friendly smiling faces. They said they were waiting for me because they already were informed by the Korean police in advance. They gave me their old civilian clothes and I gave them my brand new American GI uniform. I got out of the house saying "thank you" and I then noticed that Korean Police man was waiting for me outside of the house. He took me to one of village leader's house located in Yong-do in Busan. I stayed in that house all day. It was the first day of my civilian life after three years of my POW's life. I could go around freely anywhere I wanted without a American GI's security guard. Strangely, at first I felt some-what of empty and insecure feeling. I even had a queer feeling that I lost something, simply because I was used to the POW life.

Thus 25,000 anti-communists POWs were released by the bold decision of Korean President Rhee. We were released and embraced in the arms of Republic of Korea. Two days later, we all were called by Korean police and forced to be enlisted to the South Korean army. Most of the college students, including myself, were sent to Military Cadet to become ROK Army officers. I also became one of the ROK Army Officer. Thereby, the ROK Army augmented more military strength and fighting forces with 30,000 anti-communist POWs who were former North Korean army soldiers.

However, for the UN authority was put in an awkward position because it signed the agreement that all non-repatriation POWs were supposed to be sent to the Neutral countries commission, India, for further disposition. UN Command had to worry much about the dispersion of the armistice. General Clark, Commanding General of 8th US Army protested and sent a complaint letter to Korean president Rhee to read "You have violated gravely the authority of the United Nations" and he also sent an excuse letter to communist side that he entirely did not know about the incidence.

At this time, the North Korea and Chinese negotiators furiously criticized the UN side and made a pressing demand to recover and re-enter all the released POWs immediately. The North Korean chief negotiator Gen. Nam Il criticized harshly and demanded to know whether the United States would be able to control South Korean Army, should an armistice be reached. UN chief negotiator then stated that the ROK Army is under control of UN Command.

In the meantime, the communists planned a retaliation attacks on ROK army positions in revenge for the release of the anti-communist POWs. They wanted to kill more than 30,000 ROKA solders for the retaliation. On the raining night of July 13, the Communist forces launched a military attack only against ROK forces positions. With the first Communists offense, ROK forces had to retreat 21 miles (34Km) at the region of 'Keumsong', but on July 16, with U.S. forces help, ROK forces advanced 5 miles (8 Km) . But this fight ended on July 20, 1953. Both sides insisted to inflict enemy more than 30,000 men killed respectively. At this point, both sides wanted the truce and the conclusion of truce treaty was very near after the POW agenda was agreed. Both sides did not want to abandon the truce agreement which they exerted hard to finish it for a long time. Eisenhower won the presidential election proposing a campaign promised to implement the Korean War armistice.

Under both political and war situations, newly elected president Eisenhower sent his special envoy, Robertson, Undersecretary, Department of State, to South Korea. He promised to Rhee "if you would agree to the armistice, the United States will consider the U.S.-Korea Defense treaty that you wished." Rhee then agreed the armistice under the following conditions;

1. After the Armistice, conclude the U.S.-Korean mutual Defense treaty.
2. Give both military and economic aids (firstly $200 million) to Korea.
3. Render an assistance to build-up ROK Army Twenty (20) divisions and strengthen ROK Air force.

Following Rhee's unilateral release of anti-communist North Korean POWs, Rhee had secured from the USA a mutual defense treaty, long term economic aid, and assistance in expanding the ROK armed forces. Additionally, the Eighth US Army remained in South Korea throughout the Cold War and until the present time. The ROK was now an important in East Asia. It was one of the few nations to provide a sizable military contributions to the American war efforts in Vietnam, Iraq and Afghanistan

4. POWs ISSUE

Korean War might have been ended as early as 1951, two years before an argument of POW issue was finally reached, if both side agreed to all for all compulsory return of all POWs at the War. Indeed, one of the troublesome issues that held up a peace agreement was the issue of the repatriation of prisoners-of-war. The Communists insisted that all POWs should be repatriated on all for all exchange, as provided by the article 118 of the Geneva Convention of 1949, which called for quick and compulsory repatriation of all POWs at the end of a war; it did not provide for POWs who did not want to be repatriated. United States announced very early in the armistice that it would abide by provision of Geneva Convention, as did North and South Korea. The UN negotiators at Panmunjom also believe that the fastest way to return UN prisoners back home was to agree to an all-for-all-exchange and that the voluntary repatriation would violate the Geneva Convention. Except for the issue of POW's repatriation, an armistice ending the Korean War might have been achieved as early as 1951, approximately two years before an argument was finally reached. Indeed, after 1951, it was the only issue holding back the signing of a truce agreement.

At the time armistice negotiation began in 1951, no one expected the repatriation of POWs would be that much complicated and headache problem, but they thought was very easy issue to be solved if would exchange all-for-all repatriation in the first place. Nevertheless, the issue delayed armistice agreement almost two more years.

During the first and second year, UN forces captured large number of Chinese and North Korean troops. Some American officials began to argue against the "forced repatriation", claiming that the prisoners return to China and North Korea against their will, especially for the POW leaders of the anti-communist compounds in the UNC camps would be punished. And therefore some POWs in UN Camps, especially the POW leaders, did not want to return home because of possible retaliation and execution. The Joint Chief of Staff had gone back and force on the POW issue. At one time favoring the forced repatriation of prisoners to get American POWs returned as quickly as possible. At another time ordering General Mathew Ridgway to prepare a proposal for the return of POWs based on voluntary repatriation. Then reversing course again and favoring the prompt repatriation of all prisoners on the basis of the Geneva Convention.

However, the Truman administration was just as determined that no prisoner should be forced to return against his will, they saw more than 30,000 anti-communist POWs in the Koje-do UN Camps. For the Chinese, it was also one of the important problems that they could make no concession. As a result, the war dragged on for two more years. Not until 1953, following a breakdown of negotiations that lasted from October 1952 to April 1953. A complex formula was agreed upon by both sides according to which POWs not wanting to be repatriated would be given a period of time to change their minds and then their cases could be turned over to a Neutral Nations Repatriation Commission, which would help relocate them. In the end, only 628 of the Communists non-repatriates elected to go home. Only 10 of the UNC non-repatriates chose to return home, 86 chose India and 51 died at Panmunjom. The rest were eventually released to the South Korea the following January.

First, The Communists attempted to reestablish the 38th parallel as a line of truce, whereas U.N. forces proposed to make the truce line with existing battle line at the time of the truce agreement. Second, the delay of the POWs repatriation (for about 22 months) issue, these two issues encountered obstacles of the negotiation and the truce talks were suspended between August and October 1951. Meanwhile, the fighting continued with each side attempting to capture more territory and to occupy better strategic positions, which demanded heavy casualties both side, during this period of the war of attrition. It is believed that all those losses were wastefully occurred because of the extended POW repatriation arguments and not establishing the armistice line at the 38th parallel line, which might otherwise have been enabled to cease fire promptly even before signing the true, thus could save many lives of both sides.

It is verified later that if the armistice line was set up at the existing 38th parallel line, there was no need to fight against each other, regardless of the date armistice signed, to get more land and better strategic positions which cost many lives and property damages.

5. THE FINAL POW REPATRIATION AT THE PANMUNJOM

Although there were still many issues that had to be resolved before the war was ended, but an agreement finally signed at Panmunjom on July 27, 1953, including South Korean president Rhee's acceptance of an armistice agreement, the most insuperable issue of the war was finally resolved.

As I mentioned before, at the time armistice negotiations began in July 1951, no one (both sides) expected the repatriation of POWs would be that much of a problem when both sides agreed to exchange all-for-all, according to the Geneva Convention. If it were the case, an armistice ending the Korean War might have been achieved as early as 1951, two years before an agreement was finally reached. However, the Korean War ended after <u>three</u> years one month and two days (1,157 days), when both sides finally signed on the truce agreement. During this wasteful time, many soldiers of both sides killed in the fierce battle fields and destroyed tremendous amount of property damages.

Now one last thing to do was a final repatriation of POWs which was agreed by both sides on June 8, 1953. Both sides agreed to commence the repatriation on August 5, at the Panmunjom truce village. North Koreans transported UN POWs by train to Panmunjom and the UN forces transported North Korean and Chinese POWs by ships and train to Panmunjom. The number of final repatriation was as follows:

1. The number of UN Forces repatriated:
2. 21,389 (including both US and ROK Army soldiers) returned.)
3. 359 ROKA and 23 U.S. Army soldiers Voluntary remained in North Korea.
4. 3,500 American soldiers were repatriated.
5. Two (2) US soldiers wanted to go to India.
6. Originally the North Koreans claimed that the ROKA POWs were 65,000 to 80,000, but most of them joined in the North

Korean Army. 1628 anti-communist POWs changed their mind and returned to North Korea. 186 POWs sent to India. 151 POWs died at Panmunjom.

The POW's repatriation was successfully completed after long and heated debates in the truce meeting. The agreement signed and the exchange started from August 5 to September 6, 1953, for 33 days. As I described before, the POWs repatriation debate took almost two years to be settled and during the time two sides continued to fight a war of attrition near 38th parallel, to try to win more advantageous positions. However, neither side won any more lands and/or prevail the war, only wasting a lot of manpower and military equipment. Therefore, looking back it now, the Korean War could have ended within a year if the POWs repatriated all-in-all package and if the armistice line was established on the already existing 38th parallel line.

The Korean War ceased by a truce since July 27, 1953, without having a peace treaty for almost 62 years. Korea is still technically remained in the state of war because the three year conflict ended in a truce but no "peace treaty" yet. The peace treaty should be signed between two Koreas, United States and China to preserve the peaceful Korean peninsula. Therefore, it still exist tensions between two Koreas and a war cloud hung over the Korean peninsula constantly. The peace treaty should be signed to maintain the peace of the Korean peninsula. It also deemed necessary to sign a Peace treaty for North Korea to abolish it's nuclear weapons. On April 27, 2011, President Jimmy Carter stated to news reporters at Seoul, Korea that "it is a tragedy there is no peace treaty singed as yet between two Koreas after more than 60 years after the Korean armistice signed." He pointed out. As we all know that the Korean War armistice set a longest record in the World War history. I firmly believe the peaceful Korean peninsula would make a great contribution to the peace of the far East Asia and the rest of the world.

A Part of Kojedo UN POW Camp

▲ 1950. 8. 8. 누가 이 아이를 버리게 했을까? ⓒ2004 미국 문서기록보관청

Crying baby Lost his mother. 1950. 8. 8. 2004 US National
                                                        · archives

▲이게 유토피아? 인천 상륙작전이 끝난 뒤 한 해병이 파괴돈 다가 어린 아이와 만난다. 치열한 전투에서 살아남은 행운아 아"(이상향)이라는 다방 간판이 폐허가 된 거리 풍경과 아이 루고있다...

A Lucky Kid alive from the fierce Inchon city street fight.

서부전선에서 체포된 중공군. 사살할 것으로 오인해 살려달라고 애앳하는
모습.(1951년)

Chinese POWs pleaded ROK soldier Not to Kill them.
(1951)

폐허속에서 노숙하는 친한민 가족(1950년 9월)
Village Houses destroyed by US Air Raid (sept 1950)

▲ 1950. 9. 16. 인천부두로 상륙하는 맥아더 장군ⓒ2004 NARA   1950. 9. 16.

General Mcarthur make a Landing the Inchon Port.
Sept 16. 1950

N. Korean civilian refugees toward South.

(1951. 1. 5.)

1951년 1월 5일, 1·4후퇴 당시 파괴된 대동강 철교위를 목숨걸고 건너 남하하는 평양시민들. 이 유명한 사진은 맥스 데스퍼(Max Destor)에게 퓨리처상을 수상하게 만들었다.

Korean Refugees

(**Opposite top**) The stern 8-inch guns of the heavy cruiser
Toledo firing in support of ROK troops in the Pohang-dong [area?]
Tuesday, 22 August 1950. (**Opposite bottom**) 16-inch guns [of the]
battleship USS Missouri blasting the North Korean port of Chong[jin]
on Thursday, 12 October, and (**below**) the Missouri paying a [?]

BATTLE HORIZONS. From the decks of the "Mt. McKinley," the invasion coordinators (above) watch as the first waves of U.S. Marines storm Inchon's beaches. They are left to right: Lt. General Shepherd, CG Fleet Marine Force, Pacific; Brig. General Edwin K. Wright, Asst. Chief of Staff, G-3, GHQ, Far Eastern Command; Rear Admiral James H. Doyle, Comdr. Amphibious Group No. 1; Maj. General Edward M. Almond, X Corps Commander, and General MacArthur.

This may be a good Book Cover Picture. one £

▲ 1951. 2. 26 부산, 군교의 임시 포로수용소 전경.
ⓒ NARA   1951. 2. 26 , BUSAN Kajeri POW camp

▲ 1950. 12. 16. 폭격에 엿가락처럼 휘어진 철교.
© NARA *A railway bridge destroyed by US Air Raid.*

Would you like to see your manuscript become a book?

CPSIA information can be obtained at www.ICGtesting.com
Printed in the USA
BVOW032025220413

318821BV00002B/194/P